P9-DGL-581

FROMMER'S TOURING GUIDE TO FLORENCE

First edition prepared by
Francois Monmarché

Translation
Michele Zamfirescu

Adaptation
Times Editions, Singapore and Hachette, Paris

Production
Times Editions, Singapore

This edition published in the United States and Canada in 1987
by Prentice Hall Press
A division of Simon & Schuster, Inc.
Gulf+Western Building
One Gulf+Western Plaza
New York, New York 10023

PRENTICE HALL PRESS is a trademark of Simon & Schuster, Inc.

This guide is adapted from *A Florence*, published by Hachette
Guides Bleus, Paris, 1986.

Copyright 1986 © by Hachette Guides Bleus, Paris.
English translation Copyright 1987 © by Hachette Guides
Bleus, Paris.
Maps Copyright 1987 © by TCI, Milan and Hachette Guides
Bleus, Paris.

All rights reserved. No part of this publication may be
reproduced, stored in a retrieval system or transmitted in any
form, or by any means, electronic, mechanical, photocopying,
recording or otherwise, without the prior consent of Hachette
Guides Bleus.

Library of Congress Cataloging-in-Publication Data

Monmarché, François
  Frommer's touring guide to Florence.
  Translation of: A Florence.
  Includes index.
  1. Florence (Italy) — Description — 1981– —
Guide-books I. Title
DG732.M5713 1987   914.5'51   86-30385
ISBN 0-13-331281-X

FROMMER'S TOURING GUIDE TO FLORENCE

PRENTICE HALL PRESS

NEW YORK

HOW TO USE YOUR GUIDE

Before leaving, consult the information given in the chapter on "Planning Your Trip" (p. 9). On arrival use addresses and practical information from the chapter entitled "General Information" (p. 33).

Names of the main sites and monuments are followed by grid references to help you locate them on the maps (see below).

At the end of the guide, you will find an index of places, sites and monuments, together with a useful vocabulary list.

SYMBOLS USED

Sites, monuments, museums, works of art

★   interesting
★★ remarkable
★★★ exceptional

Hotel classification

▲   simple and comfortable
▲▲   very comfortable
▲▲▲   first class hotel
▲▲▲▲   luxury hotel

MAPS

Location map (Guides Bleus map) (6)
General map of Florence (T.C.I. map) (36-37)
Center of Florence (T.C.I. map) (40-41)
Uffizi Gallery (Guides Bleus map) (82)
Fiesole (T.C.I. map) (144)

▬ CONTENTS

Photo credits: ENIT, Paris: pp. 19, 22, 117. — C. Boisvieux: p. 14. — C.P. Rémy: pp. 27, 31, 45, 49, 56, 61, 70, 75, 78, 83, 87, 90, 120, 124, 136. — P. Milleron: pp. 100, 104. — M. Guillet: p. 140.

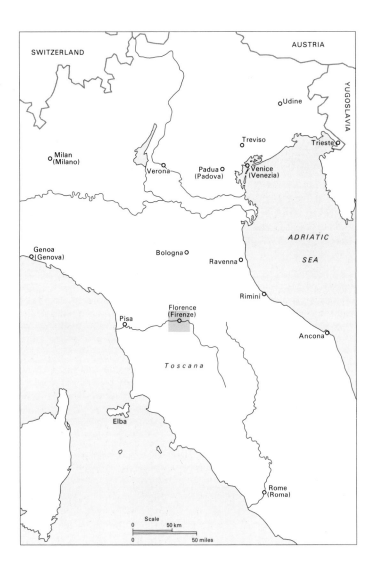

Florence, on the River Arno, is situated about 60 miles/100 km from the Tyrrhenian Sea. It is approximately 150 miles/250 km from both Rome and Venice.

APPROACH TO FLORENCE

Most of us arrive in Florence with a clearly-defined idea of the city, as seen through art books and albums: a series of well-known images, reproduced so frequently that they fall into place in our minds like pieces of a jig-saw. Florence is the face of Botticelli's "Primavera", the smile of Filippo Lippi's "Madonna", or the masculine and resolute expression of Michelangelo's "David". It is also the familiar silhouette of the Ponte Vecchio and the perfection of Brunelleschi's cupola with its range of ochres and bluish-greens which evoke the frescoes of Masaccio.

Thus, Florence appears like a perfect little universe – an ideal world, which belongs to that most privileged chapter in human history: the Renaissance. Its birthplace is here, between the banks of the Arno and the cypresses of Fiesole; here it flourished, its language expressing moderation, reason and sincerity of feeling. Florence is possibly the world's greatest example of man's ability to create beauty in harmony with nature.

In a world so often subject to doubt, Florence carries a message of hope. It symbolizes an ideal balance between the natural and instinctive forces and those of knowledge. Florence does not offer the exotic color of a visit to Nepal or Peru. There is not much of the marvelous or mysterious. Nevertheless, it takes us further into the realms of the mind and heart; and the visitor to Florence will soon discover how this city of the imagination finds an echo in reality. Having imagined Florence as it was, we see it as it is, amid the many images which animate the city's everyday life.

There is a dryness about the urban landscape of Florence which is exacerbated by the harsh light, the austerity of the houses and the feverish activity of the streets. All this may come as a surprise. The best way to take a first look at Florence is to climb up through the vineyards and olive groves to the terraces of Fiesole. From here, whether in the shadowy light of morning or evening, or under a blinding midday sun, the view is breathtaking. Domes and bell-towers, city walls and old roofs are jumbled together in a confined space below, as if to summarize the history of the city and the Renaissance. If the word "beauty" still means anything in current language, it means something here. In the heart of this landscape, suffused with light, the eye perceives the colors and the panoramic surroundings that inspired the painters of the great era.

Coming out of the cathedral or the Uffizi Gallery, our imaginations stimulated by masterpieces, we plunge into the more intimate atmosphere of the street. This, too, is Florence, with its noises and smells, its overcrowded buses and milling crowds: the elegant Florence of the Via de'Tornabuoni, the popular Florence of the San Lorenzo market.

Sitting outdoors at a café in the Piazza della Signoria, among the flocks of pigeons, we may feel the need for solitude, a yearning to have Florence all to ourselves. This is possible once night has fallen and the streets are emptied of Florentines, who have gone to dine in the *trattorie*. Then everything is calm and pleasant. Even the warm air loses its smell of exhaust fumes and carries the perfumes of the surrounding countryside and the city's many hidden gardens. This is the best moment to begin exploring the city, not for its night life, which is negligible, but for its mystery.

Once we know Florence, it becomes a lifelong friend. And when we leave, each one of us takes away a private key to the city, a personal experience of special places charged with emotion and happy memories.

PLANNING YOUR TRIP

This chapter provides all the necessary information you need to plan your trip: how to get there, passport information, currency, the climate and useful addresses.

▬ WHEN TO GO

The tourist season in Florence lasts from March to November and any long holiday weekend fills up the hotels. This is why it is always necessary to book a room in advance (see p. 39 for selecting a hotel).

Naturally, as in many other big cities, the hottest months (July and August) are to be avoided. During these months Florence loses its usual animation. It is the time when schools are closed and you are likely to hear any language on earth other than that of Donatello.

Spring and autumn are the best seasons to visit Florence because the light is then of a rare quality. Winters are said to be mild but do not depend on it; while it snows very seldom, Florence in winter can be bitterly cold. When the snow actually settles, it is a big event.

Average Temperatures (low and high for each month)

	January		February		March
Fahrenheit	35.2–48.7		36.3–52.8		40.2–59.9
Centigrade	1.8–9.3		2.4–11.6		4.6–15.5
	April		May		June
Fahrenheit	45.8–68.3		53.2–74.6		58.3–83.6
Centigrade	7.7–20.2		11.8–23.7		14.6–28.7
	July		August		September
Fahrenheit	62.8–89.2		61.8–88.1		58.1–81.5
Centigrade	17.1–31.8		16.6–31.2		14.5–27.5
	October		November		December
Fahrenheit	51.2–69.2		42.4–58		37–50.3
Centigrade	10.7–20.7		5.8–14.4		2.8–10.2

Before you decide on a date, keep in mind the calendar of the various festivities: *Scoppio del carro* on Easter day or *Festa di San Giovanni* on June 24, as well as all the cultural events (see p. 50). If you have three days, five days or more in Florence, see "Using your time wisely" (p. 35).

▬ PASSPORT INFORMATION

Visas are not required for citizens of the U.S., Canada, U.K. and most Commonwealth countries. A valid passport, however, is required. Cars are free to enter the country but do not forget your green insurance card.

▬ *MONEY*

The Italian monetary unit is the *lira* (plural: *lire*).

The U.S. dollar is about 1500 lire, and the rate for sterling is approximately 2300 lire.

Coins: 50, 100, 200, 500 lire.

Notes: 1000, 2000, 5000, 10,000, 50,000 and 100,000 lire.

Your budget

The cost of living in Florence is high. If you are not on an inclusive tour, allow between 150,000 and 200,000 lire a day for two persons. This includes hotel room and restaurants, as well as museum tickets and sundries.

▬ *HOW TO GET THERE*

Exploring Florence is a personal experience which may not lend itself to group tours. However, independent holidays are more expensive. Work out costs: plane, train or car, plus hotel. Hotels are fairly expensive. Make use of package tours inclusive of plane or train tickets and hotels (bed and breakfast) in order to get group prices while keeping your freedom. Whatever you decide to do, apply to your travel agency and book in advance.

By plane

Florence, like other Tuscan towns, is served by *Galilei Airport,* 1¼ miles/2 km south of Pisa. There is a fast train service (1 hour) from inside the airport to the center of Florence (52 miles/83 km) arriving in the main Santa Maria Novella station.

By train

It is easy to get to Florence from many European towns because the city is on the Milan–Bologna–Rome line, which is served by many international trains. You will arrive in the heart of the city at the Stazione Centrale di Santa Maria Novella.

There are some special ticket rates for touring Italy by train, starting in Venice, Rome, Milan, Turin, Pisa or Naples and ending in any other city.

By road

By using the *"pacchetto Italia"* petrol coupons you can save considerably on the price of petrol. They also entitle you to free tickets at motorway tolls and free repair service from the **A.C.I.** (Italian Automobile Club) by calling number 116 on normal roads and from the emergency telephones on the motorways.

These petrol coupons are available in certain banks, Banco di Roma and Italian Tourist Company offices in your country. Apply to your nearest Italian Tourist Office. In Italy, they are available at the A.C.I. offices and have to be paid for in foreign currency.

▬ *BEFORE YOU LEAVE: SOME USEFUL ADDRESSES*

The larger cities of the English-speaking world have an Italian consulate or a consular agent; some have a branch of the Italian State Tourist Office (E.N.I.T.) or of the airline Alitalia which often acts as E.N.I.T.'s representative. They can provide you with information about traveling to Italy, but most travel agencies and airlines should be able to give you details on current requirements (valid passport, visa if applicable, etc.). The C.I.T., or Italian Tourist Co., is the official representative of the Italian railways and one of Italy's most important tourist organizations.

Australia

Embassy:
Canberra, 12 Grey St., Deakin, ACT 2000, tel: (6) 73-33-33

Consulates:
Adelaide, 186 Grenhill Rd., Parkside, SA 5063, tel: (8) 27-20-344
Brisbane, 158 Moray St., New Farm, QLD 4005, tel: (7) 35-84-344
Melbourne, 34 Anderson St., South Yarra, VIC 3141, tel: (3) 26-75-744
Perth, 31 Labouchere Rd., South Perth, WA 6151, tel: (9) 36-78-922
Sydney, 100 William St., NSW 2000 (P.O. Box 295), tel: (2) 35-82-955

E.N.I.T.:
Sydney, c/o Alitalia, AGC House, 124 Philip St., NSW 2000, tel: (2) 22-13-620

C.I.T.:
Melbourne, 500 Collins St., VIC 3000, tel: (3) 61-27-74
Sydney, 123 Clarence St., NSW 2000, tel: (2) 29-47-54

Canada

Embassy:
Ottawa, 275 Slater St., tel: (613) 232-2401

Consulates:
Montreal, 3489 Drummond St., tel: (514) 849-8351
Toronto, 136 Beverly St., tel: (416) 977-1566
Vancouver, Suite 505-1200 Burrard St., tel: (604) 684-7288

E.N.I.T.:
Montreal, Montreal Store 56, Plaza 3, Place Ville-Marie, tel: (514) 866-7667

C.I.T.:
Toronto, 13 Balmuto St., tel: (416) 927-7712

Great Britain

Embassy:
London, 14 Three Kings Yard, Davies St., W1Y 2EH, tel: (01) 629-8200

Consulates:
London, Heathcote House, 20 Savile Row, W1X 2DQ, tel: (01) 235-9371
Edinburgh, 6 Melville Crescent, EH3 7JA, tel: (031) 226-3631
Manchester, St James Building, 79 Oxford St., W.C.1, tel: (061) 236-9024

E.N.I.T.:
London, 200 Regent St., W.C.1, tel: (01) 734-4631
1 Princess St., W1R 8AY, tel: (01) 408-1254

C.I.T.:
London, 50/51 Conduit St., W1R 9FB, tel: (01) 434-3844

Hong Kong

Consulate:
801 Hutchison House, 10 Harcourt Rd., tel: (5) 220-033

E.N.I.T.:
c/o Alitalia, Hilton Hotel, Queen's Road Central, (P.O. Box 1514) tel: (5) 237-041

Ireland

Embassy:
Dublin, 12 Fitzwilliam Square, Dublin 2, tel: (353) 76-03-66

Consulate:
Belfast, 2 Kincraig Park, Newtownabbey, BT36 7QA, tel: (232) 77-83-53

New Zealand

Embassy:
Wellington, 34 Grant Rd., tel: (4) 73-66-67

E.N.I.T.:
Auckland, c/o Alitalia, 95 Queen St., tel: (9) 79-44-55

South Africa

E.N.I.T.:
Johannesburg, London House, 21 Loveday St., Johannesburg 2000 (P.O.Box 6507), tel: 83-83-247

United States

Consulates:
Boston, 101 Tremont St., MA 02108 tel: (617) 542-0483
Los Angeles, 11661 San Vicente Boulevard, Suite 911, CA 90049, tel: (213) 826-5998
New York, 690 Park Avenue, NY 10021, tel: (212) 737-9100
San Francisco, 2590 Webster St., CA 94115 tel: (415) 931-4924

E.N.I.T.:
New York, 630 Fifth Avenue, NY 10111, tel: (212) 245-4961
Chicago, 500 N. Michigan Avenue, Ill 60611, tel: (312) 644-0990
San Francisco, 360 Post St., CA 94108, tel: (415) 392-6206

C.I.T.:
Los Angeles, Suite 819, 15760 Ventura Boulevard, CA 91436, tel: (213) 783-7245
New York, 666 Fifth Avenue, NY 10103, tel: (212) 397-9300

FLORENCE TODAY

Florence, the birthplace of the Renaissance, is timeless in its unique blend of past and present. Along the Via de'Tornabuoni, the most elegant of Florence's shopping streets, old fortified palazzos now house, with no apparent discord, such great names of Italian fashion as Ferragamo and Gucci. Near by, in the Via dei Pucci, dressmakers for the couturier Marquis Emilio Pucci work in a setting of frescoed walls and gilt coffered ceilings.

FLORENTINE SPECIALTIES

Florence is still one of the principal centers of Italian fashion, although the wool and silk industries are no longer the source of the city's wealth as they were in the Middle Ages. The hallmark of Florentine haute couture today is still clothing made of hand-woven silk. Other Florentine specialties much sought after on the international market include men's shirts, lingerie, household linen, and leather goods – notably luggage and fine footwear. To maintain its importance in the world marketplace, the city regularly hosts numerous fashion trade fairs (Pitti Uomo, Pitti Lingerie, Prato Espone) to show its products to both foreign and Italian buyers.

Crossing the Arno on the Ponte Vecchio, where goldsmiths and jewelers have prospered ever since Duke Cosimo I banished the unsightly butchers' shops, you enter the old narrow streets of the Oltrarno (left bank). Here the city's artisans hold sway. In their dimly lit workshops and tiny courtyards, there are pieces of furniture waiting to be restored, gilded wooden frames, madonnas and fat-cheeked cherubs. Florentine artisans excel at reproducing the treasures amassed over the centuries in the city of the Medici. Their skill is evident in wood, marble and stone – the *scalpellini* (stone carvers) of Florence are particularly renowned. Another local craft specialty is *pietre dure* work, in which semi-precious stones are inlaid on marble table-tops, sometimes forming little pictures.

Outside the boundaries of the historic city center, still marked by the ancient ramparts and gates, are the new urban areas served by road and rail where industry has taken over from craftsmanship. This industry consists, for the most part, of small or middle-sized businesses manufacturing traditional products: leather and suede items, ready-to-wear clothing, furniture and footwear.

The origins of the ceramics industry date back to the beginning of the 18th century, when the first ceramics factory opened at Doccia, on the outskirts of Florence. Since then, it has expanded

considerably and produces porcelain tableware, faience and ceramic parts for the electrical and chemical industries.

The larger industries are represented by two firms: the Pignone foundry, which opened in 1845 and is now part of the ENI group (Ente Nazionale degli Idrocarburi), specializing in excavating equipment; and the Galileo group, founded in 1831, which manufactures optical instruments, electrical supplies, looms and medical instruments.

Finally, it goes without saying that Florence derives a large part of its wealth from tourism. Its population of 500,000 inhabitants almost doubles in the summer months. Florence is the third most visited city in Italy.

The spirit of Florence: the grandeur of the past blended with the everyday life of today.

FLORENCE THROUGH THE AGES

The breathtaking panoramic view from Fiesole or San Miniato, with the great dome of the cathedral rising out of a sea of terra-cotta roofs, is everyone's idea of Florence. From here, the whole of Florence's history is spread before us, framed in one enchanting prospect. Along the valley of the Arno, an endless sequence of domes and towers, red tiles and ochre walls bear witness to a unique adventure in knowledge and creativity: the Renaissance. The Renaissance began on the banks of the Arno and it lingers here still, as though the intervening centuries had never happened.

THE "FLOURISHING CITY"

During the Renaissance, when the taste for imaginative etymology was rife, a hundred ways of explaining how Florence came by its name were put forward: some said it was a reference to the Roman general, *Fiorinus*, who founded the city; others, that the name referred to the abundance of flowers growing around the city and on the banks of the Arno. Today, it is thought that Florence means *"flourishing city"* because of the wealth of the surrounding countryside.

The first knowledge we have of Florence is of a Roman camp established at the narrowest point of the Arno. This was destined to replace Fiesole, the Etruscan town about 5 miles/8 km away. The center of Florence still retains traces of the grid pattern of Roman streets.

Little or nothing is known of this period except that *San Miniatus* was martyred in A.D. 250 during the persecutions of *Decius*, and the present-day church of San Miniato al Monte was built on the site of his grave. The Barbarians arrived, followed by the Lombards, then the Franks. In the time of *Charlemagne*, Florence was still a small town but was already trading with the Orient. Merchants from Greece and Syria came up the Arno to offer their wares. Trade was already an important factor in the life of the town and was eventually to become its *raison d'être*.

To protect and extend their dominance over the trade in the region, the Florentine rulers fought the feudal barons who held the surrounding countryside, waged war on Pisa, Arezzo and Siena and declared Florence a commune. The city walls, which had originally encircled the Roman camp, were extended to enclose a greater area. At the same time, the various districts of the city, between which there was incessant rivalry, began to bristle with newly-erected towers, the strongholds of various magnates.

In the 12th century, the town was ceded to the pope by the wife of Guelph IV, Duke of Bavaria. The pope's supporters, known as the *Guelph* party, set themselves up in opposition to the supporters of the emperor, who were known as the *Ghibellines.* The former would rule one day, the latter the next. This quarrel resulted in much bloodshed and, frequently, enemies of the prevailing party were exiled – this was Dante's fate. It became an excuse for murders committed for quite different motives: an unsuccessful marriage, lovers' quarrels, and the like. "What's going on?" asks a newly arrived traveler in a story dating from that time, who finds himself being jostled by armed men. "Nothing," comes the reply, "they're nominating the magistrates and public officials of the city."

THE FLORIN, THE EUROPEAN COIN

What is really extraordinary is that all this violent squabbling apparently did little to inhibit Florence's economic expansion. Political rivalry could not undermine the patriotic sentiment of the Florentines for their commune, which they were determined to make into a city-state and the foremost town of Italy. According to the *Ordinamenti di Giustizia* (a form of constitution) of 1293, in order to have citizenship it was necessary to be a member of a guild. This law was applicable to everyone, including the nobility. The real aristocracy of Florence was the aristocracy of trade. It was on trade that the Florentines founded a city-state which even their ceaseless internal strife could not destroy. The strength of the Guelphs lay precisely in their having the guilds on their side, and in the end, the Guelphs became the State.

Wool was at the center of economic activity and the wool guild comprised the artisans whom commerce had transformed into bourgeois. Wool came in, in 375-lb/170-kilo bales, from Flanders, Champagne, Burgundy, England, Spain and Portugal. Enormous workshops for the washing and drying of wool employed 30,000 workers – one-third of the population. The silk trade, which reached its peak during the 15th century under the Medici, was already developing by the early 13th century.

In 1252, as a sign of economic power and to facilitate commerce, Florence abandoned the silver standard in favor of a gold piece, the *florin*, which immediately became an international coin.

If the *Ordinamenti di Giustizia* of 1293 could be considered a first attempt at instituting legal controls over work, they fell far short of achieving this. The prosperity of Florence spawned a proletariat which soon clashed with the bourgeoisie of trade, and this was an occasion for new conflicts and uprisings which won little for the rioters but gave the wealthiest families the opportunity to impose their power on the city while ostensibly insuring civil peace. It was at this time that the *Medici*, who later changed the course of history, rose to prominence.

POLITICS, AVARICE AND PATRONAGE

The Medici were known in Florence even before their rise to power. They had been involved in a number of political intrigues and, on one occasion, had taken part in a revolt. The family even went into exile for a while but was able to secure its return because of its popularity with the people. Resident in Florence since the 13th century, the Medici had managed, by the beginning of the 15th century, to acquire control of a significant proportion of the city's affairs. Since they also knew how to manipulate public opinion, these capitalists, who ruled the banking network, ended up by ruling the entire city.

Cosimo the Elder (1389–1464), the son of *Giovanni di Bicci* (1360–1429), was the real founder of the Medici dynasty. His activities caused him to be imprisoned and exiled in 1433 on suspicion of fomenting discontent. A year later, he returned to Florence to assume supreme power. As a high functionary, he had sufficient personality and authority to govern, while managing to create the illusion of being a citizen like any other. Cosimo was habitually dressed as a peasant and he lived in a house which gave the outward appearance of austerity but masked a luxurious interior. He was almost as miserly in small matters as his grandson *Lorenzo* later proved to be but he lent colossal sums of money to anyone who applied to him, even to *King Edward IV* of England.

Cosimo knew better than to reclaim his debts, and thus his debtors remained under obligation to him. In this way he gained power. Despite his avarice, he was a great patron of the arts and a collector; he employed the sculptor *Donatello* as his advisor and commissioned a number of works.

A thirst for knowledge, a taste for beauty and constant restlessness were characteristics that Cosimo shared with many others of his time; he was also an astonishingly able politician who pioneered the politics of the balance of power. Florence, busy destroying itself through internal strife and always deeply preoccupied with profit, maintained no standing army. In times of necessity, the city had recourse to *condottieri*, mercenaries who would fight on its behalf for gold. Military weakness engendered diplomacy; Cosimo applied it, greatly to Florence's advantage, by basing his political calculations on the exigencies of trade. The lesson, once learned, was never to be forgotten and out of it came Florence's later security and prosperity.

Cosimo's son *Piero*, known as "the Gouty", lacked the brilliance of his father who was hailed on his death as "The Father of his Country", but he did have the wisdom to educate his son Lorenzo in the style of Cosimo the Elder. Lorenzo was 15 when his grandfather died, and 20 on the death of Piero. The new heir began badly, exhibiting a clumsiness and cruelty unexpected in one who was later to be renowned for his great sensitivity and intelligence. However, it was not long before he was able to reconcile his roles of prince and poet.

LORENZO THE MAGNIFICENT

Lorenzo dei Medici was not interested in power. He said so himself. He was, in a way, forced to take it after the *Pazzi Conspiracy* (1478). The Pazzi, long-standing allies of the Medici, had planned to install themselves in the Signoria and re-establish a liberty which (according to them) no longer existed. During the high mass of April 26, 1478, a man in their pay, *Bernardo Baroncelli*, led a group of conspirators in the assassination of Lorenzo's brother *Giuliano*. Two priests had been assigned to kill Lorenzo on the same occasion but he escaped and took refuge in the sacristy, where he washed his wounds at a fountain until his friends came to his aid. Lorenzo emerged the victor and the assassins were

Every year on St. John's day, the Florentines play the traditional game of football in livery.

hanged. The pope, who was a supporter of the Pazzi, was furious. He excommunicated Lorenzo, "that son of iniquity", and sent his troops into a holy war with Florence; this threat was beaten off, and peace was re-established.

As head of state, Lorenzo became "the Magnificent": he wanted Florence to be the model city of the new era that was to begin with him. He organized competitions, attracted artists to the city and paid them generously; curious behavior from a man who tended to count every penny! New buildings began to spring up all over the city and artists' workshops multiplied. In the ferment of new ideas, art and knowledge were transformed. The chief movement was towards science and realism. Scholars looked back to the Greeks for reference and inspiration but they were also forging ahead into the future. Florence was certainly not the only city to produce this spiritual rebirth but it was one of the most important centers of it and undoubtedly the first. Lorenzo the Magnificent made his city the artistic and intellectual capital of the world.

Lorenzo's policies were not universally appreciated and *Savonarola*, an impassioned and ascetic priest, warned the Florentines that they would pay dearly for their extravagance. In 1492, Lorenzo died and was succeeded by his son *Piero*. In 1494, *Charles VIII*, King of France, invaded Italy and his march upon Florence was seen as the confirmation of Savonarola's prophecy. Piero ignominiously fled but the Florentines refused to give in to Charles. Savonarola, whom Charles respected, managed to negotiate with him and spare the city from bloodshed. The priest now became the veritable ruler of Florence, and spent his time preaching absolute piety and condemning excesses – including those of the pope. This proved to be his undoing and, on May 23, 1498, Savonarola and two of his disciples were hanged from a cross and burned for heresy.

In spite of Piero's cowardice, the Medici family continued to exercise great influence amid a succession of wars and upheavals; exiled one day, they were acclaimed as leaders the next. They gave popes to the Church and queens to France, finally annexing the whole of Tuscany after the death of *Alessandro I*, who was assassinated by *Lorenzaccio* (1537). Florence became a duchy, proclaimed the grand duchy of Tuscany in 1569.

However, a string of degenerate Medici impoverished Florence and by the beginning of the 18th century, little more than the buildings bore witness to its past magnificence.

BIRTH OF THE ITALIAN NATION

The last of the Medici grand dukes was *Gian Gastone*, who died without issue in 1737. It had been decided some years before that he would be succeeded by *François*, Duke of Lorraine and husband of *Maria-Theresa von Hapsburg*, heiress apparent of the Austrian Empire. At the death of *Charles VI* of Austria in 1740, François left Italy for Vienna and the Austrian throne. For the next 27 years, Tuscany was ruled by a series of foreign regents. When François died in 1767, he was succeeded as Grand Duke of Tuscany by his son *Leopold*, who moved to Italy. Under Leopold's reforms, Florence once again prospered, but the French Revolution brought an end to that.

Leopold was followed by his son, *Ferdinand III*, who tried to maintain neutrality between Italy and France, but, in 1799, the French forces which had set out to conquer Europe under *Napoleon Bonaparte* entered Florence and Ferdinand was forced to flee. In 1807, Tuscany was ceded to France and Florence became the capital of the new French *département*, the Arno. From 1809 until the fall of Napoleon, *Elisa*, Napoleon's sister, held the title of Grand Duchess and resided in the city. In 1815, after the battle of Waterloo, the conquering allies restored Ferdinand to his heritage.

Ferdinand died in 1833 and was succeeded by his son *Leopold II*. In 1848 there was general political unrest in Europe, and Florence was no exception; Italy was now at war with Austria. Leopold was caught between his two conflicting loyalties and finally, in 1859, he left Tuscany. In 1861, the kingdom of Italy was proclaimed, and in 1865 the capital was transferred from Turin to Florence, where it remained until 1871 when it was transferred to Rome.

From 1871 until the present, the history of Florence has followed the history of Italy. The beginning of the 20th century saw the First World War and the rise of fascism, followed by the Second World War and the fall of Mussolini – fortunately, Florence was spared except for some bridges which were mined by the Germans. Under the Marshall Plan, Italy and Florence recovered spectacularly, but, in 1966, the city suffered a terrible disaster: the Arno, swollen by heavy rains, burst its banks. The Ponte Vecchio was almost swept away, while the Baptistry, Santa Croce, and the National Library sustained serious damage.

The Italian Renaissance

The Renaissance, the rebirth of European culture, marks a crucial period of about 100 years which we recognize today as the transition from the Middle Ages to modern times. Its origins can be traced to Tuscany in the 14th century; its high point was attained in the various city-states of Italy in the 15th century; and by the early 16th century, its influence had spread like wildfire all over Europe.

Basically, the Renaissance was a cultural revolution and a rediscovery of the glories of Classical antiquity. At the heart of this change was the concept of humanism: the study of philology, languages and ancient literature outside the constraints of religion, which had dominated European thought for so long. Medieval thought had viewed man as a miserable creature, the shameful product of original sin. Humanism annihilated this gloomy perspective, placing man at the very center of the universe as a being whose possibilities were infinite.

Men like Pico della Mirandola, Erasmus, Thomas More, Rabelais and Montaigne mocked medieval teaching methods with devastating effect, and humanist concepts quickly and permanently penetrated all the great European centers of learning, but of all its effects perhaps the most profound and symbolic was upon the plastic arts. The artist imitated nature, which he viewed as beautiful and wholesome. The naked figures in Renaissance paintings and sculptures are the fruit of divine love, no longer of bestial sin. According to the principles of humanism, the artist was now free to study his subjects in terms of anatomy, color, perspective and proportion: it was his business to imitate and glorify nature. He was treated as an equal by great princes, his work was signed for the first time with his own name and the complete artist, like Leonardo da Vinci, was revered as the ideal, universal man.

Major events

1304–74 Life of Petrarch, father of Italian humanism.

1440 Cosimo dei Medici found his Platonic Academy in Florence.

1453 Fall of Constantinople.

1462–92 Lorenzo dei Medici rules Florence; zenith of the Florentine Renaissance.

1486 Pico della Mirandola publishes "De Hominis Dignitate".

1492–1500 Expedition of Charles VIII to Naples opens Italy to French, Spanish and German influence.

1497 Leonardo da Vinci paints his "Last Supper".

1501 Michelangelo's "Pietà" is installed at St. Peter's, Rome.

1504 Michelangelo sculpts "David".

1516 Machiavelli publishes "The Prince"; Thomas More publishes "Utopia"; Erasmus publishes the "New Testament".

1527 Sack of Rome by Charles V, Holy Roman Emperor.

1541 Michelangelo's "Last Judgement".

1550 Publication of Vasari's "Lives", the first systematic history of Art.

1558 Death of Charles V.

Uffizi Gallery: "Madonna in trono" by Duccio di Buoninsegna.

FLORENCE
OR THE PERFECT UNIVERSE

Florence has often been compared to Athens, and with good reason. Though separated by an interval of 2000 years, the same phenomenon occurred in both cities: a search for an ideal image of man through art, philosophy and poetry. The Renaissance was launched when people openly began to question established theories of religion, freedom, truth, evolution and death. The seeds of this intellectual revolution had existed in Florence for many years: for example, in the art of *Arnolfo di Cambio* (*d.* 1302), of *Giotto* (1266–1337) and of *Orcagna* (1344–68). It can be seen, too, in the work of those precursors of the new art, *Brunelleschi* (1377–1446), *Alberti* (1404–72), *Michelozzi* (*d.* 1472), and the goldsmith and sculptor *Ghiberti* (1378–1455). *Donatello* (1386–1466) was the master sculptor of a Renaissance which was by then in full flower; meanwhile, *Luca della Robbia* (1400–82) was giving terra-cotta the expressive force of marble, and *Verrocchio* (1435–88) was fashioning his revolutionary equestrian statue of Colleoni in Venice. All of these artists questioned the meaning of art, by questioning its language, its forms and its purpose.

IN SEARCH OF THE TRUTH ...

We may look to the Etruscans, who lived in neighboring Etruria, for the secret of an art which, from the Middle Ages to the Renaissance, was never to cease interrogating Man and the universe. They, too, had come up against questions of life, death and immortality. They, too, influenced by the Greek tradition, had sought after the truth, or the relevation of it, in the transformation of reality. Where there is experimentation with forms, there is necessarily an attempt at reaching beyond appearances through those forms. Etruscan art, as far as we can judge, deals with everyday subjects; it is an art of revelation. Tuscan art, from *Giotto* to *Michelangelo*, was to travel in the same direction. The *Macchiaioli*, who have something in common with the French Impressionists, are much more closely related to the Etruscan tomb painters and the Florentine artists in the way they made colors vibrate in their attempt to reach reality by surpassing it. Florentine art transfigures the world while rejecting the materialistic, the fantastic and the mystic. It exalts it, poeticizes it and organizes it. Tuscany and Florence represent a kind of *Terrestrial Jerusalem* for many observers, rather than the *Città del Sole* of the great Renaissance philosopher *Thomas Campanella* (1568–1639).

... AND OF OURSELVES

It is difficult to grasp what constitutes the depth and unity of Florentine art, from its Gothic origins to its conclusion, without first understanding the city in which it developed and what it meant to all those who lived and worked there. Florence was seen as the perfect universe, rendered visible; it was the harmonious society chosen by man, the realization of all his hopes. In Florentine philosophy and literature, as in art and politics, we find a judicious mixture of the pagan and the Christian. God and the gods exist side by side, the Virgin and Venus, *St. Mark* or *St. John* and *Plato* or *Aristotle*. Rarely in the history of humanity has such a degree of fusion been reached. It is here that we can guess at the meaning of Florentine art. It is not an end but a means. It helps us to live; it is an instrument which enables man to become himself, as are suffering and joy, pleasure and love, work and rest. It is playing the everyday game of existence but exalting it. The man who looks at the churches, palaces, sculptures and paintings of Florence, knows that he is again being asked the same questions that have been asked since the time of the prehistoric cave painters, the questions of what he is and what he is to become. As always, and everywhere, the answer is doubtful. The city never ceases to incite spiritual anxiety through the work of its artists and thinkers. Architects, sculptors and painters, this tumultuous crowd among which we discover *Benvenuto Cellini* or *Masaccio, Botticelli* or *Filippino Lippi, Leonardo da Vinci* or *Raphael, Ghirlandaio* or *Michelangelo*, to name but a few. They did not come to reassure us but to interrogate us. To see Florence through their eyes is to try and find ourselves.

FLORENTINE PALACES

It was the discovery in 1414 of an architectural treatise by Vitruvius which animated Renaissance architecture. His work was a source of profound inspiration to Italian architects and served as a guide for their followers throughout Europe. The position of the architect within 15th-century society was radically transformed. The ecclesiastical authorities who continued to commission works were joined by princes, wealthy merchants and bankers. The palaces which prominent citizens of the era had built in Florence have some common characteristics: a rectangular plan with a central arcaded courtyard, the horizontal lines of the facades, usually in bossage, accentuated by deep cornices.

The *Palazzo Strozzi* (1489) is one of the most remarkable examples of this type of building. It has an entrance on each of its four sides and a vast central courtyard. Another excellent example of Florentine Renaissance architecture is the arcaded courtyard of the *Spedale degli Innocenti*, built at the beginning of the 15th century.

THE GREAT FLORENTINE MASTERS

Most of the artists from *Giotto* to *Michelangelo*, though not all belonging to the Renaissance period, played a part either in its birth or its flowering. Apart from their personalities and their private careers, they contributed to the depth and the unity of Florentine art. They were continually seeking an ideal image of man and an expression of his mysterious life force, but were anguished by his limitations. Today, we are still asking ourselves the same questions.

Angelico (*Guido* or *Guidolino di Pietro*, religious name *Fra Giovanni da Fiesole*, known as *Il Beato* and *Fra Angelico*; 1387–1455)

Born around 1387 at Vicchio di Mugello, this Florentine artist entered the Dominican order in the monastery of Fiesole around 1407. His early work seems to have been influenced by *Gentile da Fabriano* and *Masaccio. Fra Angelico* was, above all, inspired by a profound Christian faith. The freshness of his art and the sweetness and serenity which pervade both his sophisticated and his naive compositions express his mysticism. The fame of this Dominican painter was considerable. He worked chiefly in Florence and Rome where he died in 1455, and he is buried in the church of Santa Maria sopra Minerva.

Works can be seen at the *Uffizi Gallery* (p. 79); the *San Marco Museum* (p. 115); the church of *San Domenico di Fiesole* (p. 141), etc.

Botticelli (real name *Sandro di Mariano Filipepi*; 1444–1510)

Painter, draughtsman and engraver, *Botticelli* was born and died in Florence. At the age of 15, he was a pupil of *Filippo Lippi* but it is likely that he was also taught by the great sculptor *Verrocchio*. Although he is generally thought of as symbolizing Florentine painting, he was a unique artist. His work, which attempts a difficult marriage between the pagan aestheticism of his time with his own mystical and tormented ideas, expresses the artist's internal conflict, torn as he was between purity and voluptuousness. His work is characterized by the clarity of his drawing, the virtuosity of his arabesques and a uniformity of light which often gives an artificial quality to his paintings. There is something of the seductive and the enchanting in them. *Botticelli* fell under the influence of the preacher Savonarola and ended his days in misery and obscurity.

Works can be seen at the *Uffizi Gallery* (p. 79); the *Palazzo Pitti* (p. 93); the church of *Ognissanti* (refectory of the convent p. 109); the *Accademia Gallery* (p. 117); the *Spedale degli Innocenti* (p. 119).

Brunelleschi (*Filippo di Ser Brunellesco*; 1377–1446)

Among the many works we owe to *Brunelleschi*, the cupola of the Duomo is one of the greatest. Trained as a goldsmith and sculptor, *Brunelleschi* took up architecture after a visit to Rome where he studied the ancient monuments. His profoundly original style combines mathematical discipline with supreme elegance. In this, we might say that he incarnates the Renaissance ideal of harmony. His work shows him to be one the great theoreticians of perspective. He was the designer of a number of monuments, both secular and religious, in Florence.

Main works in Florence include: the *Duomo* (p. 60); the museum of the *Opera del Duomo* (p. 63); the church of *San Lorenzo* (p. 66); the *Palazzo di Parte Guelfa* (p. 92); the *Palazzo Pitti* (p. 93); the church of *Santo Spirito* (p. 102); the church of *Santa Maria Novella* (p. 110); the *Piazza Santissima Annunziata* (p. 119); the rotunda of *Santa Maria degli Angeli* (p. 119); the *Bargello Museum* (p. 126); the *Pazzi chapel and cloister* (p. 131).

Buontalenti (*Bernardo*; 1536–1608)

Renaissance architecture reached its peak under *Francesco* and *Ferdinando I dei Medici*, with the extraordinary *Bernardo Buontalenti*. He is responsible for a great many of the most important buildings in Florence. At the Palazzo Pitti (Silverware Museum), you can see some of the superb pieces which, among many others (vases, cups, alabaster tables, etc...), he designed for the Medici court. His contemporaries used to say there was something magic in his ability. He also designed clockwork figures, water displays, spectacular scenic effects, fêtes and firework displays.

Works in Florence include: the *Medici chapel* (p. 68); the *Loggia della Signoria* (p. 73); the *Sala della Tribuna* in the *Uffizi Gallery* (p. 85); the *Boboli Gardens* (p. 98); the church of *Santa Trinita* (p. 107); the *Forte di Belvedere* (p. 135).

Cellini (*Benvenuto*; 1500–71)

This strange Florentine character was an adventurer, a sculptor and a writer. An exponent of the Mannerist style of the late Renaissance, he was one of the few artists of the period who did not follow *Michelangelo*. His work shows a refinement and a mastery of relief work which undoubtedly derive from his training as a goldsmith (he made the famous saltcellar for François I of France). It also shows an equally remarkable psychological finesse which gives his sculpted portraits an unusual vivacity.

Works can be seen at the *Loggia della Signoria* (p. 73); the *Bargello Museum* (p. 126).

Cimabue (real name *Cenni di Pepi*; 1240/50–1302)

Little is known of his life, and some works have been mistakenly attributed to him by Renaissance chroniclers. *Cimabue*, who taught *Giotto*, remained faithful to the Byzantine heritage of central Italy, but his experiments with volume and color tended towards a sculptural concept that heralded the style of the painters of the 15th century.

Works can be seen at the *Baptistry* (p. 58); the *Uffizi Gallery* (p. 79); the museum of the *Opera di Santa Croce* (p. 131).

Della Francesca (*Piero*; 1410/20–92)

Piero was born in Borgo San Sepolcro, a village in the Tuscan Apennines, the son of a shoemaker. Having discovered the frescoes of *Masaccio* in Florence, he embarked on an itinerant career that took him to most of the artistic centers of northern and central Italy. From his contacts with the various painters (*Mantegna, Andrea del Castagno*) and schools (particularly the Flemish), he absorbed many ideas which he then integrated perfectly in an original style of his own. He combined the "rational" tendencies of his time with a realism of peasant origin.

Piero della Francesca's painting has little grace about it. The world he created is impassive and monumental. To this wonderfully constructed universe, touched with solemnity, the naturalistic setting adds a note of familiarity and warmth.

Works can be seen at the *Uffizi Gallery* (p. 79).

Della Robbia (*Luca; c.* 1400–82)

Luca della Robbia was born in Florence around 1400 and was the

Bargello Museum: "Pietà" by Giovanni della Robbia (detail).

head of a family of artists specializing in ceramic work. He was the first to work in terra-cotta with colored slip-decoration. It has been said that he gave terra-cotta the expressive force of marble. His nephew, *Andrea*, and Andrea's son, *Giovanni*, continued Luca's work though they never equaled it.

Works can be seen at *Giotto's Campanile* (p. 60); the *Duomo* (p. 60); the museum of the *Opera del Duomo* (p. 63); the church of *Santa Trinita* (p. 107); the *Bargello Museum* (p. 126); the *Pazzi chapel* (p. 131); the church of *San Miniato al Monte* (p. 134); the church of *Santa Maria dell'Impruneta* (p. 144). Works by *Andrea* and *Giovanni della Robbia* can also be seen at these places.

Donatello (real name *Donate di Betto Bardi*; 1386–1466)

This sculptor in marble and bronze was born and died in Florence. He is considered the greatest Tuscan sculptor of the 15th century. A friend of *Brunelleschi's*, he was the first artist to apply the rules of linear perspective to sculpture. He applied the classical rules of proportion to his works which are animated with an intense life. He had considerable influence on the painters and sculptors of the Renaissance.

Works can be seen at the *Baptistry* (p. 58); the *Duomo* (p. 60); the museum of the *Opera del Duomo* (p. 63); the church of *San Lorenzo* (p. 66); the church of *Orsanmichele* (p. 71); the *Palazzo Vecchio* (p. 74); the *Bargello Musuem* (p. 126); the church of *Santa Croce* (p. 129); the museum of the *Opera di Santa Croce* (p. 131)

Ghiberti (*Lorenzo*; 1378–1455)

A Florentine goldsmith, sculptor and architect, *Ghiberti's* bas-relief work marks the transition between the Gothic tradition of the 14th century and the Classical current of the Renaissance, the naturalistic trend being followed by artists like *Donatello*. *Ghiberti's* masterpiece is undoubtedly the celebrated east door of the Baptistry, which *Michelangelo* called the "Gate of Paradise" because of its great beauty. *Ghiberti*, here, inaugurated the technique known as *schiacciato* which, with its pressed modeling and its foreshortened treatment of the subject, gives the scenes represented an astonishing depth.

Works can be seen at the *Baptistry* (p. 58); the *Duomo* (p. 60); the church of *Orsanmichele* (p. 71); the church of *Santa Maria Novella* (p. 110); the *Bargello Museum* (p. 126).

Ghirlandaio (real name *Domenico di Tommaso Bigordi*; 1449–94)

In his birthplace, Florence, *Ghirlandaio* had a studio where his two young brothers, *David* and *Benedetto*, worked with him. The family was noted for its production of the silver garlands that Florentine girls wore in their hair. It is from this occupation that the artist's surname was derived. The brothers' early works are in the tradition of *Giotto* and the goldsmiths' art. However, *Ghirlandaio's* own work soon took on the decisive and measured style associated with the monumental fresco paintings of the period. Using an original narrative technique, *Ghirlandaio* was the first artist to transpose the biblical scenes he depicted in Florentine churches into a contemporary setting. The figures and their clothes belong to the 15th century of which *Ghirlandaio*, like the Flemish realists, gives us a faithful and detailed record.

Works can be seen at the *Palazzo Vecchio* (p. 74); the *Uffizi Gallery* (p. 79); the church of *Santa Trinita* (p. 107); the church of *Ognissanti* (and the refectory p. 109); the church of *Santa Maria Novella* (p. 110); the *Spedale degli Innocenti* (p. 119).

Giotto di Bondone (1266–1337)

Giotto was born of a peasant family in Colle di Vespignano. His artistic training was in the Byzantine tradition of painters like *Cimabue* and *Cavallini*. He was a painter, mosaicist and masterbuilder. He is best known for the three groups of frescoes which he painted in Assisi ("Life of St. Francis"), Padua and Florence, and which introduced a new kind of pictorial representation. He broke away from the Byzantine canon, and began to make use of space in a way that suggests a theater stage. His figures are animated and expressive. *Giotto's* work has the naturalism and emotional intensity typical of all Florentine art.

Works can be seen at *Giotto's Campanile* (p. 60); the *Uffizi Gallery* (p. 79); the church of *Santa Maria Novella* (p. 110); the church of *Santa Croce* (p. 129); the *Horne Museum* (p. 132).

Leonardo da Vinci (1452–1519)

Vinci is a small village in the Tuscan countryside; you can still see the house (reconstructed) in which one of the greatest geniuses of all time was born. At the age of 17, *Leonardo* was apprenticed to *Verrocchio* and then moved to the court of *Ludovico il Moro* in Milan. Later he lived in Mantua, Venice, Florence and Rome. The last years of his life were spent in France at the invitation of King François I.

Painter, architect, sculptor, engineer and scientist, *Leonardo* undertook research in every field of science and art. In this he can be said to embody the spirit of universality and the thirst for knowledge associated with the Renaissance man. His numerous works bear witness to his great genius, and his many drawings and studies show a strong feeling for movement. In painting, he preferred a pyramidal structure of composition and he developed the technique known as *sfumato*, in which the contours of the painting seem to dissolve. The inner light which bathes the figures and landscapes, the delicate modulation of values and the perfect balance of the scenes he depicts give a sublime vision of reality which reveals a world of extraordinary beauty.

Florence possesses only two of *Leonardo's* works, the "Annunciation" and the "Adoration of the Magi", both of which are in the *Uffizi Gallery* (p. 79). His immense fresco of the "Battle of Anghiari" (1503) painted for the *Salone dei Cinquecento* in the *Palazzo Vecchio* has unfortunately been lost. Only some preparatory sketches remain.

Lippi (*Fra Filippo*; 1406–69)

Lippi was born in Florence; when still very young, he entered the Carmelite monastery where, at the same time (1426), *Masaccio* and *Masolino* were painting the famous frescoes in the Brancacci chapel. The realism of this revolutionary work was to have a great influence on the young Florentine painter, to whom success came quickly. To a sense of space inherited from *Masaccio* he added his own preoccupation with light and a remarkable talent as a colorist. His painting is joyful and serene and he prefers subjects like the "Nativity of the Madonna" to dramatic ones like "Christ's Passion". At times, his Madonnas have the features of *Lucrezia Buti*. After a terrible scandal, this young nun and the artist renounced their religious vows. They had a child, *Filippino*, who in turn became an artist.

Works can be seen at the church of *San Lorenzo* (p. 66); the *Uffizi Gallery* (p. 79); the *Palazzo Pitti* (p. 93).

Lippi (*Filippino*; 1457–1504)

Not to be confused with his father, Filippo, *Filippino* was born in Prato, near Florence. From the age of 15, he worked in the studio of *Botticelli* to whom he remained close throughout his career. Filippino was also largely influenced by *Masaccio*, particularly by the frescoes in the Brancacci chapel in the church of Santa Maria del Carmine, which he finished. His taste for archeology is evident in a number of his paintings where a knowledgeable use of light gives the architectonic elements a fantastic aspect.

Immensely talented, this painter from Prato was admired by the whole contemporary Florentine school and left a legacy of works which demonstrate his sure pictorial instinct, and show that he absorbed all the artistic trends of the 15th century. The graceful charm of his work only partly conceals a nervous unrest.

Works can be seen at the *Uffizi Gallery* (p. 79); the *Santo Spirito* (p. 102); the *Santa Maria del Carmine* (p. 102); the *Santa Maria Novella* (p. 110); the *Badia* (p. 126).

Masaccio (real name *Tommaso di Giovanni*; 1401–28/29)

Despite the brevity of his life, this painter, who was born in San Giovanni Valdarno, played a very important part in the story of Florentine art. His research into space and perspective opened the way to the Renaissance, and he was one of the founders of modern painting. He studied the works of *Donatello* and *Brunelleschi* and translated their architectural and sculptural concepts into the language of the painter. *Michelangelo* was to study the frescoes of this revolutionary young prodigy. For *Masaccio*, the world he depicted had to be an extension of the real world. Thus, he tended towards a linear composition which took into account the position of the spectator in relation to the work. Such concepts, along with a naturalism often inspired by classical works, gave a human dimension even to the most sacred subjects, rendering them more familiar. Even his choice of coloring (green-violet, blue-orange) broke with tradition and contributed to the "secularization" of his art.

Masaccio's work already bears the seeds of the revolution in a form that would take place in European painting at the end of the 19th century.

Works can be seen at the *Uffizi Gallery* (p. 79); the church of *Santa Maria del Carmine* (p. 102); the church of *Santa Maria Novella* (p. 110).

Michelangelo (*Buonarroti*; 1475–1564)

Like *Leonardo da Vinci*, *Michelangelo* has transcended his century. His creative force was astounding. He was born in Caprese, a small Tuscan village, and was apprenticed to *Ghirlandaio*. He studied classical art under the protection of *Lorenzo dei Medici*. With extraordinary creative energy, his genius extended beyond sculpture and painting to architecture and poetry. He divided his time between Florence and Rome, where works commissioned by various popes were carried out (the tomb of Julius II, the Sistine chapel). Even in his paintings, it is evident that *Michelangelo* was first and foremost a sculptor. In his representation of the human body and the colossal power of his nudes which seem to throb with pent-up energy, he has given form to his dreams and also to his sorrow, anguish and anger. The forms he wrests from marble seem to carry the stigmata of his own lifelong struggle.

Works can be seen at the museum of the *Opera del Duomo* (p. 63); the *Biblioteca Laurenziana* (p. 68); the *Medici chapel* (p. 68); the *Palazzo Vecchio* (p. 74); the *Uffizi Gallery* (p. 79); the *Accademia Gallery* (p. 117); the *Bargello Museum* (p. 126); the *Casa Buonarroti* (p. 131); the church of *San Miniato al Monte* (p. 134).

Pollaiuolo (real name *Antonio di Jacopo Benci*; 1431/32–98)

Florentine painter, engraver and goldsmith, *Antonio*, together with his brother *Piero*, was head of a prosperous studio. His style of painting, typical of the 15th century which exalted man in the pagan manner, shows an extraordinary knowledge of anatomy. There is a Flemish influence in the use of color but the line has all the arabesque qualities of the Florentine school.

Antonio del Pollaiuolo showed equal skill in sculpture and

Uffizi Gallery: "Tobias and the Angel" by Botticini and Verrochio.

engraving. There is the same nervous and vibrant dynamism which gives such an unusual energy to his paintings.

Works can be seen at the *Uffizi Gallery* (p. 79); the *Bargello Museum* (p. 126); the church of *San Miniato al Monte* (p. 134).

Uccello (real name *Paolo di Dono*; 1397–1475)

Despite *Vasari's* opinion: "his compositions are far from harmonious because he thinks he can paint blue landscapes and houses in red and other colors", *Uccello* was a genius who belonged to no school and, today, he is recognized as one of the great innovators of the Renaissance. Although, like his contemporaries, he studied the problem of space, he seems to have amused himself with it, mixing several perspectives in one picture. He was a profoundly original artist who gave his imagination and poetic sense full rein, according sculptural values precedence over narrative evocation. In this, *Uccello* is a modern artist who created a language of painting detached from reality, a language which can only be understood in its own terms and which shows us not the universe itself but man's idea of it. At this early date, he was already taking liberties with form which foreshadow those implemented by the Cubists and abstract artists of the 20th century.

Works can be seen at the *Duomo* (p. 60); the *Uffizi Gallery* (p. 79); the cloisters of *Santa Maria Novella* (p. 112); the church of *San Miniato al Monte* (p. 134).

Verrocchio (real name *Andrea di Michele Cioni*; 1435–88)

Verrocchio was a sculptor, goldsmith, painter and also ornamentist, musician and organizer of sumptuous parties, a universal man such as only the Renaissance produced.

His first occupation as a goldsmith left him with a taste for clean chiseled forms. His work is characterized by its supreme elegance and its classical style. Many painters worked under him in his studio: *Leonardo da Vinci, Perugino* and *Lorenzo di Credi.*

Works can be seen at the church of *San Lorenzo* (p. 66); the church of *Orsanmichele* (p. 71); the *Palazzo Vecchio* (p. 74); the *Uffizi Gallery* (p. 79); the *Bargello Museum* (p. 126).

GENERAL INFORMATION

The house numbering system in Florence needs a few words of explanation. First of all, it may be helpful to know that, as in many cities built on a river, numbers on streets running parallel to the river grow higher as you walk in the direction the river flows. On perpendicular streets, numbers start at the river and increase as you walk away from it.

You may be disconcerted to come to a number you're looking for and find that it is not the place you wanted to go to. Shops, restaurants and other businesses generally have red numbers, whereas private houses and apartments are numbered in blue or black. This makes for a very bizarre order in the numbering of the buildings because each color follows sequentially. The "even" side of a typical street might be numbered: 2, 4, 6 red, 2 blue, 8, 10, 12 red, 4, 6, 8 blue, and so on. So always check the color of the number, and if you're not at the place you intended to come to, look down the street until you find the same number in the other color. In this guide, those numbers followed by an "r" are definitely red ...

▬ GETTING AROUND FLORENCE

Getting around the city isn't easy and when it comes to trying to park your car, parking lots are few and invariably full. However, the historic center is so small that it can be easily traversed on foot. You are advised to leave the car in your hotel garage or, if you are staying some distance away, to look for a parking space on the left bank of the Arno in the area around Forte di Belvedere (MAP I DE-4).

Buses

Apart from walking, the best way to get around in Florence is to use the buses, which run quite frequently.

Main bus lines:

N° 7, from the Stazione Centrale (MAP II A2) to Fiesole, through the Piazza San Marco;

N° 13, from the Stazione Centrale (MAP II A2) or the Duomo (MAP II C4-5) to the Piazzale Michelangelo (MAP I E5) and Viale dei Colli;

N° 17, from the Stazione Centrale (MAP II A2) and the Duomo (MAP II C4-5) to the Youth Hostel.

Don't forget to buy your ticket beforehand (either in a bar or a tobacconist's shop) and then get it stamped on the bus.

To find out more about the various bus services apply to the **Information Service** (A.T.A.F.), 57r Piazza del Duomo (tel: 21-23-01).

Car rental

If you want to tour Tuscany, you will probably need to rent a car.
Avis, 128r Borgo Ognissanti, (MAP II C1) tel: 21-36-29.
Budget, 113r Borgo Ognissanti, (MAP II C1) tel: 29-30-21.
Hertz, 33r Via M. Finiguerra, (MAP II C1) tel: 28-22-60.

Taxis

Main taxi stands:
Stazione Centrale (MAP II A2) tel: 21-72-71.
Piazza San Marco (MAP II A5) tel: 28-41-24.
Piazza della Libertà (MAP I B4-5) tel: 48-31-19.
Piazza della Repubblica (MAP II D4) tel: 29-62-30.
Taxi Radio tel: 4798.
Taxi Radio CO.TA.FI. tel: 4390.

Public parking lots

There are a few paying parking lots in the center of the city (from 8 am to 8.30 pm): 700 lire for the first hour, 1200 lire for each succeeding hour.
Piazza Brunelleschi (MAP II B5) ; Piazza dell'Indipendenza (MAP I B4) ; Piazza Ognissanti (MAP II C1) ; Piazza Pitti (MAP II F3)

Problems with your car

Automobile Club Firenze, at the head office of A.C.I., 36 Viale Amendola (tel: 27-841).

If your car breaks down, call 116 for the A.C.I. service (Automobile Club of Italy). This service is free if you have the petrol coupons booklet (see p. 10).

Car repair

Alfa-Romeo, 44 Via Ponte a Quaracchi (tel: 37-06-45).
Austin Rover, 54 Poggioli, Via Finlandia (tel: 68-84-97).
Citroën, De Cesare, 220 Via Sansovino (MAP I C1) tel: 70-45-32.
Ferrari/Mercedes, Campagnano Automobili, 148/C Via Francesco Baracca (MAP I A1) tel: 41-26-11.
Fiat, 51 Viale Belfiore (MAP I B3) tel: 47-921, and other branches.
Ford, Autofficina Ronchi, 8 Via Crimea (tel: 48-98-55).
Peugeot-Talbot, Aglietti, 294 Via Lanzi (tel: 47-62-13); Autowega, 199 Via Francesco Baracca (MAP I A1) tel: 41-55-75; Simcar, 101/C Via Pietro Toselli (MAP I B2) tel: 36-05-02.
Renault, Buratti, 43 Lungarno Ferrucci (MAP I D6) tel: 681-04-51; and in 15 Viale Corsica (MAP I A2-3) tel: 35-21-31.
Volkswagen, Porsche, Audi, Ignesti, 166 Via Pratese (tel: 37-37-41).
Volvo, 131 Via Lunga (tel: 71-57-41).

Horse-drawn carriages

If you feel like it, do not hesitate to go for a ride around the center of Florence or along the Arno but fix the price beforehand.

GUIDED TOURS OF FLORENCE

Throughout the year, daily coach tours of the city are organized. Departure at 9 am from main hotels, return at about 12.30 pm. These visits also take place in the afternoon from 2 pm to 6 pm. For more information, apply to any of the travel agencies listed below.

In April, May and June, there are guided tours of "Florentine Villas", departure every day at 2.30 pm in Piazza Santa Maria Novella (MAP II C2-3).

You can also take a half-day excursion to Pisa or a full-day excursion to Siena and San Gimignano. Further information is available from travel agencies.

Main travel agencies

Arno Travel Service, 7r Piazza Ottaviani (tel: 29-52-51).

Centro Turistico Universitario, 12r Via San Gallo (MAP I A4-5) tel: 29-65-86.

C.I.T., 57/59r Via de'Cerretani (MAP II C4) tel: 29-43-06.

Globus Travel Service, 2r Piazza Santa Trinita (MAP II D3) tel: 21-49-92.

Italturist, 8r Via Nazionale (MAP II AB3) tel: 28-34-36.

Tourist Travel Service, 2 Via Calimala (MAP II D4) tel: 28-33-48.

Chiariva, 26r Via Vacchereccia (MAP II D4) tel: 21-19-68.

Wagons-lits/Turismo c/o Gemini, 27r Via del Giglio (MAP II BC3) tel: 21-88-51.

Official tourist guides

If you require the services of an official guide, apply to their office at 9/A Viale Gramsci (tel: 247-81-88).

USING YOUR TIME WISELY

Whether you plan your visit beforehand or leave everything to chance is up to you. Following a prearranged plan can be tiresome, especially if you are rigid about it. In any case, however long you stay, you won't manage to see everything, so console yourself by remembering that Florence is a city to which everyone returns, a characteristic it shares with Venice, Rome and Paris.

Five days is a happy medium for a first visit. A long weekend is the minimum. Some people solve the time problem by rushing from the *Duomo* to the *Uffizi Gallery* in an effort not to waste a minute. We recommend taking a first, more general look at Florence as a Renaissance landscape from up on the *Piazzale Michelangelo* or nearby *San Miniato al Monte*; or else from *Fiesole*, or (even better) from *Bellosguardo*.

Some further advice: after this first look, park your car and walk. The museums, palaces, churches and convents are all within a geographically limited space with often only a 10-minute walk between them. In any case it is almost impossible to park in the town center (see the list of parking lots on p. 34). Remember that most museums close at 2 pm and all day Monday, so use these hours to visit the *Galleria dello Spedale degli Innocenti*, the monumental apartments in the *Palazzo Vecchio*, the *History of Science Museum* or the museum of the *Opera del Duomo*, all of which remain open in the afternoon.

Remember also that the museums begin to empty about midday, leaving you the last two hours to look around them in peace without being crushed

FLORENCE (I)

| 0 | 200 | 400 | 600 m |
| 0 | 200 | 400 | 600 yds |

Motorway 4.5 miles (7 km) – Siena 43.5 miles (70 km)

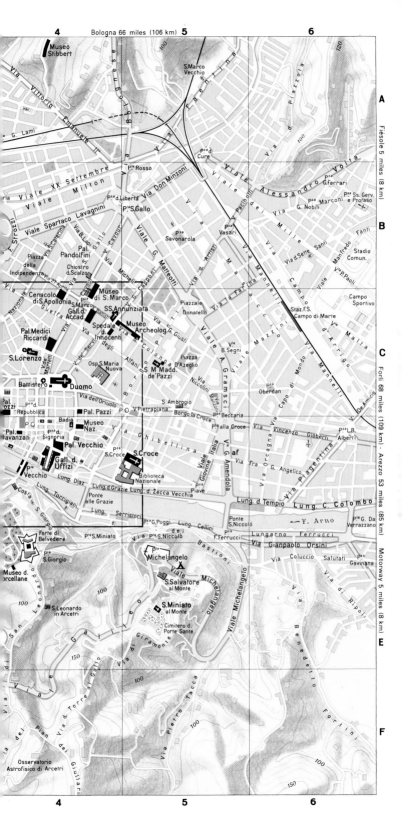

— but don't go too late because most of them will not admit visitors after 1 pm, especially the larger ones.

Leave window-shopping until late afternoon. Most shops stay open until 7.30 pm in summer and as late as 8 pm in winter. The days are long so take your time and even waste a little as you go along. Avoid culture fatigue by alternating visits to churches and museums with walks around the historic center, in the gardens or the surrounding hills.

Winter or summer, Florentine sunsets are always sublime because of the way the ochre buildings take on the rosy glow of the sky. If you are in the center, watch the sun go down from the banks of the Arno or on the Ponte Vecchio.

Two or three days in Florence

After a drive on the hills of Florence, along the *Viale dei Colli*★★ (p. 133), you will want to go straight to the heart of the city, the historic center on the banks of the Arno, which forms a vast square, the corners of which are: the church of *Santa Maria Novella*, the convent of *San Marco*, the church of *Santa Croce* and the *Pitti Palace.*

The *Duomo*★★★ (cathedral) (MAP II C4-5), the *Baptistry*★★★ and the *Piazza della Signoria*★★★ (MAP II D4), are also in the heart of the city.

Among the museums to be visited, give priority to the *Uffizi Gallery*★★★ (MAP II E4), where you should concentrate on the major works of art: early Tuscan school, *Filippo Lippi, Botticelli, Leonardo da Vinci,* Flemish school. etc... Your next visit should be to the *Galleria dell'Accademia*★★ (MAP II A5) to see the original "David" by *Michelangelo* as well as other unfinished sculptures by him.

Besides the *Duomo,* try to see the following churches: *San Lorenzo*★★★ and the *Medici chapel*★★ (sacristy) (MAP II B4); *Santa Croce*★★ (MAP II E6); *Santa Maria Novella*★★ (MAP II B2-3), and (late in the afternoon) *Orsanmichele*★ (MAP II D4).

The convent of *San Marco*★★★ (MAP II A5) should be visited because of the magnificent frescoes there by *Fra Angelico.*

You may not have sufficient time to visit the *Pitti Palace*★★★ (MAP II F3) which contains the splendid collections of the Medici (paintings from 16th, 17th, 18th centuries, and silverwork in the *Museo degli Argenti*) but, in the late afternoon, do not miss a walk through the *Boboli Gardens*★★ (MAP II F3).

If you have time left, go to the *Medici–Riccardi Palace*★★ (MAP II B4) to see the frescoes by *Gozzoli,* or go to the enchanting *Davanzati Palace*★ (MAP II D3) to understand how people lived in Florence in the Middle Ages.

There is a lot to do. Don't forget that you are on holiday! Break up this program with pauses in cafés or in some of the excellent restaurants of the city (see list on p. 46). Remember that Florentine food in itself is worth the trip.

Five days in Florence

Five days are adequate for a first visit to Florence. You can spend more time in the museums (particularly in the *Uffizi Gallery*) and add to your program the *Pitti Palace*★★★ (MAP II F3), the *Bargello Museum*★★★ (MAP II D5), the *Opera del Duomo Museum*★★ (MAP II C5), the *History of Science Museum*★ (MAP II E4), and the *Opificio delle Pietre Dure* (inlaid and mosaic work in semi-precious stones) (MAP II B5) where you can admire the products of a typically Florentine craft.

There are also the *house of Michelangelo*★ (Casa Buonarroti, MAP II D6), the refectories of *Sant'Apollonia*★ (MAP II A4-5), and of *Santo Spirito* (MAP II E2), as well as the monumental apartments of the *Palazzo Vecchio*★★ (MAP II DE4)

You can see more churches: *Santa Trinita*★ (MAP II D3), the *Badia*★ (MAP II D5), *Santissima Annunziata*★ (MAP II A6), *Santo Spirito*★★ (MAP II E2)

Santa Maria del Carmine★ (MAP II E1). Go (or go back) to *Fiesole*★★ by way of the Viale Alessandro Volta (MAP I A6) and to *San Miniato*★★★ (MAP I E5): Florence looks so beautiful seen from those nearby hills.

You should also go and see the Florentine villas or the Certosa (Carthusian monastery) of Galluzzo. You can take more time to visit the places recommended and be sure not to miss the opportunity of going to a concert or to the opera if you are in Florence at the right time. Make your stay even more enjoyable by getting to know Tuscan food better.

ACCOMMODATION

From April to October, it is very difficult to find a room in Florence if you have not reserved ahead.

To reserve before you arrive, call: **Florence Promhotels** (tel: 21-11-60 or 21-97-94) or **Toscana Hotels** (tel: 24-78-543, 544, or 545). From abroad, the code for Italy is 39, the code for Florence is 55. The area code 055 must be dialed if calling from elsewhere in Italy.

On arrival you can reserve a room by telephone or in person at: **I.T.A.**, Stazione Centrale (MAP II A2) tel: 28-28-93, or on the motorway A11 (Firenze – Mare) at the A.G.I.P. petrol station (**Area di servizio**) of Peretola (tel: 44-07-90).

The prices of hotel rooms vary widely. They range from 500,000 lire (per night) for a double room in a luxury hotel, to 30,000 lire in a simple hotel. You can calculate an average price of 80,000 lire for a double room with bath in a comfortable hotel. Half-board costs about 160,000 lire a day for two persons.

Usually taxes and service are included. To find out whether breakfast is included as well, check with the receptionist. By law, prices must be on display in the rooom.

Hotels
Luxury hotels

▲▲▲▲ **Augustus e dei Congressi**, Vicolo dell'Oro (MAP II E4) tel: 28-30-54. Near the Ponte Vecchio, pleasant rooms with balconies and view of the *Duomo* and the *Campanile*.

▲▲▲▲ **De la Ville**, 1 Piazza Antinori (MAP II C3) tel: 26-18-05. Situated among the palaces of the famous Via de'Tornabuoni. Traditional but charming.

▲▲▲▲ **Excelsior**, 3 Piazza Ognissanti (MAP II C1), tel: 26-42-01. Traditional distinguished hotel with a beautiful view over the Arno. Elegant décor. All the qualities and services offered by the hotels from the CIGA group. In summer, the terrace restaurant is open, overlooking the whole city.

▲▲▲▲ **Grand Hotel Baglioni**, 6 Piazza Unità Italiana (MAP II B3) tel: 21-84-41. Near the station. Most appreciated by people who like hotels that have history and charm. In summer, the terrace restaurant, offering the most beautiful view over Florence, is open.

▲▲▲▲ **Lungarno**, 14 Borgo San Iacopo (MAP II E3) tel: 26-42-11. As the name suggests, the Arno runs right by this hotel with the Ponte Vecchio and the historic center in the background. Good service but the rooms are small.

▲▲▲▲ **Savoy**, 7 Piazza della Repubblica (MAP II D4) tel: 28-33-16. Right in the center, a very plush hotel but a bit too noisy, particularly in summer. Avoid rooms overlooking the square because bands play there late at night.

▲▲▲▲ **Villa San Michele**, 4 Via Doccia in Fiesole, 4 miles/7 km north-east of Florence (exit from city, MAP I A6), tel: 59-451. This historical building, the facade of which is attributed to *Michelangelo*,

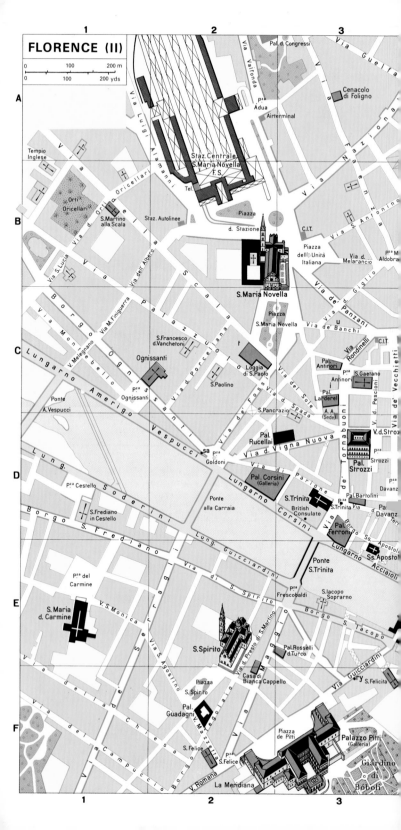

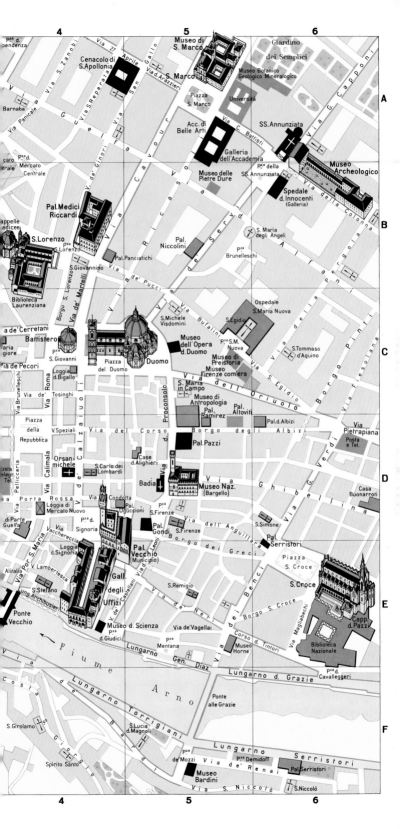

stands among cypresses, overlooking the domes of Florence. The rooms look like very good copies from *Carpaccio's* painting "The Dream of Saint Ursula" You will find polite service and elegance as well as a good selection of food and wine. Swimming pool.

First class hotels

▲▲▲ **Alba**, 22 Via della Scala (MAP II B1-C2) tel: 21-14-69. If you have forgotten your toothpaste, go to n° 16 in this street and you will find the most beautiful pharmacy in Italy.

▲▲▲ **Aprile**, 6 Via della Scala (MAP II C2) tel: 21-62-37. Close to the pleasant Piazza Santa Maria Novella. Don't miss the chance to visit the beautiful pharmacy at n° 16 of this street.

▲▲▲ **Balestri**, 7 Piazza Mentana (MAP II E5) tel: 21-47-43. On the banks of the Arno, close to *Santa Croce* and the *Uffizi Gallery*. 19th-century building.

▲▲▲ **Beacci Tornabuoni**, 3 Via de'Tornabuoni (MAP II D3) tel: 21-26-45. This comfortable hotel is in a palace in one of the most beautiful streets in the world. Lovely roof-top terrace.

▲▲▲ **Mona Lisa**, 27 Borgo Pinti (MAP II C6) tel: 247-97-51. The decoration of this old palace is superb. Ask for a room overlooking the garden.

▲▲▲ **Porta Rossa**, 19 Via Porta Rossa (MAP II D4) tel: 28-75-51. Located in one of the small streets of the center. Large bedrooms. Victorian décor.

▲▲▲ **Rapallo 999**, 7 Via Santa Caterina d'Alessandria (MAP I B4) tel: 47-24-12. Florentines often recommend this comfortable hotel on the edge of the historic center of town.

▲▲▲ **La Residenza**, 8 Via de'Tornabuoni (MAP II D3) tel: 28-41-97. The attraction of Via de'Tornabuoni and of staying in a Renaissance palace will make a stay here most enjoyable.

Very comfortable hotels

▲▲ **Bencista**, 4 Via Benedetto da Maiano in Fiesole, 4 miles/7 km north-east of Florence. tel: 59-163. Aristocratic building, antique furniture. Wonderful view over Florence.

▲▲ **Crocini**, 28 Corso Italia (MAP I C2) tel: 21-29-05. Near the theater.

▲▲ **Pitti Palace**, 2 Via Barbadori (MAP II E3) tel: 28-22-57.

▲▲ **Tirreno**, 21 Via Lupi (MAP I B4) tel: 49-06-95.

▲▲ **Villa Bonelli**, 1 Via Francesco Poeti in Fiesole, 4 miles/7 km north-east of Florence. tel: 59-513/59-89-41. The access road is not easy but you will forget this slight inconvenience once you have tried the excellent food served at the restaurant which has a panoramic view over the hills.

Simple and comfortable hotels

▲ **Adria**, 4 Piazza Frescobaldi (MAP II E3) tel: 21-50-29.

▲ **Cestelli**, Borgo Santissimi Apostoli (MAP II DE3) tel: 21-42-13.

▲ **Elisa**, Via delle Oche (MAP II C4) tel: 29-64-51.

▲ **Ottaviani**, 1 Piazza degli Ottaviani (MAP II C2) tel: 29-62-23.

▲ **Palazzo Vecchio**, 4 Via Cennini (MAP II A3) tel: 21-21-82.

Youth hostels (Ostelli della Gioventu)

Casa dello Studente, 15 Piazza dell'Indipendenza (MAP I B4) tel: 47-15-81. July and August only.

Casa di Ospitalita, 11 Viale dei Mille (MAP I B5-6) tel: 57-62-98.

Santa Monaca, Centro di Ospitalità, 6 Via Santa Monaca, tel: 26-83-38.

Villa Camerata, 2-4 Viale Augusto Righi, tel: 60-14-51.

Camping sites

Autosole, in Calenzano, tel: 88-23-91.

Italiani e stranieri, 80 Viale Michelangelo, tel: 681-19-77.

Panoramico, in Fiesole, Via Peramonda, tel: 59-90-69.

FLORENTINE FOOD

Despite its great simplicity, Florentine cuisine is among the most varied and refined of the whole Italian peninsula. It has a long history and is based on a variety of traditions. It is the fruit of a lengthy evolution beginning with the Etruscans who are thought to have invented the famous *bistecca alla fiorentina*. If we are to believe what we see on the frescoes in their tombs, they kept fine tables, making use of plates and glasses, and dined to musical accompaniment.

The Florentine culinary art we know today, however, dates back only as far as the 14th century, when a period of political stability permitted the Tuscan Renaissance culture to mature. We even have a recipe book from the first years of that century containing 57 recipes (a number of them still in use today). It gives various ways of serving pasta, grilling fish from the Arno, preparing sauces and making desserts and cakes.

In 1439, the Ecumenical Council was moved from Ferrara to Florence, and this heralded a great period in the development of Tuscan cuisine. The banquets held for *Pope Eugenio IV* by *Cosimo dei Medici*, descriptions of which fill contemporary journals, gave rise to the creation of many new dishes which have since become traditional. Some of the legends relating to their origins are worth mentioning here. It may be remembered that the Greek Orthodox Church was represented at the council. The result was that there tended to be some confusion or adaptation of languages between the Greek and the Italian. The nomenclature of Florentine cuisine had its starting point here. Thus, *vino santo* (a sweet dessert wine) has nothing saintly about it (though it is often used during mass) but gets its name from an exclamation "Ma questo è Zantho!" (from the name of the Greek island of Zanthos which produces a similar wine). Another exclamation from one of the Greek priests of the council gave the name *arista* to a roast loin of pork. "Aristos" means excellent in Greek. The famous *bistecca*, of course, derives from the English but from a later period, the 16th century, when some English travelers watched the public distribution of roast beef in the Piazza San Lorenzo.

In this brief history of Florentine cuisine, the works of Lorenzo dei Medici dedicated to this subject ("Nencia da Barberino" or "Canto de Cialdonai") are worth a mention, as is the appearance on the Florentine market of some new products, following the discovery of America: potatoes, tomatoes, white beans (it is said that *Catherine dei Medici* set out for France with a package of the precious beans), turkey and, later on, chocolate that was introduced by the Florentine merchant *Francesco Carletti*.

The invention by the Florentines of the ice-house, the league known as the *Compania del Paiolo* which gathered together all the artists of the city to promote the enjoyment of good food, and the establishment of the *buche* (restaurants set up in the cellars of noble houses) at the end of the 19th century, all give an indication of the importance given to local culinary tradition.

The pleasures of the table, of good company and good wines are an important part of Florentine life. This is an aspect of the city which you should not overlook during your stay.

The Florentine menu

The Italians, and especially the Florentines, have a reputation for eating abundantly and at their leisure. A meal consists of several courses: appetizers (*antipasti*), then the first dish (*primo piatto*) of either pasta, rice or soup; followed by the main dish (*secondo piatto*) together with vegetables (*contorni*). Next comes a sweet course followed by coffee and a liqueur which may be *grappa*, a type of brandy made from wine lees, or *amaro*, a bitter digestive liqueur. In Florence, pears are sometimes served with the cheese and, before dessert, a glass of *vino santo* may be served along with hard biscuits with almonds made in Prato, called *cantuccini*, to "help down" the main course.

The great variety of *antipasti* or starters served in Florence includes the *affettati*, which is a selection of dry-cured Italian hams (*prosciutti*) and sausages such as the *salami toscano* or the *finocchiona*, which is flavored with fennel seeds. The *crostini di fegatini* are small slices of bread spread with chicken liver paté. In summer, you can choose *prosciutto* with either melon or figs. There are also the *antipasti misti* (mixed starters) which will differ from one place to the other but always include a large selection of salads with either seafood or vegetables. A traditional summer salad is the *panzanella* made with bread crumbs, fresh onions and tomatoes, sprinkled with basil leaves and delicious Tuscan olive oil.

For a *primo*, pasta can be dressed in a hundred different ways; however, you will most frequently be presented with: *spaghetti alla carrettiera* (spaghetti with garlic and hot peppers), *penne strascicate* (short pasta with a sort of bolognese sauce) and *ravioli al burro e salvia* (ravioli with butter and sage). The *risotto* will often be cooked with mushrooms (*funghi*). Among the soups, try not only the *minestrone* but also some of the others like the *pappa al pomodoro* (bread and tomatoes) or the famous *ribollita* (with bread and various vegetables).

For the main dish, the most famous *secondo* is the *bistecca alla fiorentina*, a grilled T-bone steak sprinkled with salt, pepper and a little olive oil. Florentines are very fond of roast or grilled meat (chicken breast, rabbit, guinea-fowl, pork, sausages) served with baked beans in tomato sauce with sage: *faggioli all'uccelletto*. Florence is not the best place for fish but on Fridays try the typical *baccalà* (salt cod) either in a tomato sauce or simply with olive oil and chick peas.

Tuscan wines

Among the wide range of Italian wines which are produced all over the country from the Veneto to Sicily, a special place must be reserved for those from the hills of Tuscany. The bouquet and color seem to take on all the natural beauty of the area. Although Tuscany is not among the most important areas of production (about 1,258,000 gallons/5,719,000 litres per annum), it is notable for the quality of its wines. Eighty percent of the production is accounted for in red wines and the best known of these is *Chianti*, which comes from the region situated between Florence and Siena.

Over the centuries since 1260, the production zone has been extended to meet an ever-increasing demand. As a consequence of this demand, a redefinition of the Chianti label was decreed in 1932 and again in 1967. The Chianti Classico label is strictly confined to a small territory to the south of Florence with its main wine-growing centers in Greve, Panzano, Castellina, Radda and Gaiole. Chianti Classico is recognizable by the black rooster label on the neck.

The Chianti label covers six other regions surrounding the Chianti Classico zone: these are Montalbano, Rufina, Colli Fiorentini, Colli Senesi, Colli Aretini and Colli Pisani.

Chianti wines must have the following content in terms of grape varieties: 50–80% *Sangiovese*, 10–30% *Canailo Nero* and 10–30% *Malvasia del Chianti*.

There is also an ancient recipe known as *governo*. In November, between 5% and 10% of *mosto* (unfermented wine) is added to the new wine and this gives a particular and unexpected though pleasant flavor to the young Chianti. The Tuscans call this special tang "bites and kisses".

Chianti can be drunk young, even during the first year, but never before the end of the spring after it has been put in the cask. At that point it is a pleasant, light table wine to be drunk at a temperature of about 62°F (17°C).

The better quality *crus* mature in the cask for two or three years and are then *vecchio* (vintage). After this period they can be given a *riserva* label; such wines should be opened a few hours before serving at a temperature of 68 to 72°F (20 to 22°C).

Chianti has a light ruby-red color which tends to darken with time. The bouquet is pronounced when the wine is young but it soon takes on a slight aroma of violets or irises, a well-defined perfume, lightly impregnated with tanin, which becomes more delicate with age.

The alcohol content is never less than 11.5°. Non-vintage Chianti is usually sold in flasks of just less than ½ gallon (2 litres). Vintage Chianti is sold in ordinary wine bottles.

Although Chianti accounts for half the wine production of the province, there are other less famous wines of high quality. *Brunello di Montalcino* (Siena area) is worth mentioning. It is more full-bodied than Chianti and with a higher alcoholic content (12.5°–13°). This wine has to mature for at least three years in the cask to achieve its delicate aroma of violets. Unfortunately it is only produced in very small quantities.

Nobile di Montepulciano takes its name from the hills in the province of Siena. It is dark in color and slightly bitter in taste and should only be drunk after a minimum of two years' maturation.

The delicate white wines account for less than 20% of production. The alcohol content is never more than 12°. Among the white wines of the region are the famous *Vernaccia di San Gimignano*, which was the subject of songs by 11th-century minstrels, and the *Bianchi Vergini d'Arezzo*, light in alcohol content and slightly acidic in taste.

Restaurants

The setting and decoration of a restaurant do not matter much to the Italians. Many restaurants are run by families and the service is often informal. The Italian restaurant is more of a meeting place for friends than a gastronomic shrine. *Trattorie* are usually simpler and less expensive than restaurants. A three-course meal in a restaurant costs between 25,000 and 30,000 lire per person. A good thing for both your figure and your budget is to have only one "Florentine" meal a day, preferably in the evening. This way, you can visit museums at lunch time (they usually close at 2 pm) when they are less crowded. For a quick snack, there are many places around the *Duomo* and the *Piazza della Signoria* offering a vast selection of excellent sandwiches. If you just want to eat a dish of pasta, try the *trattorie*, especially those off the beaten track in the Oltrarno area (MAP II EF1-2-3)

In any case, if you only want a light meal, don't go to a restaurant because you will be expected to eat a full meal there.

From 40,000 to 60,000 lire.

Enoteca Pinchiorri, 87r Via Ghibellina (MAP II D5-6) tel: 24-27-77. Certainly the most sophisticated restaurant in Florence. You can enjoy eating inside this magnificent restaurant, or, in the summer, in the charming courtyard. Wines are of the best quality and the cellar stocks about 70,000 bottles. Expensive.

Lo Zodiaco, 2r Via delle Cesine (MAP I D5) tel: 67-23-19. Good fish and seafood. This elegant restaurant has a mostly Florentine clientele.

Sabatini, 9r/A Via de'Panzani (MAP II BC3) tel: 21-15-59. Florentines like this traditional and classic restaurant where both service and food are always faultless. Elegant décor. Excellent Tuscan wines.

From 30,000 to 40,000 lire

Al Campidoglio, 8r Via del Campidoglio (MAP II C3) tel: 28-77-70.

Al Lume di Candela, 23r Via della Terme (MAP II D3) tel: 35-39-74.

Cammillo, 57r Borgo San Iacopo (MAP II E3) tel: 21-24-27. Florentines, as well as foreigners, appreciate this traditional *trattoria* known for its speciality of *Trippa alla fiorentina* (tripe in the Florentine style) served with excellent Chianti.

Da noi, 46r Via Fiesolana (MAP II C6) tel: 24-29-17. Reservations are necessary because the place is very small. The cooking is original and of good quality. Marvelous pasta and meat (rabbit, lamb). Not to be missed.

Giannino in San Lorenzo, 37r Borgo San Lorenzo (MAP II BC4) tel: 21-22-06.

Oliviero, 51r Via delle Terme (MAP II D3) tel: 28-76-43.

Paoli, 12r Via dei Tavolini (MAP II D4) tel: 21-62-15).

From 20,000 to 30,000 lire

Angiolino, 36r Via di Santo Spirito (MAP II E2) tel: 29-89-76. Good food and a warm atmosphere, set in a vaulted room.

Antico Fattore, 1r Via Lambertesca (MAP II E4) tel: 26-12-15. Good traditional cooking. Pleasant setting.

Centanni, 7 Via Centanni, in Bagno a Ripoli (tel: 63-01-22). You can eat out in the garden in summer. Good food.

Latini, 6r Via Palchetti (MAP II D2) tel: 21-09-16. Reasonable prices for good food including roast meat and fish. Politicians and artists among the clientele.

La Loggia, 1r Piazzale Michelangelo (MAP I E5) tel: 28-70-32. From the terrace you will see one of the best panoramas of Florence. Good food and fair prices.

La Sostanza, 25r Via della Porcellana (MAP II C2) tel: 21-26-91. A real high spot where Florentine dishes are served in a lively atmosphere. Try to go there at least once during your stay.

La Vecchia Cucina, 1r Viale De Amicis (MAP I C6) tel: 67-21-43. Original variations on international cuisine. Elegant décor. Reservations necessary.

Osteria del Cinghiale Bianco, Borgo San Iacopo (MAP II E3) tel: 21-57-06. Recommended if you like roast boar.

Trattoria La Carabaccia, 190r Via Palazzuolo (MAP II C2) tel: 21-47-82. This is the perfect place to taste traditional Tuscan cooking, beautifully prepared by the chef. Reservations necessary.

Trattoria Omero, 11r Via Pian dei Giullari in Arcetri, a hill above Florence (tel: 22-00-53.). Florentine families go there on Sundays to enjoy an excellent *bistecca alla fiorentina*.

Tredici Gobbi, 9r Via della Porcellana (MAP II C2) tel: 29-87-69. A good and classic restaurant known for its excellent Florentine and Hungarian cuisine. Good selection of Chianti wines and beers from northern Europe.

Enoteche and mescite

Apart from the normal snack-bars, you can have a break, in between two museums, in one of the inexpensive *mescite* or *enoteche* (wine bars). They are often located in cellars and they sell all sorts of sandwiches, *prosciutto*, olives and cheeses, to eat while drinking local wines. You will find them in the center, usually in the small streets off larger squares. Here are a few addresses:

Borgioli, Piazza dell'Olio (MAP II C4).

Fratellini, Via dei Cimatori (MAP II D4)

Lo Sgranocchiatoio, 12r Via Canacci (MAP II C2), open in the evening after 8 pm. Friendly atmosphere, good selection of Italian wines, cold buffet, run by a family.

Nicolino, under the Volta dei Mercanti (MAP II D4)

Pane e vino, 48 Via Poggio Bracciolini (MAP I E6). Serves a cold buffet only, but the menu is comprehensive and there is an interesting wine list.

Cafés and ice-cream shops

Young Florentines and tourists like to meet and gather in the large cafés on the Piazza della Repubblica (orchestras play there in summer). The famous **"Rivoire"** café in Piazza della Signoria has a more traditional atmosphere, especially in the winter.

You can eat the best ice-creams at: **Vivoli**, Via Isola delle Stinche (MAP II D6) and **Perché no**, Via Tavolini (MAP II D4)

■■■ *PRACTICAL GUIDE*

Time

In winter, Italy is G.M.T. + 1 and it is G.M.T. + 2 in summer. Italy is therefore 1 hour ahead of Britain, 6 hours ahead of New York and Montreal, and 9 hours ahead of Los Angeles and Vancouver.

Opening hours

Banks are normally open Monday to Friday, from 8.30 am to 1.20 pm, and from 2.45 pm to 3.45 pm. A few exceptions:

American Service Bank, 2r Via della Vigna Nuova (MAP II D2-3) tel: 21-81-41. Open from 8.30 am to 6.30 pm, Monday to Saturday.

Cassa di Risparmio di Firenze, Agenzia 16, 14r Via degli Speziali (MAP II D4) tel: 29-67-61. Open on Saturday from 9 am to 1 pm and from 2.30 pm to 4.45 pm in addition to normal banking hours.

Credito Romagnolo, 11 Via Brunelleschi (MAP II C4) tel: 21-63-12. Open Saturday morning in addition to normal banking hours.

Museums

Florentine museums have different hours according to whether they are run by the state, the city or privately.

State-run museums are generally open from 9 am to 2 pm from Tuesday to Saturday, and from 9 am to 1 pm on Sunday and holidays. They are closed Monday. This is the case for the *Academy Gallery*, the *Palatine Gallery*, the *Pitti Palace*, the *Uffizi Gallery*, the *Bargello Museum*.

Many private or local collections are open to the public in the afternoon including Monday: *Galleria dello Spedale degli Innocenti, Bardini Museum, museum of the Opera del Duomo.*

Museum hours are given with the itineraries in this guide.

Churches usually open every day from 7.30 am to 12 noon and from 3 pm to 7 pm.

Shops: Shopping hours are generally from 9 am to 1 pm and 3.30 pm to 7.30 pm. Shops are closed on Sunday, as well as on Monday mornings in winter and Saturday afternoons in summer (June 15 – September 15). There are three pharmacies which are open 24 hours a day:

Farmacia comonale n° 13, in the Santa Maria Novella Station (MAP II AB2).

Farmacia Molteni, Via de'Calzaiuoli (MAP II CD4)

Farmacia Taverna, Piazza San Giovanni (MAP II C4)

Newspapers, periodicals, books

These are available at the Santa Maria Novella Station and at many newsstands and kiosks in the center.

For local information on shows, concerts and theaters in Florence, buy *La Nazione* or *La Città*.

Post office and telephone

The easiest way to receive mail is to have it sent to your hotel; otherwise, have it sent to the General Delivery Post Office where you can go and collect it; **Ferma Posta**, 53–55 Via Pietrapiana (MAP II D6); for information dial 160. Stamps (*francobolli*) may be purchased either at the post office or at tobacconists' shops.

The main phone service is in the Via Pellicceria (MAP II D4); for information dial 184. Remember that it's cheaper to call in the evening or at weekends. The country codes for the major English-speaking countries are:

Australia: 61	New Zealand: 64
Great Britain: 44	South Africa: 27
Ireland: 353	U.S. and Canada: 1

Traditional meeting place of the Florentines, the Piazza della Signoria is now also a tourists' stopping place.

FLORENCE, CRADLE OF THE ITALIAN LANGUAGE

Italian is a musical, cheerful-sounding language based on late Latin. However, the political division of the peninsula gave rise to different ways of speaking, each of which developed autonomously. Because of this, the Sicilian and the Neapolitan dialects are almost incomprehensible to an Italian from Piedmont or Venice.

Tuscan, on the other hand, soon became a fully developed language, pure and grammatically well-structured. Thanks to the influence of an enlightened cultural policy, between the 13th and

14th centuries Tuscan established itself as the language on which Italian literature was founded. The works of Boccaccio, Petrarch and, above all, Dante testify to this.

Between 1860 and 1870, after the unification of Italy, Tuscan became the official language of the newly-founded state. The Florentines are proud of this fact and maintain that only they speak the true Italian language.

Latin (and Greek) origins are still evident in the vocabulary. The grammar is particularly complex and foreigners will find an added difficulty in the accentuation of the words. The accent hardly ever falls on the first syllable. Usually it falls in the middle of the word, but there is no inflexible rule.

At the end of this guide you will find a useful list of commonly used words.

▬ ENTERTAINMENT

Festivals, exhibitions and special events

Although the government has tried to limit them, there are many one-day holidays in Italy, not only national ones but also religious and local festivals.

Calendar

April: At Easter, the big event is the *scoppio del carro*, literally, "the explosion of the cart". The festival dates back to the end of the 11th century when a Florentine knight brought back fragments of the Holy Sepulchre after the First Crusade. Every year on the day before Easter, the archbishop of Florence used pieces of this sacred stone to relight the holy flame which had been put out on Good Friday. Nowadays, the tradition is kept alive during mass on Easter Sunday (at 12 noon). A giant cart, the *Brindellone*, is covered with firecrackers and placed in front of the cathedral. A steel cable connects it to the high altar. During the "Gloria in Excelsis", a rocket in the shape of a dove runs along the cable and sets fire to the cart. If the flight of the *colombina* and the lighting of the firecrackers is successful, it is regarded as a good omen, especially for the harvest.

April/May: Exhibition of craft work in the *Fortezza da Basso* (MAP I B3); flower show in the Piazza della Signoria (MAP II D4). In the *Cascine Park* (MAP I B1), on Ascension day, there is a spring festival of pagan origin, the *Festa del Grillo* (cricket): parade, orchestras, picnic. Children carry crickets in brightly colored little cages.

May: Beginning of the *Maggio Musicale Fiorentino*, an international music festival which goes on until July. Reservations can be made at the theater.

June: Summer festival in Fiesole until September. On June 24, the feast day of Saint John, who is patron saint of the city, the game of *Calcio Storico Fiorentino* (historical soccer) is played in 16th-century costumes.

Originally, *Calcio* was a military game more violent than today's soccer, which, to some extent, derives from it. *Calcio* was played in the streets and squares of Florence as early as the 15th century. The streets had to be wide enough for the two teams of 27 players, each divided on three lines. The aim of the game was to send the ball over the opponent's line. The tradition is kept alive every year in June when formidable matches are played to defend the honor of the four districts of the old city center: White for Santo Spirito, Blue for Santa Croce, Green for San Giovanni and Red for Santa Maria Novella.

The rules of the game have hardly changed: the game usually takes place in the Piazza Santa Croce, and as in the past, a marvelous parade in 16th-century costumes, with drums and trumpets, precedes the game.

September: On the 7th, the *Rificolona* takes place – a procession to the sanctuary of Santissima Annunziata. Today, the *rificolona* are colored paper lanterns carried by the children. On the 28th, do not miss the bird market in Porta Romana.

September/October: Every two years, on the odd-numbered years, the Palazzo Strozzi (MAP II D3) houses the famous Antiques Biennial Show, which displays pieces (and prices) of a high level.

In the winter: The Opera season. Information on the program can be obtained from the Azienda Autonoma di Turismo, Via de'Tornabuoni (MAP II C3) tel: 21-74-59.

Florence by night

Do not expect much night life in Florence. Like other inhabitants of Italian cities with a high tourist population, the Florentines prefer to meet in a restaurant or in a private home. Sometimes they go to night clubs in the suburbs.

Some addresses:

Jackie O', 24 Via Erta Canina.

Mach 2, 4 Via Torta.

Oberon, 12r Via Erta Canina.

Space Electronic, 37 Via Palazzuolo.

Yab Yum Club, 5r Via Sassetti.

▬ SHOPPING

Florence is one of the most important centers in Europe for luxury goods and artisans' products. A tradition of craftsmanship over the centuries has given Florence a reputation for products in leather, gold and silver, wool and silk.

You will probably be shopping mostly for leather goods, lingerie, shoes, silverware, jewelry, clothes ... but you will also find interesting old books, prints, marble copies, and inlaid pictures in semi-precious stones, not to mention local wines. You will probably spend a lot of time shopping, as the shop windows are most attractive and tempting.

The main shopping area is in the center of the town along *Via de'Tornabuoni* (MAP II D3), *Via de'Calzaiuoli* (MAP II CD4), *Via della Vigna Nuova* (MAP D2-3), *Via Calimala* (MAP II D4), *Via Por Santa Maria* (MAP II E4) and *Via Roma* (MAP II C4). *Via de'Panzani* and *Via de'Cerretani*, which connect the central station to the Duomo, are also interesting but less elegant.

There is another Florence, closer to the tradition of fairs and markets from the Middle Ages and the Renaissance. Stalls outside the church of San Lorenzo (MAP II B4), for example, sell cheap clothing, handbags and all sorts of leather ware, along with equipment from American surplus stores. Prices are very reasonable but, everywhere, bargaining is expected.

Because living in Florence is expensive, visitors should be more careful than usual and should check the price and quality of goods before buying. Apparently similar articles can be sold in different places with a difference of 50% in price, but this does not mean that the price is not justified in both cases. Fashion changes fast in Italy, especially for young people, and many articles will only last one summer.

You always pay for quality, but here it is offered to you together with an unrivaled elegance of shape and line.

Antiques

The best antique shops are along *Via Maggio* (MAP II EF2) and *Via de'Fossi* (MAP II CD2).

Walk along *Via di Santo Spirito* (MAP II E2) and all the small streets of the Oltrarno between the churches of *Santa Maria del Carmine* (MAP II E1) and *Santo Spirito* (MAP II E2). Prices are high.

Jewelry and silverware

First of all, go to the *Ponte Vecchio* (MAP II E4) where the shops have kept their atmosphere from the past. Have a look at **Melli, Settepassi** and **Piccini**, who also has another shop in the *Via Por Santa Maria*. For silverware, the oldest firm established in Florence is **"T.U."**, 9 Via di Santo Spirito (MAP II E2): walk under the arch and turn right. Take the opportunity to go and have a look at the next courtyard.

Luxury stationery

This, together with prints, is one of the traditional products of Florence.

Pineider, 14 Piazza della Signoria (MAP II D4) and 76r Via de'Tornabuoni (MAP II D3)

Il Papiro, 24r Piazza del Duomo (MAP II C4)

Bottega Artigiana del Libro, 40r Lungarno Corsini (MAP II D2-3)

Ducci, 24r Lungarno Corsini (MAP II D2-3), and also posters of works of art and gadgets.

Semi-precious stones

Another Florentine speciality is *pietre dure*: inlaid and mosaic work in marble and semi-precious stones (table tops, small pictures). You might be tempted by a view of Florence. Minimum price about 200,000 lire.

G. Ugolini, 66/70r Lungarno Acciaioli (MAP II E3).

La Bottega del Mosaico, 126r Via Guicciardini (MAP II EF3)

Gilt and carved wood

Bartolozzi e Maioli, 13r Via Maggio (MAP II E2-3)

Marble

If you want to buy a life-size reproduction of a work of art, or if you want a marble bust of yourself to put on your mantelpiece at home, make a note of the following addresses:

R. Romanelli, 72r Lungarno Acciaioli (MAP II E3)

Antonio Frilli, 24/26r Via de'Fossi (MAP II CD2)

Bazanti, 46r Lungarno Corsini (MAP II D2-3)

Shoes

Shoe-making is an old Florentine traditional craft, and many shops offer their own creations for sale.

Ferragamo, 2 Via de'Tornabuoni (MAP II D3). Luxury shoes, handbags, scarves and clothes.

Mantellassi, 3r Via Rondinelli (MAP II C3) and 25r Piazza della Repubblica (MAP II D4).

Zanin, 4r Via dei Panzani (MAP II C3). Original creations at reasonable prices.

Leather goods

Gucci, 73 Via de'Tornabuoni (MAP II D3). Luggage, handbags. International reputation.

Leather goods and handbags in Florence's central market.

Giotti-Bottega Veneta, 3r Piazza Ognissanti (MAP II C1)

Saccardi, 8r Piazza Goldoni (MAP II D2)

Cellerini, 9 Via del Sole (MAP II C3)

Ottino, 60r Via de'Cerretani (MAP II C4)

Gherardini, 13 Via della Vigna Nuova (MAP II D2-3) and another shop a little farther away in Via dei Strozzi (MAP II D3)

Gloves

Ugolini, 20/22r Via de'Tornabuoni (MAP II D3) Gloves, shoes, ties.

Madova, 1r Via Guicciardini (MAP II EF3) A small shop where you will find a broad selection of high quality; reasonable prices.

Old books and prints

Libreria Antiquaria Luigi Gonelli, 14 Via Ricasoli (MAP II B5)

Stampe Artistiche Albizo degli Albizi, 22 Piazza del Duomo (MAP II C4-5)

Alinari, 46r Via della Vigna Nuova (MAP II D2-3). A famous shop selling old prints and photographs.

Unusual addresses

Bizzarri, 32r Via Condotta (MAP II D4). An old-fashioned herbalist's shop where you can find anything under the sun.

Farmacia di Santa Maria Novella, 16 Via della Scala (MAP II BC2). Creams, powders and cosmetics made according to old recipes and presented in attractive packaging. Wood paneling and antique jars.

▬ USEFUL ADDRESSES

Airline companies

Although there is no airport in Florence (Pisa serves the whole of the area), many airline companies have an office in town.

British Airways, 36r Via della Vigna Nuova (MAP II D2-3) tel: 21-86-55.

T.W.A., 2r Piazza Santa Trinita (MAP II D3) tel: 28-46-91.

Air France, 15 Via de'Tornabuoni (MAP II D3) tel: 26-32-08.

Alitalia, 10/12r Lungarno Acciaioli (MAP II E3) tel: 26-30-51.

Consulates

Great Britain, 2 Lungarno Corsini (MAP II D3) tel: 28-41-33.

United States of America, 38 Lungarno Amerigo Vespucci (MAP I C3) tel: 29-82-76.

Central railway station

Santa Maria Novella (MAP II AB2); for information tel: 27-87-85.

Tourist information

Azienda Autonoma di Turismo, 15 Via de'Tornabuoni (MAP II D3) tel: 21-74-59.

I.T.A. Office, Santa Maria Novella Station (MAP II AB2); for hotel reservations, tel: 28-28-93.

Medical emergencies

The easiest way to get medical help is to ask the receptionist of your hotel to call a doctor; otherwise call the police by dialing 113 Monday to Saturday and 47-78-91 on Sunday and holidays.

Public lavatories

Public lavatories are scarce in Italy and particularly in Florence (there are some in the Santa Maria Novella Station). Most bars and cafés in town do not have lavatories. You will find some in the museums and in the cafés on the Piazza della Repubblica.

Religious services

Most Italians are Catholic. On Sundays and on days of religious celebration, Mass is between 7 am and 12 noon. There is also a service at 6 pm in the main churches.

You will find English-speaking priests in the main churches of the town (Duomo, Santa Croce, Santa Maria Novella).

Non-Catholic houses of worship:

Italian Orthodox church, 27 Via Casentino.

Greek Orthodox church, 76 Viale Mattioli (service in Greek).

Anglican church, 15 Via Maggio (service in English).

American church, 13 Via B. Rucellai (service in English).

Lutheran church, 11 Lungarno Torregiani (service in German).

Apostolic church, 134 Via Ponte alle Mosse.

Synagogue, 4 Via Farini.

Miscellaneous

Associazione Amici della Musica, 49 Via Sirtori, tel: 60-84-20.

Chamber of Commerce, 3 Piazza dei Giudici (MAP II E4) tel: 27-951.

Centro di Firenze per la Moda Italiana (Fashion fair), 109 Via Faenza (MAP II B3) tel: 21-93-31.

Lions International Club, 8 Via Guerrazzi, tel: 57-84-49.

Rotary Club Firenze, Circolo Borghese e della Stampa, Via Ghibellina, tel: 28-49-21.

TAXI

ITINERARY A
THE PIAZZA DEL DUOMO

**The Baptistry, Giotto's campanile, The Duomo,
The Museo dell'Opera del Duomo.**

The Piazza del Duomo is one of those privileged places
that seem to give expression to the human ideal of
beauty. Yet when construction started, the ultimate design of
this beautiful church with its polychrome marble facade was
not even dreamed of. It is difficult to see more than a small
section of the building from any one spot and complicated
gymnastics are required to achieve a complete view of
Brunelleschi's cupola.

The baptistry is thought to date back to the 4th/5th
century, the marble facade and interior decoration having
been added between the 11th and 13th centuries. The
campanile was built in the 14th century. The cathedral,
which was begun in 1296, was not completed until the
mid-15th century. *Arnolfo di Cambio* was the first architect
and, upon his death, around 1302, work on the building
slowed to a stop. In 1334, *Giotto* was appointed in his place
but he occupied himself almost exclusively with the campanile, and it wasn't until 1357 that work began again in earnest
on the Duomo itself, this time on a new and more grandiose
design. The Piazza del Duomo from then on became the
center of frenetic activity. On the foundations laid by an
earlier age, architects, sculptors, painters and goldsmiths
began the construction of a new universe — that of the
Renaissance.

Today, in the shadow of the Duomo, noise and chaos
make us long for peace and solitude. All the main commercial thoroughfares open onto the Piazza del Duomo, filling
the square with crowded buses, swerving taxis and buzzing
mopeds. Florence mixes its past and its present with a
splendid Italian nonchalance that contributes greatly to its
atmosphere of vigor and vitality.

In front of Santa Maria del Fiore, better known as the Duomo.

THE BAPTISTRY★★★

(MAP II C4)

Visit: 9 am to 12.30 pm and from 3 pm to 6.30 pm.

"Mio bel San Giovanni" was how the exiled *Dante* referred to his beloved baptistry which is dedicated to St. John the Baptist (San Giovanni). Its early history is uncertain. The original church was built on the site of an earlier Roman structure and some elements are included in the present building, work on which was begun around the 5th century and continued until the 11th century. The building is octagonal in form and is an interesting example of the Roman architecture of Tuscany. The mixture of styles and techniques in no way detracts from the unity of inspiration which predominates, nor does it blemish its faultless elegance. The dazzling white of the wall surface is striped with a green marble from Prato of so deep and rich a color as to make it seem almost black. The roof is pyramidal. At the end of the 13th century, the rectangular apse or *scarsella* (pocket) was constructed. The building has three sets of magnificently decorated bronze doors on the north, south and east facades. It may become necessary to remove these celebrated doors to the museum of the Opera del Duomo for their protection.

The south door★★ was the first monument in bronze to be made in Florence. It was executed by Andrea da Pontedera, known as *Andrea Pisano* (1290–1349), and he completed it in about 1330. It has 28 compartments containing reliefs within Gothic quatrefoil frames, portraying the life of St. John the Baptist, and allegories of the theological and cardinal Virtues. In spite of the Gothic style, there is a pervasive ease and naturalness about this work, especially in the representation of the Virtues. The door was to have considerable influence on the art of the following century.

The north door★★ was made between 1403 and 1424 after a competition held in 1401 between the principal artists of the city. The rules required that the door should repeat the structure of *Andrea's* south door of three-quarters of a century before and should be divided into 28 compartments in the same way. Among the candidates were such great masters as *Jacopo della Quercia* but the final choice was between two very young artists, *Brunelleschi*, who was 24, and *Lorenzo Ghiberti*, 23. It was Ghiberti (1378–1455) who won the commission. He was a goldsmith and architect whose bas-relief work on this door and on the sarcophagus of San Zanobi in the Duomo is without equal, even in the epoch with its well-earned reputation as the golden age of sculpture.

The panels of the north door show episodes from the "Life and Passion of Christ". There are also panels showing the "Evangelists" and the "Doctors of the Church". The whole work is in the medieval tradition. The bronze figures of "St. John the Baptist Preaching", a Levite and a Pharisee on the architrave above are by *Giovanni Rustici* (1511).

Near by stands the column of *St. Zanobi* (1384), who was one of the first bishops of Florence (4th century). Many miracles were attributed to him. He is said to have raised a small boy from the dead after he had been run over by a cart. The bishop-saint was first buried outside the city walls, but his body was later brought into Florence to be buried in a style more worthy of him (his tomb is now in the Duomo). When the coffin bearers were passing by a withered elm, the tree burst suddenly into leaf.

This legend seems to symbolize a Florence dead in paganism and brought back to life by Christianity. The column by the baptistry was erected in memory of this last miracle of St. Zanobi. On the top of it, there is a bronze branch recalling the resurrection of the withered elm.

The Gate of Paradise★★★ (east door) opens onto the facade of the Duomo. The commission was again given to *Ghiberti* in 1425. The door is his greatest masterpiece and took him 25 years to complete. He had full autonomy and was at the height of his powers as an artist. *Ghiberti* divided the surface of each side of the double door into five panels, each showing a different scene from the Old Testament. The 10 panels from left to right (beginning at the top) show:

1) The Creation of Adam and Eve and Original Sin;
2) Cain and Abel;
3) The Story of Noah;
4) Abraham and the Angels and the Sacrifice of Isaac;
5) The Story of Isaac, Rebecca and Esau;
6) Joseph Sold by his Brethren;
7) Moses Receiving the Tablets of Stone on Mt. Sinai;
8) Joshua and the Fall of Jericho;
9) David and Goliath;
10) Solomon and the Queen of Sheba.

Tiny figures of prophets and sibyls alternate with portraits of contemporary artists on the cornices of the two sides. Among these is the bald-headed *Ghiberti* himself (left side, right cornice between the third and fourth panels counting from top to bottom); level with this, on the left cornice of the right side is *Bartoluccio*, his father-in-law and master. It was recently discovered that the whole surface of the doors was originally gilded.

It should be remembered that *Ghiberti* was a goldsmith before he was a sculptor, and his Baptistry doors are the work of a goldsmith. It is a work of extraordinary precision, detail and realism. Whole crowds of peasants and bourgeois are placed within a relatively small space, invading and animating it in a way similar to medieval miniatures or certain Flemish altarpieces. The art of *trompe-l'oeil* makes its debut here with astounding effect. The door-frame with flowers, fruit and animals is also by *Ghiberti*. On the architrave is a bronze group, "The Baptism of Christ" by *Andrea Sansovino* (1502), and an "Angel" by *Spinazzi* (1792).

Once you have admired the doors, look at the interior of the Baptistry.

The immensity of the interior is surprising and somewhat reminiscent of the Pantheon in Rome. It should be remembered that a building of this type was designed to hold large crowds because baptisms were only given once a year. The walls are decorated with colored marble and the floor is in mosaic (1209). The most striking feature of the interior is the cupola, a very complex structure for its period, decorated with **mosaics★**. It is divided into eight sections. The decoration is in the Byzantine tradition, like the famous mosaics of Ravenna and Venice; it was begun in the middle of the 13th century and not completed until the 14th century. The duration of the work explains the variations in style; it is easy to see how, as the work progressed, the artists liberated themselves from the aesthetic limitations of eastern iconography. In seeking other means of expression, they developed new artistic formulae.

The first mosaicists to work on the cupola were *Jacopo da Torrita* and *Apollonio Greco*; they were followed by *Gaddo Gaddi, Andrea Tafi* and others. Later came some unknown artists, one of whom came to be known as the "Maestro della Maddalena", and another the "Maestro del San Francesco Bardi". A more important artist who worked on the mosaics was *Cenni di Pepi*, better known as *Cimabue*. Beneath an image of the "Creator", there are scenes from "Genesis", the "Story of Joseph", scenes from the "Life of Christ" and, lower down, the "Life of St. John the Baptist". Above the *scarsella* (apse) is the **Last Judgement★** with a huge and terrifying figure of Christ in the center like the one in the church of Daphnis in Greece. He is surrounded by the Angels of the Resurrection, the Virgin, the Apostles and the Saints. Other scenes show "The Resurrection", "The Inferno" and "Paradise".

The baptismal fonts were made in 1371. To the right of the altar stands the tomb of the antipope, John XXIII, deposed by the Council of Constance at which he himself acknowledged the sovereignty of *Pope Martin V*. The latter nominated him Cardinal of Florence; he died in 1419. His tomb is the work of *Donatello*, assisted by *Portigiani* and *Michelozzo* (1427).

Facing the Baptistry, at the corner of Via dei Calzaiuoli, stands the **Loggia del Bigallo** (MAP II C4), a Florentine Gothic building of the 14th century. Lost or abandoned children were shown to the public here. In the chapel there is a "Virgin and Child between Two Angels" by *A. Arnoldi* (1364); the predella is by *R. Ghirlandaio* (1515).

GIOTTO'S CAMPANILE★★

Visit: winter, 9 am to 5 pm; summer, 9 am to 7 pm.

The Florence campanile stands 278 feet/84.7 m high and is surely one of the most beautiful in Italy. It was begun by *Giotto* in 1334, three years before his death, and continued by *Andrea Pisano* (the two levels with double arched windows are by him). It was completed by *Francesco Talenti* between 1350 and 1359. The attraction of this building lies chiefly in its airy gracefulness. The Florentine style of alternating different colors of marble, the windows which lighten the structure on three of the levels and the bas-relief work decorating the base, all serve to give the tower much grandeur and charm.

The 28 **bas-reliefs★** on the base (both these and the statues have been replaced by copies; the originals are now in the museum of the Opera del Duomo, see p. 63) are set within hexagonal frames and show allegorical or mythological scenes representing the **Creation of Man and the Arts and Industries★**. They are thought to have been designed by *Giotto*. The sculptures are by *Andrea Pisano* and *Luca della Robbia*. The upper register has reliefs which may have been partly the work of *Pisano* but were more probably done by his pupils and those of *Andrea Orcagna*. The figurines represent "The Planets", "The Virtues", "The Liberal Arts" and "The Sacraments". Above them are niches with statues of the prophets and sibyls.

If you have enough courage to climb the 414 steps to the top of the campanile, you will not regret it. Once you have caught your breath, you will be able to enjoy one of the most beautiful **panoramas★★** in the world.

THE DUOMO★★★

Santa Maria del Fiore (MAP II C4-5)
Visit: 7.30 am − 12 noon and 2.30 − 6 pm.

In the 10th century, the church of Santa Reparata stood on this site. It served as a cathedral for almost three hundred years. The development of the city and a corresponding increase in population persuaded the authorities to pull down the church and build a monument more worthy of Florence.

Arnolfo di Cambio (c.1240–1302), who had already been responsible for a number of the city's important buildings, was given the task of building the cathedral. *Arnolfo* had planned to build a basilica with three naves and three polygonal apses. Unfortunately, although he had designed Santa Maria del Fiore, he died before it was completed.

Giotto, who succeeded him, occupied himself chiefly with the campanile until 1337 when his death once again interrupted building work.

Francesco Talenti, the next appointee, enlarged and developed the original design considerably over the next 15 years. The cathedral was to be 508 feet/155 metres long and 295 feet/90 m wide at the transept. It was one of the largest buildings of the Christian world at that time. Only St. Peter's in Rome, built some 200 years later, could match it in sheer scale. Unfortunately, the development of building techniques was not as rapid as had been hoped: in 1380, the naves were finished and the

From almost every street in Florence you can see a narrow "slice" of Brunelleschi's dome.

vaults covered; between 1380 and 1421, the three tribunes around the octagon were completed. Between 1420 and 1434, *Brunelleschi* built his **cupola**★★ over the octagonal drum. The lantern was put in place in 1461 and the summit is at a height of 351 feet/107 m.

The construction of a cupola was a major problem. There was no lack of suggestions: an attempt was made at building an octagonal tower over the drum but the attempt failed. Engineers proved mathematically that columns in place of wooden supports would hold up the dome they would install at the summit of the building. The more ingenious of them claimed that the only real problem was the weight of the cupola and that if they built it of pumice stone from Vesuvius it would be light enough to stand.

Brunelleschi's dome. *Filippo Brunelleschi* (1377–1466) was a sculptor and goldsmith but his chief interest was architecture. If we are to believe *Vasari*, he went to Rome and spent a long time studying the ancient monuments there, taking their exact measurements to establish their proportions. In 1417, *Brunelleschi* offered to build a cupola for the Duomo of Florence. His design was ovoid in form and had double walls. The structure was to be supported by a stone chain. This balancing act smacked of the miraculous to his contemporaries. *Brunelleschi's* studies of ancient monuments had taught him that architecture could be translated into geometry. He was convinced that by mathematical means he could resolve the difficulties posed by the Florentine architects who had preceded him. According to him, the resistance of materials and dynamic pressures could be calculated in numbers. He made designs and even models of the structure in its intended setting to give an idea of how the finished work would look. The cupola has a diameter of 148 feet/45 m. The whole thing could have collapsed during the course of its construction, but *Brunelleschi* knew that the base he was building on allowed him to do without scaffolding or props. This was a source of general amazement. No such dome had risen towards the skies since Roman times. A century later, *Michelangelo* went to Rome to make the cupola of St. Peter's Cathedral with this Florentine original in mind.

There remained only the western facade. The original project by *Arnolfo* and *Talenti* was abandoned as being unsatisfactory. The part that had already been built was demolished in 1588. It was not until the end of the 19th century, between 1881 and 1888, that *Emilio de Fabris*, taking his inspiration from the 14th century, built the present facade. While not absolutely unworthy of the cathedral, it can only be said to be an academic pastiche of earlier styles. Of the bronze doors on this facade, *G. Cassioli* (1899) built the one on the right, *A. Passaglia* (1897–1903) those at the center and on the left.

The exterior of the dome is decorated with a geometric design of green, white and pink marble.

On the southern facade, behind the campanile, the doors known as the **porta dei Canonici★** are decorated in the Gothic style with sculptures by *Lorenzo di Giovanni d'Ambrogio* and *Piero di Giovanni Tedesco* (1397). Inside the apse you will find a balcony at the base of the cupola. The balcony is an unfinished work by *Baccio d'Agnolo* (1506–15).

On the north side, the small **porta della Mandorla★** was decorated under the direction of *Giovanni d'Ambrogio* between 1395 and 1408. Here the Gothic is beginning to give way to the Renaissance style, as we see from such works as the "Annunciation", a mosaic in the lunette by *Domenico* and *David Ghirlandaio* (1490), the **Assumption★** in relief by *Nanni di Banco* (1421) in the gable, and the two busts of prophets in relief on the inside of the gable (1408) which are thought to be early works of the great Tuscan sculptor *Donatello*.

The interior of the Duomo can best be described in two words: grandeur and simplicity. It is difficult for a building so large and grandiose to be at the same time so visually contained but the judicious placement of the pillars divides the space to create a feeling of uplifting harmony.

The decorations are with few exceptions, more profane than sacred. This is symptomatic of changes in the concept of art which was moving away from religious spiritualism towards humanism.

The nave. The mosaic in the ogival tympanum of the central portal is attributed to *Gaddo Gaddi* (14th century); the stained glass windows were designed by *Lorenzo Ghiberti*. *Paolo Uccello* painted the prophets which decorate the clock.

To the right of the doors is the **tomb of Bishop Antonio d'Orso★** (1321) with a statue attributed to *Tino di Camaino*. This artist had a great influence on sculpture in the 14th century, both in Tuscany and the south of Italy.

The crypt of Santa Reparata★. *Visit: 9.30 am – 12.30 pm; 2.30 – 5.30 pm; Sun 9.30 am – 12.30 pm (Free admission Sun)*. Steps lead down from the nave to the excavations of the former church of *Santa Reparata* which, itself, was built on the site of a Paleo-Christian basilica (5th century). The excavations have revealed three naves and five apses, the remains of the original floor, some fragments of decoration in stone and several tombs including that of *Filippo Brunelleschi*, discovered in 1972.

The south aisle. Here you can see a bust of Brunelleschi by his pupil *Buggiano* (1447); a statue of the prophet Isaiah by *N. di Branco*; and a bust of Giotto by *B. di Maiano* (1490). A Gothic stoup (1380) is near the pillar. On the second altar are two painted sepulchral monuments by *Bicci di Lorenzo* (15th century). Near the side door you will see a bust of Marsilio Ficini by *A. Ferrucci* (1521).

The octagonal marble rail enclosing the choir is by *Bandinelli* and *G. Bandini* (1555). The high altar, also by *Bandinelli*, is dominated by a crucifix in wood by *Benedetto da Maiano* (1497).

Access to the area beyond the choir is not usually permitted.

The cupola (height 299 feet/91 m) is decorated with a "Last Judgement" begun by *Vasari* in the last years of his life (1572–74) and finished by *Federico Zuccari*. This great cupola merited something better. The stained glass windows in the roundels were designed by *Uccello, Donatello, Andrea del Castagno* and *Ghiberti*.

Farther back, the three apses are separated by the sacristy doors decorated with bas-reliefs in bronze and, on the lunettes, terra-cotta. The latter are by *Luca della Robbia* and show the **Ascension**★ (right) and the **Resurrection**★ (left). This "Resurrection" is the first known example of slip-decorated ceramic work (1444). This was the door, leading to what was known as the new sacristy, through which Lorenzo dei Medici escaped the assassins who attacked him on April 6, 1478.

In the chapel of the central apse is the **bronze reliquary urn**★ of the first bishop of Florence, San Zanobi (*d.* 417) by *Ghiberti*. The "Pietà" of Michelangelo which once stood in the first chapel of the left apse is now in the museum of the Opera del Duomo (see below).

The north aisle. In the north aisle itself, you will see a painting on wood by *Domenico di Michelino* (1465) showing Dante with a copy of the Divine Comedy in his hand and a view of Florence in the background; the Inferno and Purgatory are to one side of him and Paradise is on the other. Two frescoes complete this exceptional group: they are equestrian portraits of two *condottieri* who fought for Florence: the first shows the Englishman **John Hawkwood**★★ (called Giovanni Acuto in Italian), painted by *Paolo Uccello* in 1436. Geometric in style, it is an experiment in the new technique of perspective, giving the impression of having been painted from a statue rather than from a live figure; the other fresco shows Niccolò Marucci da Tolentino, painted by *Andrea del Castagno* in 1456. Nearby, there is a statue of Joshua attributed in part to Donatello.

The north aisle gives access to the cupola (*visit: 8.30 am – 12.30 pm. and 2.30 – 5.30 pm. Closed Sun. Sale of tickets stops 40 mins. before closing)*. The 463 steps are arduous but climbing them will enable you to take a closer look at *Brunelleschi*'s methods of work and, at the top, you can admire the Florentine landscape from a height of 351 feet/107 m.

▬ *MUSEUM OF THE OPERA DEL DUOMO*★★
Museum of the Opera di Santa Maria del Fiore, 9 Piazza del Duomo (MAP II C5)
Visit: winter 9 am – 6 pm; summer 9 am – 8 pm; Sun 10 am – 1 pm.

The museum was opened in 1892 and contains many important works of Florentine sculpture, particularly of the 14th and 15th centuries. Most of these works were once in the Duomo or the Baptistry. As well as sculptures and bas-reliefs, there are plans and drawings relating to the Duomo and the Baptistry. There are also terra-cottas by *Andrea* and *Luca della Robbia*, sculpted fragments and a lunette with San Zanobi and angels by *A. della Robbia* and some of the original statues from the first facade of the Duomo which was never completed: **St. John the Evangelist**★ by *Donatello*; "St. Matthew" by *Ciuffagni*; **St. Luke**★★ by *Nanni di Banco*; "St. Mark" by *N. d'Arezzo*; **Virgin and Child with Saints**★ and **Santa Reparata**★ both by *Arnolfo di Cambio*. The statues of **Pope Boniface VIII**★ and of the **Virgin of the Nativity**★ are also by *A. di Cambio*. Two small rooms show material relating to *Brunelleschi* and the building of the cathedral (including the equipment used).

The octagonal chapel contains a fine collection of reliquaries from the 14th to the 18th century. On the landing is a **Pietà**★★★ by *Michelangelo*. This is one of his last works, dated around 1550 when the artist was 80 years old, and it was intended for his own tomb. He never completed it. It is a highly dramatic work in which the figures seem to be rooted in the earth and to be engaged in an internal struggle between a natural human horror of death and faith and hope in the life to come. The head of "Nicodemus" is a self-portrait of Michelangelo with his chiseled features, beard, and wearing a hood over his head. He is straining to support the dead Christ. The expression and pose are charged with emotion. Rarely has the mystery of death been treated with such a feeling of truth and grandeur. Unsatisfied with his work, the sculptor destroyed the arm and left leg of Christ. *Tiberio Calcagni* repaired the arm and finished the figure of Mary Magdalen.

On the first floor you can see the famous wooden sculpture of **Mary Magdalen**★★, by *Donatello* (it was once in the Baptistry). The 16 statues from the niches of the campanile are also here, notably the **Habbakuk**★★ and **Abraham and Isaac**★, both by *Donatello*. These two figures have such force of expression that they give the impression of being portraits of real people. The **choir stalls**★ on the walls were once above the sacristy doors of the Duomo. The one on the left is by *Luca della Robbia* and the one on the right by *Donatello*.

The next room has the original bas-reliefs which decorated the two lower registers of the campanile. The lowest register by *Andrea Pisano* (from designs by *Giotto*) contains the **Creation of Adam**★, the "Creation of Eve", the **Labors of Adam and Eve**★, **Hunting**★, **Navigation**★, etc.; the last five are by *Luca della Robbia* (1439). The plaques from the register above are by pupils of *Andrea Pisano*. At the end of the adjoining room there is a remarkable silver gilt and enamel **altar**★★ showing scenes from the life of St. John the Baptist made by 14th- and 15th-century Florentine goldsmiths.

ITINERARY B
THE SAN LORENZO DISTRICT

**Palazzo Medici-Riccardi,
the church of San Lorenzo,
the Biblioteca Laurenziana, the Medici chapel.**

San Lorenzo is only a few minutes' walk from the Duomo.
Stop on the way to visit the Palazzo Medici-Riccardi
which is a perfect example of Renaissance magnificence.
Piazza San Lorenzo brings a sudden change of atmosphere
with its bustling, colorful central market. Here you can buy
everything that Tuscan craftsmanship produces in wood,
leather or cloth at modest prices; it is also the central food
market. Here you can observe the everyday life of Florence
against the backdrop of the austere facade of Brunelleschi's
church of San Lorenzo, which has all the restrained elegance
of Renaissance architecture. Members of the famous Medici
family are buried in the chapel behind San Lorenzo which
bears their name. The tombs and much of the decoration of
the chapel are by Michelangelo, who treated the theme of
death in a spirit not far removed from Baroque pathos.

Via de'Martelli (MAP II BC4) is one of the busiest and
liveliest streets in Florence. It passes in front of the
Renaissance church of San Giovannino, built by Ammannati
in the 16th century.

━━━ *PALAZZO MEDICI-RICCARDI*★★
Via Cavour, facing San Giovannino (MAP II B4)
*Visit: 9 am – 12.30 pm and 3 – 5 pm; Sun 9 am – 12 pm. Closed Wed.
Admission free.*

This is one of the most extraordinary palaces of the Florentine Renaissance. It was built for *Cosimo the Elder* in 1444 by *Michelozzo* and was the
residence of the Medici until 1540 (in 1537, *Cosimo I* left the palace and
installed himself in the Palazzo Vecchio). In 1655, the Medici, having settled
permanently in the Palazzo Pitti (p. 93), sold their former residence to the
Riccardi family who enlarged it by building over part of the garden. It is now
the police headquarters and also houses the Biblioteca Riccardiana.

The palace, which was to influence later buildings, is a successful amalgam
of differing styles, showing the influence of *Brunelleschi* and the medieval
tradition, especially in the ground floor arcades. Once walled in, the ground
floor now has windows designed by *Michelangelo*.

The courtyard of the building is a masterpiece; the continuous colonnade which surrounds it gives it an exquisite grace and, at the same time, lightens the mass of the building above it. It is decorated with a frieze of roundels inspired by antique gems in the Medici collection. In the garden there is a statue of Judith by *Donatello*; the trees were trimmed in the shapes of animals according to Renaissance taste. The marriage of *Lorenzo dei Medici* to *Clara Orsini* was celebrated here.

The first floor is reached by a staircase on the right of the courtyard. The **chapel★** is by *Michelozzo* who also designed the ceiling and floor. The inlaid seats are probably the work of *Giuliano di Sangallo*. The "Nativity" on the altar is a copy of *Filippo Lippi's* 'Navity" which is now in Berlin. It is the work of *Pseudo Pier Francesco Fiorentino*. The **frescoes★★** on the walls of the chapel are by a then little known artist, *Benozzo di Lese*, called *Benozzo Gozzoli* (1420–98). Painted between 1459 and 1460, they show the "Adoration of the Angels" (on each side of the altar) and the "Procession of the Magi". An "oriental" world is depicted here, prompted, no doubt, by the Ecumenical Council held in Florence in 1439 in which the Church of Rome and the Byzantine Church attempted a reconciliation. The oriental garb of the figures was probably inspired by the clothes of the Arab merchants who came to buy and sell along the banks of the Arno. All the members of the Medici family are recognizable in the procession, including Piero the Gouty and Lorenzo in a magnificent white robe, riding an equally white horse and representing one of the Magi. The procession winds its way through the Tuscan countryside before a silent and wondering populace. Toward the top, in the middle of the procession, there is a self-portrait of the painter, with his name on his cap.

The next door on the right in the courtyard opens onto stairs leading to a gallery decorated by *Luca Giordano* (1670). This is in a completely different style and, in the "Apotheosis of the Medici", it attains a Baroque effervescence as seductive in its drawing and composition as in its richness of color.

The **Piazza San Lorenzo** (MAP II B4) is one of the most animated squares in the city. The small streets leading into it are crowded with people squeezing between food stalls and stands selling cheap clothing. This is the site of the central food market, and its feverish activity contrasts with the beautiful church of San Lorenzo which dominates the piazza. The statue rising above the market stalls was sculpted in 1540 by Bandinelli; it depicts Giovanni dei Medici (*Giovanni dalle Bande Nere*), mercenary and the father of Cosimo I. In the nearby Borgo San Lorenzo is the Albergo dell" Agnolo (n° 14 black) where the French essayist, Montaigne, stayed in 1580 and 1581.

▬▬ *THE CHURCH OF SAN LORENZO★★★*
(MAP II B4)

This is one of the most beautiful buildings of the early Renaissance. It was the parish church of the Medici, which explains not only why the name Lorenzo was so common in their family, but also why they took such an interest in this church. An earlier chapel was built on this site in about the 4th century, close to a cemetery which stood outside the city walls. Another sanctuary was consecrated there in 1060. In 1423, *Giovanni di Bicci*, founder of the Medici dynasty, commissioned *Brunelleschi* to build a monument worthy of his family which was then coming into power. The work took a long time, from 1425 to 1446. On the death of *Brunelleschi*, the architect *Antonio Manetti* took over. The facade was never completed. *Michelangelo* later offered to decorate it but his offer was never put into effect. *Michelangelo* did, however, decorate the library vestibule, the staircase and the New Sacristy.

The church of San Lorenzo has a three-nave basilica plan but *Brunelleschi* added a new dimension to the building by using materials of contrasting colors: bluish gray and white. To the new flexibility and clarity he brought to architecture, he added a décor inspired from ancient Greece and Rome. Function and ornament are effortlessly combined. *Brunelleschi* was an abstract artist, given by nature to reflections on the meaning of architecture, and this building could well be considered his spiritual testament. Just as, for Renaissance man, the world was becoming comprehensible and subject to reason, so for *Brunelleschi* the same reasoning must be applied to the world of art, and especially to architecture.

The nave. Under the last two arches, there are two **pulpits★** with bas-reliefs in bronze of the "Passion of Christ". They date from around 1465 and are the last works by *Donatello*, who died before finishing them; they were completed by his pupils, *Bertoldo* and *Bellano*.

Right aisle. In the second chapel you will see a **Marriage of the Virgin★** by *Rosso Fiorentino*, one of the principal exponents of Mannerism. This cannot be said to be a representative work (1523); at the end of this aisle there is a **tabernacle★** by *Desiderio da Settignano* which served as a model for other works of this type.

Right transept. The modern tomb of the Danish geologist *Niels Stenson* (1638–86) can be seen in the chapel on the right.

The choir. Three grilles in the pavement indicate the crypt where *Cosimo the Elder* is buried (*d.* 1464). On the high altar is a 16th-century crucifix by *Baccio da Montelupo*.

Left transept. A 14th-century statue of the Virgin in polychrome wood can be seen in the first chapel on the right; a painting of "Three Saints", from the school of *Ghirlandaio*, is in the second chapel.

At the end of this transept, inlaid doors give access to the **Old Sacristy★★**; one of the most beautiful works of the Renaissance, built by *Brunelleschi* (1420–29) and decorated by *Donatello* (1435–43). The *Old Sacristy* is a geometric form in its purest state, an abstraction. The tondoes in the pendentives and lunettes of the cupola depict the **Life of St. John the Baptist★** and the **Four Evangelists★** by *Donatello*. Below is a frieze of cherubs' heads also by *Donatello*. Note the **bronze panels★★** on the doors of the two small chapels which open onto the sacristy: they constitute the most important work of this great precursor of the Renaissance. The 10 scenes on each leaf show, on one side, "Discussion between the Martyrs", and, on the other, "Discussion between the Apostles and the Doctors of the Church". Above the doors are bas-reliefs in terra-cotta of the saints, also by *Donatello*. In the small chapel on the left, there is a lavabo in marble designed by *Donatello* and made by the workshop of *Verrocchio*. To the left of the entrance of the Old Sacristy is the **sarcophagus of Piero and Giovanni dei Medici★**, sons of Cosimo the Elder. It is in porphyry and bronze and was made in 1472 by *Verrocchio*. In the center, there is a marble table, under which can be seen the sarcophagus of Giovanni di Bicci and Piccarda Bueri (parents of Cosimo the Elder) by *A. Cavalcanti* (1434). Set upon the cupboard to the right of the entrance is a very realistic terra-cotta bust of **San Lorenzo★**. It has been attributed to *Donatello* but also to *Desiderio da Settignano*.

Returning to the transept, go into the Martelli chapel which borders the nave on the right. Here you will see a **monument to Donatello★** (*d.* 1466); the artist is buried in the vault below and the funerary monument dedicated to him was made in 1896 by *Guidotti* and *Romanelli*. The chapel, which houses the tomb of N. Martelli (school of Donatello), has an altarpiece with the **Annunciation★** by *Filippo Lippi* (1440) which is unusual in having two angels behind the figure of the angel Gabriel.

Left aisle. A fresco by *Bronzino* (1559) shows the martyrdom of San Lorenzo. The Cantoria beside it in polychrome marble was once attributed to *Donatello*.

The **cloister**★ can be entered by a door in this aisle. It was built in 1457 in the style of *Brunelleschi*. It can also be entered from an independent door from the exterior (n° 9 Piazza San Lorenzo). Since no city noise penetrates this enclosure, it provides a peaceful and refreshing pause. The cathedral dome is visible from here, dominating the roofs and their tangle of television aerials. A stairway leads to the Biblioteca Laurenziana.

▬▬ *BIBLIOTECA LAURENZIANA*★★
9, Piazza San Lorenzo (MAP II BC4)
Visit: 9 am – 5 pm. Closed Sun and holidays.

The Biblioteca Laurenziana is a library founded by *Cosimo the Elder* who wanted to keep all the products of human thought under one roof. It is named after *Lorenzo* who enlarged it.

Pope Clement VII, who was a Medici, wanted to have the library decorated in a more worthy manner and, in 1523, he asked *Michelangelo* to design the staircase and vestibule. The whole complex, which was realized in 1599 by *Ammannati*, to *Michelangelo's* design, has a Baroque feeling which gives a foretaste of the style of the next generation. *Ammannati*, sculptor and architect, designed the library's great reading room. The wooden ceiling, desks and chairs were also designed by *Michelangelo*.

Among the treasures of this prestigious library are 4th- to 5th-century manuscripts of Virgil, a 6th-century Syriac Bible, the works of Horace annotated by *Petrarch*, signed writings by *Leonardo da Vinci* and letters of *Napoleon*, etc. Exhibitions are also held in the library.

▬▬ *THE MEDICI CHAPEL*★★
Piazza Madonna degli Aldobrandini, behind the church of San Lorenzo. (MAP II B4)
Visit: 9 am – 2 pm; Sun 9 am – 1 pm. Closed Mon.

The vast crypt contains the tomb slabs of numerous members of the Medici family. A staircase leads to the first floor and the **chapel of the Princes**★. This chapel was begun in 1604 by the architect *M. Nigetti* on a plan by *Don Giovanni dei Medici*, illegitimate son of Cosimo I.

It is a large domed octagon, Neo-Classical in style, with walls covered in dark colored marble and semi-precious stones. The cupola, which was to have been inlaid with lapis lazuli, was painted with frescoes by *Pietro Benvenuti* (1828). The altar in *pietre dure*, the mosaic marble floor, the sarcophagi of the Grand Dukes in Egyptian granite, green jasper from Corsica and oriental granite combine to make a decor which is funereal, grand and impressive. The tombs of Cosimo II and Ferdinand I are surmounted by gilded bronze statues by *Ferdinando Tacca*.

Behind the altar in the Capelle delle Reliquie e del Tesoro, there are some fine rock crystal vases, reliquaries and goldsmiths" work of the 17th and 18th centuries.

A corridor leads from the left of the entrance of the New Sacristy, so-called because, architecturally, it balances the Old Sacristy on the other side of the transept (though it no longer communicates with the transept). The New Sacristy was built by *Michelangelo* a century after the old one of *Brunelleschi* and contains the **Medici tombs**★★ by the same artist. Unlike the Old Sacristy, which is severe and geometric, the New Sacristy is lyrical and magnificent in its beauty, and *Michelangelo* has treated the theme of death in a Baroque, theatrical manner. He began work on it in 1520 but, angered by political strife, he left Florence for good without finishing it. His work was completed by *Montorsoli* and *Triboli*, his pupils.

The **tomb of Lorenzo II**★, Duke of Urbino (*d.* 1519) who was the grandson of *Lorenzo il Magnifico*, can be seen on the left. The duke is shown in a pensive attitude and the statue is commonly known as The Thinker. This was no doubt the inspiration for Rodin's (French sculptor) famous piece of the same name. On the sarcophagus are two allegorical figures; Dusk and Dawn. Opposite stands the **tomb of Giuliano★**, Duke of Nemours (*d.* 1515), son of Lorenzo the Magnificent, showing the young man in his armour. At his feet are the two allegorical figures of "Night" and "Day". "Day" is incomplete. **Night★** is represented by a sleeping woman in a languid and elegant pose. The figure is very sensual, though the limpness of the flesh suggests an imminent decadence. The feeling expressed by this monumental group is one of despair. Time is dragging man inexorably towards the abyss of death. The triumph of Death is all the more forcefully emphasized here because the two princes buried in these tombs died very young. Michelangelo is posing a question on the nature of death. For an answer we must look at the tombs of Giuliano and Lorenzo which are together in the sacristy. Here the only decoration is a **Virgin and Child★** by *Michelangelo* who, though he did not finish the tombs, completed this statue; it is a hymn to hope and an act of faith in the Resurrection. On either side, there are statues of St. Cosmos (by *Montorsoli*) and St. Damien (by *Raffaello da Montelupo*). Some drawings by Michelangelo and his school can be seen in the apse.

Work carried out in 1975 in a basement chamber of the New Sacristy revealed a previously undiscovered underground passage. The walls and ceiling are decorated with drawings attributed to *Michelangelo* (visits in small groups; inquire at the entrance). The artist, who had to divide his time between the various building works entrusted to him in Florence and Rome, and was disturbed by the political turmoil in the city of the Medici, was not able to work with any regularity. It is probable that the 50 or so sketches found in San Lorenzo, one of which is a head of Christ, form part of a project as yet unidentified. Barely a year goes by without the discovery of preliminary sketches or even finished works easily attributable to him in the places where he worked.

ITINERARY C
THE PIAZZA DELLA SIGNORIA

Via de'Calzaiuoli, Orsanmichele,
Piazza della Signoria,
Palazzo Vecchio.

If stones could speak, the group of beautiful buildings which form the Piazza della Signoria could recount much of the history of Florence and not just stories of Renaissance elegance; the austere, feudal Palazzo Vecchio is a reminder of an age of plot and counter-plot and years of vicious struggle between rival factions.

Today, the tourists who visit the square can enjoy the more peaceful events which now take place in front of the sensual nymphs of Giambologna and Buontalenti. In fine weather, the restaurants put out their tables and multi-colored umbrellas, and the pigeons gather round to beg for a scrap of pizza.

▬▬ VIA DE'CALZAIUOLI
(MAP II CD4)

This street connects the Piazza del Duomo with Piazza della Signoria. It was widened in 1841 according to a plan by *G. del Rosso*. Artisans" workshops have given place to cafés and shops selling artisans' wares which are now made in neighborhoods away from the city center. There are also large and very elegant fashion shops.

Coming from the Piazza del Duomo you will pass the 14th-century Gothic **church of San Carlo dei Lombardi** on the left, and the **church of Orsanmichele.**

▬▬ ORSANMICHELE★
(MAP II D4)

This square, two-story building occupies the site of a Carolingian monastery, San Michele ad hortum, from which it inherited the name. It has played its part in both the civil and religious history of Florence.

Loggia della Signoria: the "Rape of the Sabine Women" by Giambologna.

In 1290, *Arnolfo di Cambio* built a grain market on this site, designed to serve the city in case of famine or siege. The building was almost completely destroyed by fire and a new, bigger loggia was begun in 1337 by *Talenti*.

An image of the Madonna decorates one of the pillars; it was said to work miracles. When the people of Florence put the tyrant, *Gautier de Brienne*, to flight on St. Anne's day in 1349, they attributed their success to this Madonna.

The loggia of the grain market, where the crowd gathered to give thanks in prayer, was made into a sanctuary. In 1380, the arcades were walled in by *Simone Talenti* who provided a glass roof to light the interior. The recesses in the pillars each hold a patron saint of one of the guilds of the city (7 major guilds and 14 minor guilds).

Beginning on the east side in Via de'Calzaiuoli, the patron saints are as follows: **St. John the Baptist★** by *Ghiberti* (1414–16) for the *Calimala* or importers and finishers of foreign cloth; **St. Thomas★** by *Verrocchio* (c. 1466–83) for the merchants' tribunal; and "St. Luke" by *Giambologna* (1601) for the judges and notaries.

Continue around to the north side and the Via Orsanmichele to see: "St. Peter", attributed to *Donatello* (1408–13) for the butchers; "St. Philip" by *Nanni di Banco* (1411) for the tanners; **Four Crowned Saints★** (*i quatro coronati*), also by *Nanni di Banco* (1413) for the masons and carpenters; and a copy of **St. George★** by *Donatello* (c. 1417), for the armourers. The original is now in the Bargello Museum.

You will now arrive in the Via dell'Arte della Lana on the west side, which shows: "St. Matthew" by *Ghiberti* (1419–23) for the bankers; **St. Stephen★**, also by *Ghiberti* (1425–29) for the wool guild; and "St. Eligius" by *Nanni di Banco* (c. 1410–11) for the blacksmiths.

Finally, on the south side, in the Via dei Lamberti, the following works are displayed: **St. Mark★** by *Donatello* (1411–13) for the linen weavers and drapers; a "St. James the Great" attributed to *Niccolò di Piero Lamberti*, for the furriers and leather workers; a "Madonna della Rosa" attributed to *Piero Tedesco* (1399) for the doctors and pharmacists; and, lastly, "St. John the Evangelist" by *Baccio da Montelupo* (1515) for the silkweavers and goldsmiths. A terra-cotta roundel, either glazed or painted and showing the coat of arms of the guild in question, is placed above each patron saint. These roundels are the work of *Luca della Robbia* and members of his workshop.

The interior of Orsanmichele has two naves. In the nave on the right is an elegant Gothic **ciborium★** by *Andrea Orcagna* (1349–59). The tabernacle in marble encrusted with mosaics in gold and lapis lazuli is decorated with reliefs and enamel plaques. It originally held a miraculous image of the Virgin that was destroyed by fire. The present painting is attributed to *Bernardo Daddi* and known as the "Madonna delle Grazie" (1366). On the other altar is a marble group of "The Virgin and Child and St. Anne" by *F. Sangallo* (1526). The Florentines had a particular reverence for the Virgin and St. Anne. Traces of 14th-century frescoes are visible on the vaults and pillars.

The Palazzo dell'Arte della Lana

This 14th-century palace, which was once the seat of the powerful Wool Guild, was completely restored in 1905 by the Dante Alighieri Society which now has its headquarters there. (Apply to the custodian for permission to visit the inside.) It is connected by a bridge to the first floor of the church of Orsanmichele.

Take the bridge to visit the two upper **salons★** of Orsanmichele which are sometimes used for art exhibitions. At one corner of the palazzo, on the Via Calimala side, is the Gothic tabernacle of Santa Maria della Tromba (14th century) containing the "Coronation of the Virgin" by *Jacopo del Casentino*. It was placed there in 1895 after the demolition of the old market.

▬▬ *PIAZZA DELLA SIGNORIA★★★*
(MAP II D4)

This square, dating in its present form from the 13th and 14th centuries, is the true heart of the city. It was the scene of many important events in Florentine history: a place for popular assembly, a center for revolution, a background for torture and for sumptuous celebrations. The square is vast and its monumental buildings form one of the most famous architectural complexes in Italy, or even in the world. It is dominated by the majestic Palazzo Vecchio flanked by the elegant arcades of the Loggia della Signoria.

The **Loggia della Signoria★** is also referred to as the Loggia d'Orcagna after the architect to whom it was first attributed, or as the Loggia dei Lanzi because of the German lancers posted there to guard *Cosimo I*. It is the work of *Benci di Cione* and *Simone Talenti* (1376–82). Many of the Signoria's important ceremonies took place here. The loggia contains a number of interesting statues which, together with the various other monuments in the square, make it a veritable open-air museum.

Standing back to the left of the Palazzo Vecchio are the **Tribunale di Mercanzia** (14th century; n° 10) and the **Palazzo Uguccioni** (n° 7) in front of which is the equestrian statue of Cosimo I, by *Giambologna* (1594) and also the immense Fonte di Piazza, also known as "Il Nettuno". This fountain was made by *B. Ammannati* between 1563 and 1575 for the marriage celebrations of *Francesco dei Medici*, son of Cosimo I and *Joanna*, the daughter of the Emperor of Austria. It was erected in the square where Savonarola was executed in the hope of discouraging pilgrims and of wiping out the memory of the man who had preached in favor of a more severe religion and a republican regime. The statue of Neptune is not particularly good. It is said that Michelangelo never failed to remark when passing it: "Ammannato, Ammannato, che bel marmo hai rovinato!" (what a beautiful piece of marble you've ruined). The Florentines derisively call it "il Biancone" (big white thing). However, the nymphs and fauns around the base of the fountain, by *Ammannati, Giambologna* and assistants, have a pleasing sensual freshness. With them, nudity, free from the associations of the sins of the flesh, for the first time made its appearance in the streets of the city. Savonarola nevertheless hasn't been eliminated entirely; a plaque marks the spot where he was burned.

In front of the Palazzo Vecchio stand the Marzocco, a copy of *Donatello's* Florentine lion; David, a copy of *Michelangelo's* statue, the original of which is in the Accademia Gallery; and a not very successful work by *Baccio Bandinelli* representing Hercules Killing Cacus (1533).

Beneath the loggia is a statue of **Perseus★** by *Benvenuto Cellini*, with which this great Florentine artist proved, despite his detractors, that he could do as well as *Donatello* and *Michelangelo*. The bas-relief on the base of Perseus shows the freeing of Andromeda (the original is in the Bargello).

A group by *Giambologna*, called the **Rape of the Sabine Women★** (1582), is on the right. Writers in the 16th century praised this work for the spiral movement which enlivens the composition. The statue of 'Hercules and the Centaur' is surrounded by Roman statues of women.

▬ *PALAZZO VECCHIO*★★

or Palazzo della Signoria (MAP II DE4)
Visit: 9 am to 7 pm; Sun 9 am to 1 pm. Closed Sat.

In the 13th century, this part of the town, which covered the site of the ancient Roman theater, was occupied by houses belonging to a powerful Ghibelline family, the *Uberti*. The political factions disputed the area until the *Guelphs*, having beaten the *Ghibellines*, destroyed the whole of it as a symbolic act. It was here, where nothing but a few ruins were left, that the new rulers of Florence decided to build the Palazzo della Signoria to match their newly increased power. *Arnolfo di Cambio* was given the task of designing the building. The state of the terrain and the remaining foundations of ancient buildings obliged the architect to give the palace an unusual asymmetrical form. This has the effect of attenuating the austerity of the design. Building began in 1299 and the first phase continued until 1314. The palace is built along the lines of a fortress and opens onto a square interior courtyard. It is surmounted by a tower, 310 feet/94 m high, known as the **Torre d'Arnolfo**★; its battlemented gallery and crenellations near the summit give the palace a feeling of great height and grandeur. The building was enlarged at various times over the years, particularly in the 16th century by *Buontalenti* and *Vasari* for Cosimo I. However, the additions made to the rear of the building did nothing to soften the stark feudal aspect of these walls, which were the background to many violent events in the city's history.

The Pazzi conspirators who killed Giuliano and almost killed Lorenzo dei Medici were hanged from these narrow windows (April 1478).

The palace was the residence of Cosimo I from 1540 to 1559. When he moved into the new Palazzo Pitti in 1560 the Palazzo della Signoria became known as the Palazzo Vecchio, the old palace. At the time of Savonarola, it was the seat of the ephemeral Florentine Republic. The Chamber of Deputies of the kingdom of Italy met there between 1865 and 1871. In 1872, the palace became the Florence town hall.

The main entrance opens onto the **Michelozzi courtyard**★ (1470; *admission free*) with a beautiful shady portico that adds to the coolness and shade provided by the high walls of the palace. In the center of the courtyard is a porphyry fountain crowned by the bronze statue by *Verrocchio* (1476) of a winged cherub clutching a fish, a copy of the one now inside the palace. Two great staircases lead to what are known as the Monumental Apartments.

The **Salone dei Cinquecento**★ is the great room where the Consiglio della Repubblica, or Council, met in Savonarola's time. It was designed by *Simone del Pollaiuolo*, known as *Il Cronaca*, in 1495. After the fall of the Republic, the Salone dei Cinquecento was used for receptions, balls and city festivities and was decorated by *Vasari* and the workshop of *Michelangelo* (1555–72). The frescoes show episodes in the history of Florence and are of more interest from a historical than an artistic point of view. The tapestries show the life of St. John the Baptist (1651). At the end of the room is the raised area from which the grand dukes used to give audiences. Around it are recesses with statues of the Medici, many of which are by *Bandinelli*. In a niche on the opposite wall stands *Michelangelo's* **Victory**★, designed by the artist for the tomb of Julius II.

A door leads to the **Studiolo di Francesco I**★ designed by *Vasari*. The prince's study shows his taste for beautiful things and his curiosity about the new discoveries of his day. The study contains, among other things, a bronze by *Giambologna* and portraits of Francesco's parents, Cosimo I and Eleonora of Toledo by *Bronzino*.

Next to the Salone dei Cinquecento is the **Apartment of Leo X,** in use as a municipal office and not normally open to the public. The rooms of this first Medici pope were decorated by *Vasari* with frescoes showing episodes in the family's history. Also note the beautiful fireplace. The chapel of

The Palazzo Vecchio dominated by the highest tower in the city. Seen from the Boboli Gardens.

Clement VII, the second Medici pope, has a beautiful floor and numerous paintings by *Vasari* and his workshop. Like most of the paintings in the palace, they have little artistic merit but are of interest historically, especially for their views of the city.

Second floor

The **Sala dei Gigli★** was designed by *Benedetto da Maiano*. The door frame is surmounted by a statue of St. John the Baptist with four cherubs by *B. da Maiano*. The ceiling is by *Giuliano da Maiano*. At the end of the room, the fresco by *Domenico Ghirlandaio* and his workshop shows scenes from Roman history and the beginnings of Christianity (1481).

To the right, the **Guardaroba** has cupboards decorated with maps (16th century). These 53 maps painted between 1563 and 1584 by *Ignazio Danti* and *Stefano Buonsignori* are of great historical interest, especially those relating to navigation.

Through the door on the left of *Ghirlandaio's* fresco in the Sala dei Gigli is the **Cancelleria.** Here you will find *Verrocchio's* original **Winged Cherub Clutching a Fish★**, the copy of which is on the fountain in the courtyard.

The **Sala dell'Udienza,** built by *Benedetto da Maiano* in 1480, has a carved and gilded ceiling by *Giuliano da Maiano*. The frescoes are by the Mannerist painter *Francesco Salviati* (1550). The doors leading into this room from the Sala dei Gigli are decorated with marquetry portraits of Dante and Petrarch by the *Da Maiano* brothers (1481). The marble portal showing an allegory of Justice is by the same artists. The bronze group **Judith and Holophernes★** by *Donatello* was placed out in front of the Palazzo Vecchio in 1495 to symbolize the freeing of Florence from the tyranny of the Medici.

The next room is the Capella della Signoria, painted by *Ghirlandaio*, which gives access to the **Apartments of Eleonora di Toledo** (wife of Cosimo I), decorated by *Vasari*. They consist of the Camera di Gualdrada (named after a young local heroine of the 13th century who refused the kiss of Emperor Otto IV), the Camera di Penelope, the Camera di Ester, which was the dining room (note the 15th-century marble lavabo and the tapestries), the Camera delle Sabine, and a chapel painted by *Bronzino*.

A gallery above the Salone dei Cinquecento leads to the **Apartment of the Elements,** built by *G.B. del Tasso* in 1540 for Duke Cosimo I. The decoration is by *Vasari*; the apartment is named after the paintings of the Four Elements which are in the first room. The five rooms, two vestibules, and a covered terrace named after Saturn contain antique furniture and tapestries.

The **Apartments of Maria Salviati,** Cosimo I's mother, are on the entresol. The *Loeser collection* is housed here. The collection has paintings from the Tuscan school of the 14th to the 16th centuries and some foreign works.

━━ *GALLERIA D'ARTE MODERNA "ALBERTO DELLA RAGIONE"*
5 Piazza della Signoria.
Visit: 9 am to 2 pm; Sun 9 am to 1 pm. Closed Mon.

This gallery has a good collection of contemporary works by great Italian artists (*De Chirico, Morandi, De Pisis, Guttuso, Manzù,* etc.)

The **Piazzale degli Uffizi** begins between the Palazzo Vecchio and the Loggia della Signoria. It is long and narrow and ends at the banks of the Arno with a good **view★** of the Ponte Vecchio and the hill of San Miniato. It is enclosed by the vast building of the **Uffizi Palace,** which houses both the famous gallery and the State Archives which contain all the documents relating to the history of Florence and Tuscany from its origins up to the present day (the Archives can be reached through one of the last doors in the left-hand portico). There is talk of moving the Archives to a new location so that the Uffizi Gallery can be enlarged to put its rich collection of Flemish paintings on show.

ITINERARY D
THE UFFIZI GALLERY

A number of times each day, the Medici used the private corridor which passed along an upper floor of the Ponte Vecchio connecting the Palazzo Pitti, their residence, to the Palazzo Vecchio, the seat of the government. To make the walk more pleasant, they filled the part of the corridor that passed above the Uffizi (offices) with paintings and other works of art from their collection. The first art gallery was born.

The **Palazzo degli Uffizi** (MAP II E4) was built by *Cosimo I* so that all the functionaries serving him could work in the same office building. In this way, the State's power was concentrated in one place. *Vasari* was put in charge of the construction which took 20 years, lasting from 1560 to 1580.

Vasari designed a vast palace centered around a courtyard (*Piazzale degli Uffizi*), which took up the space between the Palazzo della Signoria and the river. To do this, the architect was forced to sacrifice part of the old church of San Piero Scheraggio (11th century; what remains can be seen at the corner of Via della Ninna and in the vestibule of the Uffizi Gallery) which had already been cut into for the building of the Signoria. The courtyard is enclosed on three sides by a continuous portico in which the offices are connected directly with one another and with the exterior, facilitating the flow of traffic and making rapid communication easy.

Today there are no office workers passing under the portico. Their place has been taken by stalls selling reproductions and cut-price art books alongside leatherwork and other goods which are not always made in Florence.

▬▬ THE UFFIZI GALLERY★★★

Entrance at n° 6 Piazzale degli Uffizi under the portico on the left coming from the Palazzo Vecchio, between the statues of Cosimo the Elder and Lorenzo the Magnificent.

Visit: 9 am to 2 pm; Sun 9 am to 1 pm. Closed Mon. Bar and toilets at the end of the west corridor after room 45.

Uffizi Gallery: "Bacchus" by Caravaggio.

The basic collections were enlarged by the dukes of Lorraine, successors of the Medici. Today the Uffizi is the richest gallery in the world as regards Italian art in general and Florentine art in particular.

About this collection

Tuscan and Florentine art naturally take first place in this collection. Early Tuscan painting is represented by *Cimabue* and *Duccio di Buoninsegna* (**rooms 2 and 3**), each of whom painted a "Virgin in Majesty". See also *Giotto's* **Virgin and Child with Angels and Saints,** and "Virgin with Four Saints", a polyptych; and *Simone Martini's* "Annunciation". In room 7 the attention is drawn by a masterpiece: the **Battle of San Romano,** by *Paolo Uccello.* In the same room can be seen the portraits of Federico da Montefeltro and Battista Sforza (possibly still being restored) by *Piero della Francesca,* and a beautiful "Virgin and Child with Saints" by *Fra Angelico.*

There are some fine works by *Filippo Lippi* and *Pollaiuolo* in **rooms 8 and 9.** **Rooms 10 to 14** now form one large room devoted to *Botticelli* and his greatest pupil, *Filippino Lippi.* The artistic connections between Flanders and Florence are illustrated by the famous triptych by *Hugo van der Goes.* The most notable of the Botticelli works are the **Birth of Venus** and the **Primavera.**

Works by *Verrocchio* and *Leonardo da Vinci* are in **room 15**; by the former, a "Baptism of Christ", and by the latter, an **Adoration of the Magi** and an **Annunciation.** The room of maps now houses paintings by *Hans Memling.*

Room 18 contains works by *Raphael* ("St. John in the Desert"), *Rosso Fiorentino* ("Cherub Musician") and, above all, by *Pontormo* ("Cosimo the Elder") and *Vasari* ("Lorenzo the Magnificent"). There is also a portrait of the beautiful Venetian adventuress, Bianca Cappello, whose romantic life is part of the chronicles of Florence.

Works by *Dürer* and the German painters of the Renaissance are in **room 20: Madonna and Child, Portrait of the Artist's Father,** and the **Adoration of the Magi** by *Dürer*; and **Portraits of Luther and his Wife,** as well as a panel showing **Adam and Eve** by *Cranach.*

Room 21 is devoted to *Bellini* and *Giorgione.* More Flemish and German paintings can be seen in **room 22**, including the "Departure" and the "Martyrdom of St. Florian" by *Albrecht Altdorfer. Raphael's* **Portrait of Perugino,** his **Madonna with a Goldfinch, Self-portrait** and **Portrait of Leo X** are in **rooms 25 and 26.**

One of *Titian's* greatest paintings, the **Venus of Urbino,** is in **room 28** along with his **Knight of Malta. Room 34,** devoted to *Veronese,* has his **Annunciation** and **Holy Family.** Paintings by *Tintoretto* are in **room 35. Room 41** contains some fine works by *Rubens*: "Henri IV at the Battle of Ivry", **Entry of Henri IV into Paris** and the portrait of **Isabelle Brandt** (the painter's wife).

Room 42 (Sala della Niobe) is temporarily closed. *Caravaggio* dominates **room 43** with his **Bacchus,** a work which is very typical of the artist. In **room 44** there are a number of paintings by *Rembrandt*; two **self-portraits** and **Portrait of an Old Man** are of particular merit. Lastly, **room 45** unites French, Italian and Spanish painters of the 18th century: *Nattier, Chardin, Guardi, Canaletto, Goya.*

Note: You may find the following details of the visit have changed, either because a given painting has been removed for restoration or because a room has been closed for repair and the paintings it housed are temporarily being shown elsewhere.

Details of the visit

Inner vestibule. The remains of the apse and choir of the church of San Piero Scheraggio contain some **frescoes**★ by *Andrea del Castagno* (1450) showing famous men such as Petrarch, Boccaccio and Dante, etc. Special permission is needed to enter.

On the left is a monumental staircase by *Vasari* decorated with Roman busts.

An elevator will take you directly to the second floor (3rd floor U.S.); pause to admire the staircase before entering the gallery. One of the entrance vestibules is decorated with porphyry busts of the dukes of Tuscany, the other with classical works.

Using the stairs you can reach the level below and the entrance to the famous **Gabinetto dei Disegni e delle Stampe★★**. These collections were begun by *Cardinal Leopoldo dei Medici*. The first room is used for temporary exhibitions of drawings and engravings by Italian and foreign artists. Continue up the stairs to the second floor and the picture galleries.

East corridor of the gallery. The ceiling is painted with grotesques by Florentine painters (1581). On the left wall, a series of excellent tapestries (some under restoration) are an indication of the rapport between Florence and Flanders in the 16th century; "Wolf and Boar Hunts" by *Squilli*, based on a cartoon by *Van der Straat*; the "Months of the Year", with lively and imaginative scenes on a yellow background, by the Flemish tapestry-makers, *Karcher* and *Roost*, based on drawings by the painter, *Bachiacca*. These artists were the founders of the Medici workshop.

The châteaux of Anet and Fontainebleau are recognizable on a series of "Fêtes and Tournaments at the Court of Catherine dei Medici and Henri II" (1580). These cartoons are attributed to *François Quesnel*. In the bay window along the corridor there are classical statues (mostly copied from the Roman) and busts (Empire period).

Room 2. The Duecento. This room contains four early Tuscan works of particular interest; a **Maestà★★** (Majestic Virgin) by *Cimabue* from the church of Santa Trinita and dated *c.*1275; another **Maestà★★** (1285) by *Duccio di Buoninsegna* from the Ruccellai chapel in Santa Maria Novella; a **Virgin and Child with Angels and Saints★★** (*c.* 1300) and a polyptych of the **Virgin with Four Saints★** by *Giotto*.

Duccio di Buoninsegna (*c.* 1255–1319) is less rigid than *Cimabue*, more sensitive to the play of forms, grace and elegance. With him, art becomes more pagan. His painting of the Virgin shows the first signs of the Renaissance to come; the Sienese style of painting began with him.

Room 3. Sienese painting of the Trecento. *Pietro Lorenzetti* (*c.* 1280 – *c.* 1348), who worked mainly in his native Siena and then in Assisi, painted the **Maestà★** here; *Ambrogio Lorenzetti*, his brother (*d.* Siena *c.* 1348), painted the **Life of St. Nicholas of Bari★** and the "Presentation in the Temple". Pietro's work is remarkable for its internal power which is also to be found, perhaps with more poetry and intimate delicacy, in *Ambrogio's* paintings.

The **Annunciation★★** (1333) by *Simone Martini* is the most important painting in this group. *Simone Martini* (*c.* 1285–1344) left some very important works in Siena. The Uffizi "Annunciation" gives a powerful image of the mysticism which must have inspired the painting. The saints on each side are by his brother-in-law *Lippo Memmi*.

Room 4. Florentine painting of the Trecento. Most of the Florentine painters of the 14th century were disciples of *Giotto* or had occasion to work with him. In this room, there are works by *Bernardo Daddi*, *Taddeo Gaddi*, *Giottino*, *Giovanni da Milano*, and *Andrea Orcagna*. Orcagna was an architect as well as a painter and sculptor and, starting in 1362, did considerable work on the Duomo, Santa Maria Novella, Orsanmichele, etc.; he was influenced by *Giotto* but was also exploring new ideas of his own.

Rooms 5 and 6. International Gothic. This room features works of the late Gothic period. At the end of the Flamboyant Gothic period there was an explosion of form and color reminiscent of the early Byzantine style. *Cimabue* and *Giotto*, however, were more austere. The late Gothic style was a culmination of the whole Gothic period but was already experimenting with new ideas. The **Coronation of the Virgin★** by *Lorenzo*

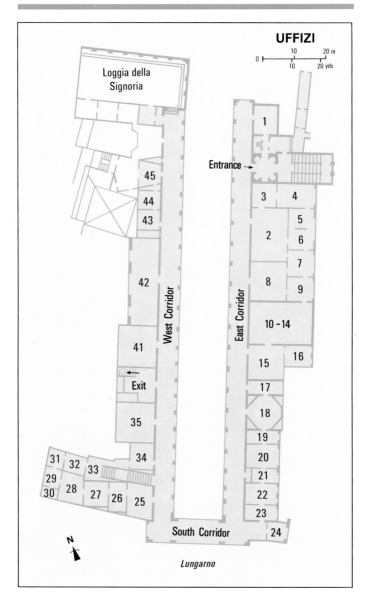

Monaco (1370–1425; master of Fra Angelico), **Adoration of the Magi★** by *Gentile da Fabriano* (1370–1427), and works by *Gherardo Starnina* (1354–1413) are among the most important here.

Room 7. Painters of the early Renaissance. *Uccello* painted the **Battle of San Romano★★★** (1456). It is an immense work. The panel we see here is the central part of a triptych. (The other two panels are in the Louvre and the National Gallery, London.) There is no attempt at realism here; rather, we are given an imaginative vision of history, a portrayal of human misery and glory.

Uffizi Gallery: "Annunciation" by the Sienese painter Simone Martini.

The **Virgin and Child with St. Anne**★ is by *Masaccio* (1401–29), but *Masolino di Panicale* (*c.* 1383–1447) also worked on it. The Gothic influence is evident but the treatment of the figures, which shows a concern with expressiveness and the play of light and perspective, is new. This work (1424) points the way to *Leonardo da Vinci, Michelangelo* and *Raphael*.

The **Madonna and Child with Four Saints**★★ is by *Domenico Veneziano* (*c.* 1400–61) and was painted *c.* 1445 for the church of Santa Lucia dei Magnoli. The famous **Portraits of Federico da Montefeltro and Battista Sforza**★★, the duke and duchess of Urbino, are by *Piero della Francesca* (1416–92). *Fra Angelico* is represented by a **Virgin and Child**★ and a "Coronation of the Virgin".

Domenico Veneziano's "Santa Lucia" shows a quality of light (on the right of the picture) which was to be frequently exploited after him, while the double portrait by *Piero della Francesca,* his pupil, shows a distant horizon behind the profiles which is both beautiful and symbolic.

Room 8. Sala di Filippo Lippi. *Filippo Lippi* (1406–69) was Botticelli's master and was himself much influenced by Masaccio. Here you will find his "Virgin and Child with Four Saints"; two paintings of the "Virgin Adoring the Child with Saints"; a **Coronation of the Virgin**★ and the famous **Madonna and Child with Two Angels**★★. Other works in this room: *Matteo di Giovanni,* "Virgin and Child with Two Saints and Two Angels"; *Lorenzo di Pietro,* known as *Il Vecchietta* (*c.* 1412–80), "Virgin and Child Surrounded by Saints"; *Alessio Baldovinetti,* pupil of *Domenico Veneziano,* **Annunciation**★. The "Resurrection of Lazarus" (above the door) was painted by *Nicolas Froment* (1435–84) who worked for Cosimo dei Medici before becoming the official painter of King René of Provence.

Room 9. Pollaiuolo and the early works of Botticelli. *Antonio* and *Piero del Pollaiuolo* are the center of interest here: six **Virtues**★ (note "Charity" by Antonio, a great sculptor and goldsmith). *Sandro Botticelli* makes his first appearance in this room. Note his **Judith**★ and **Fortitude**★, which are part of a series of panels made on the occasion of the competition for seats in the Tribune of Merchants.

On comparing the "Virtues" by *Antonio del Pollaiuolo* and *Botticelli's* "Fortitude", the different results which the artists have obtained while using the same vibrant, volume-creating line can be seen. *Botticelli*, the typical representative of Florentine art, has already, in his earliest works, attained an extraordinary expressive beauty which was to become habitual with him. But there is also emotion, restlessness and mystery, along with the pagan mysticism that we find in his greatest works.

Also in room 9 can be seen "Young Man in a Red Hat", attributed to *Filippino Lippi*; a portrait of Maria Sforza; "St. Vincent, St. James and St. Eustace" and two works by *Antonio* and *Piero del Pollaiuolo*.

Rooms 10-14. The Botticelli rooms. Here you can see the **Madonna with the Pomegranate★**; the **Portrait of an Unknown Man Presenting a Medal to Cosimo the Elder★**; the **Virgin of the Magnificat★★**; the **Minerva and the Centaur★**; the **Adoration of the Magi★** (among the figures in this painting are three generations of Medici and Botticelli himself in a yellow cloak); and the **Annunciation★** (1481).

The **Birth of Venus★★★** and the **Primavera★★★**, ("Springtime") are the two most famous and popular Botticelli paintings. The two works were commissioned by *Lorenzo di Pierfrancesco*, a relative of Lorenzo dei Medici who lived in the town of Castello. The "Primavera" was painted in 1478, the "Birth of Venus" in 1485. According to Jean Delumeau, a French historian specializing in the Renaissance, the visual link between the two is the spring veil which is about to cover Venus as she rises from the water. In Delumeau's words, Venus is "born of the water, pushed towards the shore by amorous zephyrs who represent the 'spirit of love' that gives shape and form to matter. The fertilization of the sea by the sky is symbolized by the mystical rain of roses escaping from the mouths of the zephyrs. Renaissance men and, in particular, Pico della Mirandola, saw this image as an allegorical interpretation of the biblical phrase: 'The soul took wing over the waters.' The relationship between the two paintings implies, as it certainly implied to educated Florentines, a distinction between the two Venuses that was proposed centuries before by *Plato*. The nude goddess appearing in all her pure splendor is Venus Urania, the inspiration of celestial love. The other, presiding over the rites of Spring, is Venus Pandemos, the incarnation of human love. Her spring gown, charming though it is, is a veil behind which her true beauty can only be guessed at. She is the shadow, the earthly image, and the representative of the other, more exalted Venus to whom she must finally lead her lovers." *Titian* dealt with the same theme in his "Sacred and Profane Love".

The symbols in the "Primavera" are no less difficult to decipher. According to some commentators, there is an allusion to the tournament of 1475 which was won by *Giuliano dei Medici*; there is also an allusion to Lorenzo's precarious victory over the *Pazzi*. The women are said to be *Simonetta Vespucci* and *Lucrezia Danti*, whose names have been linked romantically with the two Medici brothers. *Botticelli* was not a realist painter. What he wanted to depict, in allegorical form, was life and death, beauty and eternity, dream and reality. The artist's domain is that of the philosophical fable; beauty is born out of the opposition between purity and the senses. The three dancing Graces are the images of Chastity, Voluptuousness and Beauty. They dance under the eye of Venus who directs their steps. Chastity is seen only from behind; her eyes are turned towards Mercury, who is pointing to Heaven, where all mysteries have their answer.

Other paintings by *Botticelli*: "St. Augustine and the Child by the Sea", and the famous **Calumny★** (c. 1495), painted during Savonarola's time. *Botticelli's* greatest pupil, *Filippino Lippi* (c. 1457–1504), the son of *Filippo*, has some paintings here: "Adoration of the Child and St. Jerome", "Self-portrait", "Portrait of an Old Man" and "Virgin and Child with Saints".

Note also the "Adoration of the Magi" by *D. Ghirlandaio*, and the "Venus" by *Lorenzo di Credi.*

Part of the room is devoted to the rapport between Flanders and Florence in the 15th century; the greatest masterpiece is the **Adoration of the Shepherds★★** by *Hugo van der Goes* (c. 1440–82), painted in Bruges (1476–78) for Tommaso Portinari who represented the Medici banks there. The work was much admired by the Florentines and had a great influence on the painters of the city, such as *Ghirlandaio, Filippino Lippi* and *Lorenzo di Credi* whose pictures are on show here to permit the comparison. Note also the **Deposition in the Sepulchre★** (c. 1450) by *Roger van der Weyden.*

Room 15. Leonardo da Vinci and Verrocchio. The Florentine painters are absent, but the Umbrian school and the school of *Leonardo da Vinci* are represented: by *Lorenzo di Credi*, an **Annunciation★**; by *Luca Signorelli*, a highly dramatic "Crucifixion" and a "Holy Trinity with the Madonna and Saints"; by *Perugino*, a "Pietà"; by *Piero di Cosimo*, the "Immaculate Conception" and "Perseus Freeing Andromeda"; by *Verrocchio* (1435–88), the famous **Baptism of Christ★**, on which it seems *Leonardo* also worked at the beginning of his career, painting one of the angels. The most important work in the room is the **Adoration of the Magi★★** by *Leonardo da Vinci* (1452–1519), a work commissioned in 1481 by the monks of San Donato at Scopeto, which the artist left at the drawing stage.

However, in this work, which is no more than a sepia drawing on an ochre background, we can already recognize the painter's style, his way of integrating masses into a geometrically organized composition and the way in which, in the light and shade of the *sfumato*, he softens the edges of his forms and gives to the light in the picture, whether visible in space or resting on flesh, a velvet softness of which the secret is his own. We find the same quality in his **Annunciation★** which is also in this room.

Room 16. The room of maps. The walls of this room are decorated with maps of Tuscany painted by *Stefano Buonsignori* in 1589. There are also several works by *Hans Memling*: **Portrait of an Unknown Man★**; **Portrait of Benedetto Portinari★★**; **Virgin between Two Angels★**. The ceiling is by *Jacopo Zucchi.*

Room 17. In this room the Hellenistic statue, "Sleeping Hermaphrodite" (2nd century B.C.) combines an Alexandrine grace with a taste for androgynous bodies. It is a fine work, albeit a little too sweet. On the wall is the "Virgin of the Grotto" (1489) by *Andrea Mantegna.*

Room 18. Sala della tribuna. Built in 1585–89 by *Bernardo Buontalenti*, this room is in the form of a small classical temple and is known as the Tribune of Venus. The polychrome decorations and mother-of-pearl incrustations go well with the antique pieces which are from the Medicis' first collection of sculptures; the **Medici Venus★** is a copy of a Hellenistic statue from the 4th century B.C. found in Rome in the 17th century and brought to Florence in 1717. Beside it is a 4th-century Apollo, a Knifegrinder, Wrestlers, etc. showing the Medici's strong interest in antiquity, and especially Greek antiquity.

Chance would have it that the greater part of these works, discovered and admired by the Medici and their contemporaries, are of a relatively late period and in a very different style from those of the Athenian Golden Age which had such a great influence on Renaissance sculpture.

Note the beautiful Florentine ebony cabinet inlaid with semi-precious stones (*pietre dure*), and the table, also in *pietre dure*. *Bronzino* (1503–72) and *Pontormo* (c. 1494–1556) painted the portraits of the various members of the Medici family on the walls. *Bronzino* painted those of Francesco I, Don Giovanni, **Lucrezia and Bartolomeo Panciatichi★**, Cosimo I and his wife, Eleonora di Toledo, with her son, and Maria dei Medici. The **portrait of Cosimo the Elder★** is by *Pontormo*. The portrait of Lorenzo the Magnificent, humanist and lover of antiquities, is by *Vasari*. You will also see here a portrait of Bianca Cappello by *Alessandro Allori*; **St. John in the Desert★** by *Raphael*; the "Madonna del Pozzo" by *Franciabigio*; **Cherub**

Musician by *Rosso Fiorentino*; "Charity" by *C. Salviati*; "Christ Carrying the Cross" by the same artist; "Virgin and Child" by *Giulio Romano*; portraits by *Andrea del Sarto* of an **Unknown Woman**★, "Unknown Man Dressed in Black", and a **Young Girl**★. **The Girl with a Book**★ is by *Bronzino*; the "Young Man" by *R. Ghirlandaio*.

Room 19. Perugino and L. Signorelli. *Perugino* (1445–1523) painted the "Virgin and Child between St. John the Baptist and St. Sebastian" and the "Crucifixion" as well as a series of **portraits**★: "Young Man", "Mario Palmezzano", "Francesco delle Opere", "Don Biagio Milanesi", "Baldassare", "Vallombrosian Monk". Other paintings include a **Portrait of Evangelista Scappi**★, by *Francesco Francia*; the **Holy Family**★, and "Virgin and Child" by *Luca Signorelli*; and works by *Lorenzo Costa, Melozzo da Forli* and *Girolamo Genga*.

Room 20. Dürer and the German painters. Here we leave Florence to discover the influence of the different schools of the Italian Renaissance on some Germanic artists. Among the more important are works by *Lucas Cranach the Elder* (1472–1533), portraits of **Luther**★, of Catherine von Bora, his wife, of Melanchthon, of John I and Ferdinand III (Electors of Saxony), "Self-portrait", "Lady with a Red Hat", **St. George**★, "Adam and Eve"; *Hans Burgkmair*; "Portrait of a Young Man"; *Albrecht Dürer* (1471–1528), the **Madonna with a Pear**★, "Portrait of the Artist's Father", "Adoration of the Magi", "The Great Calvary", "St. James the Apostle", "St. Philip the Apostle"; *J. Brueghel V*, "Portrait" (on the back, a "Calvary" inspired by Dürer's engraving); *Hans von Kulmbach*, "Lives of Saints Peter and Paul".

Room 21. Bellini and Giorgione. First place must be given to the Venetian painter *Giovanni Bellini* (c. 1430–1516), known as *Gianbellino*, with his "Pietà", **the Sacred Allegory**★★ and the "Portrait of a Gentleman". Beside his works are those of *Giorgione* (c. 1477–1510) in which we can see the mode of expression basic to Venetian painting: the light, in works such as the **Test of Gold and Fire before the Pharaoh**★, the "Judgement of Solomon" and "Warrior with a Sword". There are also works here by *V. Carpaccio*, "Halberdier and Lancer"; *B. Vivarini*, "St. Louis, Bishop of Toulouse"; *Giovanni Mansueti*, "Christ Teaching in the Temple"; *Cima da Conegliano*, "Virgin and Child", *Cosimo Tura*, "St. Dominic".

Room 22. Flemish and German masters. The main works in this room are: *Lucas van Leyden*, "Christ Crowned with Thorns"; *Hans Holbein the Younger* (1497–1543), **Self-portrait**★ and, by his school, "Thomas More" (?); *Albrecht Altdorfer* (c. 1480–1538), the "Departure and Martyrdom of St. Florian"; *Joos van Cleve*, "Portrait of a Man and his Wife", **Mater Dolorosa**★★; *Gérard David* (c. 1460–1523), "Descent from the Cross" and the "Adoration of the Magi"; *Bernard van Orley*, "Man and his Wife"; *Maestro della Virgo inter Virgines*, "Crucifixion".

Room 23. Correggio. The painters grouped together here are followers of *Leonardo da Vinci*. They include *Antonio Allegri*, known as *Correggio* (c. 1489–1534), **Adoration of the Child**★, "Virgin with Angels", the "Flight into Egypt", already in some aspects close to the Baroque style; *Il Sodoma*, "Christ Captured"; *Bernardino Luini*, *G.A. Boltraffio*, and *G. de Predis*. There are also two panels attributed to *Raphael*: a portrait of Guidobaldo della Rovere and a portrait of Elizabetta Gonzaga.

Room 24. Miniatures. Collection of miniatures dating from the 15th to the 18th century (usually closed).

You will now cross the south corridor which links the two wings of the Uffizi. Note the 16th-century ceiling and the many sculptures (some classical, others copies), including the Boy Removing a Thorn and Young Girl Preparing to Dance.

As you cross, you will see one of the most beautiful **panoramas**★★ of Florence: on the right are the Piazza della Signoria, the Palazzo Vecchio and the Duomo; on the left, the hills, the river, the bridges and the Ponte Vecchio through which passes a corridor linking the Uffizi with the Palazzo Pitti, which is visible in the distance against the hill of the Boboli Gardens.

Uffizi Gallery: 'Venus of Urbino' by Titian.

The south corridor of the Uffizi, known as the **Vasari Corridor,** was built by *Vasari* in 1564 and contains the famous gallery of **self-portraits★** (*for conducted tours, apply to the administration*) which date from the 16th century to the present day. The self-portraits of *Titian, Andrea del Sarto, Vasari, Rubens, David, Ingres, Corot,* and *Canova* are particularly interesting. (*Raphael's* self-portrait hangs with his other works in room 26.)

West corridor. There are numerous Roman busts and classical sculptures, as well as three series of 16th- and 17th-century tapestries: "Scenes from the Passion" (manufactured in Florence); the "Story of Jacob" and "Battle Scenes" (two series from Brussels). The ceiling is decorated with 17th-century frescoes restored after the last war.

Room 25. Michelangelo, Raphael and the Florentines. Here we encounter the full flowering of the Renaissance, not only in Italy, but throughout Europe. *Raphael* (1483–1520) and *Michelangelo* (1475–1564) dominate the group. Take special note of *Raphael's* **Portrait of Perugino★★** and *Michelangelo's* **Holy Family★★** (1504–45), an astonishingly sculptural composition. The arrangement of colors, forms and masses give it a rhythmic dynamic force. This work was painted shortly before Michelangelo was commissioned to paint the Sistine chapel. The room also houses the work of various artists whose work is close to that of the two masters: *M. Albertinelli,* the "Visitation", the "Annunciation", the "Nativity" and the "Presentation in the Temple" (the last three are on the predella); and *Rosso Fiorentino* (1495–1540); "Moses Defending the Daughters of Jethro". There are also paintings here by *Berruguete* and *Fra Bartolomeo.*

Room 26. Raphael and Andrea del Sarto. Here again you will see a number of masterpieces by *Raphael:* **Madonna of the Goldfinch★★, Self-portrait★★, Leo X★★** flanked by Cardinal Giulo dei Medici (his cousin, the future Clement VII) and Cardinal Luigi de' Rossi, and **Francesco Maria della Rovere★★**. These vigorous works show a strong Florentine influence. The Tuscan Mannerists are represented by *Andrea del Sarto*

(1486–1530): "Madonna of the Harpies" (so called because of the two harpies sculpted on the pedestal of this altarpiece); and *Pontormo*: "Portrait of a Lady", "The Abbot St. Anthony", and "Adam and Eve Expelled from Paradise".

Room 27. Pontormo and Rosso Fiorentino. *Pontormo* (c. 1494–1556) was a pupil of *Andrea del Sarto*. Lorenzo dei Medici entrusted the decoration of his villa at Poggio a Caiano, near Florence to him; he was certainly influenced by *Dürer* and had a taste for dramatic representations and excess. His works in this room include the **Portrait of Maria Salviati★**, the "Virgin and Child with the Infant St. John", the "Portrait of a Musician" and the **Supper at Emmaus★**. Among the other paintings in this room, note the "Holy Family" and the "Dead Christ between the Virgin and Mary Magdalen" by *Bronzino*, and the "Life of St. Acacio", by *Bachiacca*.

Room 28. Titian. Michelangelo admired Titian but criticized his methods on the grounds that he had not had good training in drawing and design. "If this man," he said, "were aided by art and design as he is by Nature, especially in copying from life, he would not be surpassed, for he has ability and a charming vivacious style." The paintings by Titian (1490–1576) shown here certainly testify to his ability to copy from life: they are the **Knight of Malta★**, **Flora★**, the portraits of Francesco Maria della Rovere and Elizabetta Gonzaga della Rovere (duke and duchess of Urbino), as well as the portraits of Caterina Cornaro and of Bishop Beccadelli, "Venus and Cupid" and, above all, the exceptional **Venus of Urbino★★★**. Here, as in all this painter's works, the woman's beauty seems to deny carnal sin while proclaiming the liberation of the spirit through sensual pleasure. *Jacopo Palma the Elder* reflects Titian's style ("Resurrection of Lazarus", "Judith", "Conversation of Saints"), but without his gracefulness.

Room 29. Parmigianino. The beginnings of Mannerism can be seen in the works of *Parmigianino* (1503–40), especially the **Madonna with the Long Neck★**; *Nicola Pisano* ("Holy Family"), *Girolamo da Carpi* and *Il Garofalo*.

Room 30. The painters of Emilia. Still in the same style: "Portrait" by *Niccolò dell'Abate*, "Rest in Egypt" by *Dosso Dossi*, "Virgin and Child with St. Anne" and paintings of saints by *Mazzolino*.

Room 31. Dosso Dossi. The evolution of Mannerism continues with *Dosso Dossi* ("Maestà", "Witchcraft"), *Sebastiano del Piombo* ("La Fornarina") and *L. Lotto* ("Portrait of a Young Man").

Room 32. S. del Piombo and L. Lotto. A continuation of the previous rooms with *Sebastiano del Piombo* ("The Death of Adonis"), *Paris Bordone* (two portraits), *L. Lotto* ("Holy Conversation"), and *Girolamo Romanino* ("Self-portrait").

Room 33. Corridoio del Cinquecento. Minor works by Tuscan and other Mannerists, such as *Ligozzi*, *Vasari*, *Allori*, *Zucchi*, *Poppi* ("The Three Graces"), etc. Note also the paintings by *F. Clouet* ("Portrait of François I of France"); *Pourbus* and other painters of the French school ("Warrior", "Portrait of a Lady"); *Luis de Morales* ("Christ Bearing His Cross"); *Antonio Mor* ("Self-portrait") and *Charles Amberger* ("Portrait of Charles Gross").

Room 34. Veronese. Some magnificent canvases by *Paolo Veronese* (c. 1528–88) including the **Annunciation★** and the **Holy Family with St. Barbara★★**. You will also find here three paintings by the great Bergamesque portrait painter *G.B. Moroni*, a "Man with a Mandolin" by *G. Campi* and a "Transfiguration" by *Girolamo Savoldo*.

Room 35. Tintoretto and Baroccio. Venice again with *Tintoretto* (1518–94) and his dramatic light and shade effects: **Christ and the Samaritan★**, **Portrait of Jacopo Sansovino★**, "Leda and the Swan", the "Apparition of St. Augustin"; *Jacopo Bassano*: the "Burning Bush"; *Baroccio* (c. 1528–1612), somewhat affected at times: **Madonna of the People★**. There are also works by *Leandro Bassano* (less well known than his father and teacher Jacopo), by *Domenico Tintoretto* (son of the great painter), and by *Palma the Younger*.

The vestibule of Buontalenti's staircase, once occupied by rooms **36–40,** has been reopened and now forms the gallery's exit. Here one can see the **marble boar★** (Roman copy of a Greek bronze), from which *P. Tacca* made a bronze copy in 1612 (known as the "porcellino") that now stands in the Mercato Nuovo. The torso of a satyr, a 2nd-century Greek statue, and some charming Florentine tapestries complete the décor.

Rooms 41 to 44 were being restored at the time of writing and you may find them closed.

Room 41. Rubens (1577–1640). *Rubens* dominates the room with two major works: the portrait of **Isabelle Brandt★**, his wife, and the **Entry of Henri IV into Paris★**. There are also paintings by *Van Dyck, Sustermans* and *Baciccia*, and a "Portrait of an Old Lady" by *Jacob Jordaens*.

Room 42. Sala di Niobe. This room contains a Roman copy of a Greek statue by the sculptor *Scopas* (4th century B.C.) representing Niobe and her sons being killed by Apollo and Diana. There are also paintings by *Chardin* and *Nattier* and views of Venice by *Canaletto* and *F. Guardi.*

Room 43. Caravaggio (1573–1610), **Adolescent Bacchus★★, Medusa★** and the "Sacrifice of Isaac"; also works by *Carracci* and *Claude Lorrain.*

Room 44. Rembrandt and the Flemish painters. *Rembrandt:* two self-portraits (1634 and 1664), and a **Portrait of an Old Man★★**. The influence of the Italian 17th century on European schools of painting, especially that of Flanders, can be seen here in works by *Jan Steen, F. van Mieris, G. Metsu, J. Molenaer* and *J. van Ruisdael.*

Room 45. 18th-century paintings. *Jean-Marc Nattier, Jean-Baptiste Chardin, Francesco Guardi, Canaletto, Francisco de Goya.*

ITINERARY E
THE ARNO, THE PALAZZO PITTI
AND OLD FLORENCE

Via Calimala, Ponte Vecchio, Palazzo Pitti, Oltrarno

Little remains of the memory of Roman Florence and, in the Piazza della Repubblica, once the ancient forum, not even a pillar or a brick wall is left to remind us of those once great builders. Nevertheless, Florence was founded here, at a narrow ford of the Arno which was easy for the Roman legions to defend. The Arno can become a raging torrent at times, as it did in 1966 when it burst its banks and flooded the city, breaking down the doors of the Baptistry and soiling the works of art with mud. Crossing the Ponte Vecchio, which was also menaced by the flood, it is difficult to imagine how such damage could have been wrought by this placid-looking river, which seems content to do nothing more than reflect the palaces which line it and the bridges which straddle it. The view is famous and justly so. The best time to look at it is towards sunset when everything blends in rosy tones of ocher and olive and it is difficult to judge whether it is the water, the sky or the stones that diffuse such an unreal light and atmosphere. The clean hard lines of the Palazzo Pitti bring us back to reality and remind us, too, of what an ordinary citizen, admittedly a very rich one, could build for himself as a residence during the Renaissance. Today, we have the pleasure of visiting the six museums housed in the palace and of strolling along the shady walks of the Boboli Gardens.

The Oltrarno, with its narrow streets encircling the huge palace, is to Florence what the Trastevere is to Rome, and it still retains an authenticity which the "rehabilitated" Roman district has lost. Among the palaces and churches, artisans" workshops open onto the street like shop windows, giving us a glimpse of a way of life which has been handed down from the Middle Ages.

View of the Arno from the Piazzale Michelangelo.

PIAZZA DELLA REPUBBLICA
(MAP II D4)

This was once the Forum. A temple, the *Capitolium*, dedicated to the three great Roman deities, once stood here. The nearby street called Via Campidoglio is named after it. The square was enlarged at the end of the last century; porticoes line the west side and the square has some beautiful shops and cafés which make it one of the most frequented centers of Florence.

VIA CALIMALA
(MAP II D4)

This street, along with Piazza San Giovanni and the Via Roma, was one of the main arteries of the ancient Roman city. It crossed imperial Florence from north to south and was called the *decumanus*. The name Calimala may thus be derived from *Callis maius* (main street), but other origins have been suggested, such as *Callis malus* (bad street) and *Kalos mallos* which is Greek for "good wool". This derivation, too, is plausible since this was the street of the cloth finishers guild. The drapers of Florence imported raw cloth from abroad and, in the 13th century, the banks and inns of Paris, Caen, Rouen, Provins, Montpellier, Avignon, Marseilles and Toulon were filled with their representatives. The city of Florence was virtually run by strictly regulated guilds, like that of the *Calimala*, and, in a way, this street was both the heart of the city and the point of departure for its great wealth. The **Loggia del Mercato Nuovo,** built by *G.B. del Tasso* in 1551, belongs to the same period. The stalls under its arcades now sell straw hats and bags, embroidered linen, sweaters and fancy leather goods. On the left side of the market stands the **Fontana del porcellino.** Porcellino (little pig) refers to the bronze statue of a boar, which is a replica made in 1612 by *Pietro Tacca* of the marble statue in the Uffizi. The coins tossed into the fountain go to a fund for orphans. Don't forget to stroke the boar on the snout, shiny from centuries of caresses, both to bring you luck and to ensure your return to the city.

Behind the market on the right, in the Piazza della Parte Guelfa, you will see the **Palazzo di Parte Guelfa,** commissioned in the 14th century and completed a century later by *Brunelleschi* and *Vasari*. Inside the building, which now houses the Università Popolare, the rooms are decorated by *Vasari* and *Brunelleschi*.

VIA POR SANTA MARIA
(MAP II DE4)

This is an extension of the Via Calimala and was almost entirely rebuilt after the last war. It gives access to some very picturesque streets such as the Via delle Terme, named after the baths of the Roman city, and **Borgo Santissimi Apostoli** with its beautiful tower-houses. A tiny street on the left leads to the **church of Santo Stefano al Ponte** (12th century); the interior, which was refurbished in the 17th century, had to undergo considerable restoration in 1947.

PONTE VECCHIO★★
(MAP II DE4)

This is the city's oldest bridge and the only one to escape destruction by the Germans in 1944 when the Wehrmacht, pursued by the Allied troops, retreated north. This story is told in *Rossellini's* film "Paisà". Although the bridge itself wasn't damaged, the old districts on either side of it were bombed. These areas have been entirely reconstructed but you can still see old structures, like the **Torre dei Consorti,** rising out of a sea of modern buildings.

The Ponte Vecchio is situated at a narrow point in the river, a little downstream from where the old Roman bridge once stood. It could well be that this narrowing accounts for the build-up of water that causes the floods from which the city has suffered. The first one occurred in 1333, the last and worst in 1966. The Ponte Vecchio dates from 1345; it is not known who the architect was but it may have been *Taddeo Gaddi* or *Neri di Fioravanti.* The bridge connects two commercial districts; it was, therefore, natural that the bridge itself quickly became covered with shops. In time, the shops expanded, overhanging the water on each side and supported by wooden consoles. At first they were butchers' shops, and their waste was thrown into the river. *Cosimo I,* concerned about public hygiene as well as the city's appearance, got rid of the butchers and their place was taken by the goldsmiths and jewelers who are still there today. In the center of the bridge, from which there is a marvelous **view★★** of the city and the river, there stands a bronze bust of Benvenuto Cellini, placed there in 1900.

When *Cosimo* moved to the Palazzo Pitti (1560), he had a long corridor built as a sort of second floor running above the shops in order to go from his new residence to the Palazzo Vecchio without the risk of mixing with the crowds in the street and perhaps of being attacked. The first Medici art collections were hung in this corridor, which was designed by *Vasari* (1565).

▬▬ *VIA GUICCIARDINI*
(MAP II EF3)

This street was largely destroyed during the war and has been rebuilt. It is named after one of the great historians of Medicean Florence, *Guicciardini* (1483–1540), who is as highly regarded as a writer of history as his contemporary, *Machiavelli* (1469–1527), is for his writings on the art of politics. Both men lived in this street: *Guicciardini* in the Palazzo Guicciardini (n°15; a beautiful garden), built at the beginning of the 15th century and renovated in the 17th century; *Machiavelli* in a house where n°18 now stands.

In a small square, on the left, at the beginning of the street, is the **church of Santa Felicità** (MAP II F3) which has two works by *Pontormo,* both works located in the first chapel on the right: a **Deposition★** (painting) and an **Annunciation★** (fresco, 1526–28). The 15th-century sacristy, in the style of *Brunelleschi,* contains some good 14th- and 15th-century paintings. The church stands on the site of a Paleo-Christian cemetery in a particularly charming district that you will enjoy exploring.

▬▬ *PALAZZO PITTI★★*
(MAP II F3)

This palace, with its 650-foot/200-metre facade and immense forecourt, is one of the most impressive buildings in Florence. It stands on the side of the hill which now constitutes the Boboli Gardens. The palace was the residence of the Medici family and their successors, the grand dukes of Lorraine, from 1560 to 1859. It then became one of the residences of the royal family (1865–1919). It now belongs to the State and contains, in addition to the royal apartments, several museums; the **Palatine Gallery** (chiefly 16th- and 17th-century paintings), the **Museo degli Argenti** (silver) and the **Galleria dell'Arte Moderna** (modern paintings). In the **Boboli Gardens** behind the palace, you will find the **Galleria del Costume** (clothes) and the **Museo delle Porcellane** (porcelain).

The Palazzo Pitti is a Renaissance building begun in 1458 by *Luca Fancelli* and based on a design by *Brunelleschi* for *Count Luca Pitti*, a rich and influential banker. The *Pitti* family were involved in the *Pazzi* conspiracy against the Medici, a mistake on their part. It caused their downfall and, from 1465, their palace remained half-built until *Cosimo I* bought it in 1540 from *Bonaccorso Pitti*, *Luca's* great-grandson, with the dowry brought him by his wife, *Eleonora di Toledo*. Eleonora made changes to the palace by enlarging it and adding the gardens.

The Palazzo Pitti was the largest palace ever built by a private citizen. Some important changes were made to the original building by *Bartolomeo Ammannati* (1558). He replaced the old roofing with a balustrade, inserted Renaissance windows into the walled-in arcades on the ground floor, and designed the courtyard and the rear facade facing the gardens. In 1560, *Cosimo I* left the Palazzo Vecchio to install himself and his court in the Palazzo Pitti.

In 1620–40, *Giulio Parigi* and his son, *Alfonso*, lengthened the facade still further. Between 1764 and 1819, *Giuseppi Ruggeri* added the two porticoed wings on each side of the palace.

The central doors lead into a doric atrium (1850) by *P. Poccianti* through which you will enter the **courtyard**★ by *Ammannati*. At the bottom of the courtyard, below the terrace, you will see the Grotto of Moses with a statue of the prophet in porphyry by *Curradi*; below is the Artichoke Fountain by *F. del Tadda* and *A. Susini* (1641). On the right under the portico of the courtyard is a chapel decorated with Neo-Classical frescoes. Also worth noting are the mosaic **altar**★ and an ivory crucifix by *Giambologna*.

The Palatine Gallery★★★

Visit: 9 am to 2 pm; Sun 9 am to 1 pm. Closed Mon.

Access to the gallery on the 1st floor is by the palace's main staircase built by *Ammannati*. The gallery was given its name on the occasion of the marriage of *Anna-Maria Lodovica* (1667–1743), the last of the *Medici*, with the *Elector Palatine Johannes Wilhelm*. The gallery has been open to the public since 1828. The collections are hung in sumptuous rooms which form a beautiful perspective with the royal apartments when the latter are open. The princely character of the gallery is emphasized by the frescoed ceilings which were specially painted, between 1637 and 1665 by *Ciro Ferri* from drawings by *Pietro da Cortona*.

The paintings in the Palatine Gallery were bought by the Medici, starting from about 1620. It is not organized according to modern standards of display but simply according to the taste of the grand dukes who, from generation to generation, collected for their own pleasure.

This is a personal collection. By contrast with the Uffizi, the Tuscan primitives are absent and paintings of the early Renaissance are rare. The Palatine is richest in works dating from the 16th, 17th and 18th centuries, among which are paintings by *Botticelli*, *Filippo Lippi*, *Raphael*, *Titian*, *Andrea del Sarto*, *Bronzino*, *Tintoretto* and *Veronese*, as well as numerous works by Flemish and Spanish artists. It is an exceptionally important collection.

The order in which you see the rooms is subject to alteration if restoration work is in progress.

From the vestibule of the great staircase you enter the statuary gallery containing classical sculptures.

Hall of Venus. There are some important works here by *Titian*: **Beautiful Woman**★★, **Portrait of Piero Aretino**★, the **Concert**★★ (once attributed to *Giorgione*); two seascapes painted by the Neapolitan *Salvatore Rosa* (1615–73); two beautiful paintings by *Rubens*: "The Peasants' Return", which depicts the countryside on a summer evening, a popular Flemish theme, and "Ulysses on the Island of the Phaeacians". Facing this is the famous "Portrait of Julius II", copied by *Titian* from a lost original by *Raphael*.

Hall of Apollo. This room contains a number of valuable works. By *Titian*: "Mary Magdalen", **Portrait of a Gentleman★★**, "Virgin of the Misericord"; by *Tintoretto*: **Portrait of Vincenzo Zeno★**; by *Rosso Fiorentino*: "Virgin and Saints"; by *Andrea del Sarto*: "Holy Family", **Deposition★**; by *A. van Dyck*: portraits of Charles I of England and his wife Henrietta of France (daughter of Henri IV and Maria dei Medici); by *Luis Morales*: "Ecce Homo".

Hall of Mars. This room contains works by Venetian painters and others who were influenced by the Venetian school. There are also works by *Rubens*: the **Four Philosophers★** (starting from the left: the artist, his brother, Philip, the philosopher *Joost Lips* and, under a bust of Seneca, his pupil *Jan van Wouwer*) and the **Consequences of War★**, painted for *Ferdinando II dei Medici*; *Murillo*: "Virgin and Child", and **Virgin of the Rosary★**; *Veronese*: "Daniele Barbaro"; *Titian*: "Cardinal Ippolito dei Medici"; *Tintoretto*: "Portrait of Luigi Cornaro"; *A. Van Dyck*: "Portrait of Cardinal Bentivoglio".

Hall of Jupiter. In the center, there is a Neo-Classical sculpture of Victory. The paintings on the walls are by *Andrea del Sarto*: "St. John the Baptist", "Portrait of the Artist and his Wife", "Annunciation", "Virgin with Four Saints" (incomplete due to the artist's death); by *Fra Bartolomeo*: **Deposition★** and "St. Mark"; by *Bronzino*: "Guidobaldo della Rovere"; by *Perugino*: "Adoration of the Child"; by *F. Pourbus*: "Portrait of a Young Man". There is also a "Battle Scene" by the French painter *Jacques Courtois*, known as *Il Borgognone* (1621–76). Near the window is a "Holy Family" by *Rubens*; the "Three Ages of Man" from the Venetian school of the 16th century, (once attributed to *Lorenzo Lotto*); and the "Madonna of the Swallow", by *Guercino*. The finest masterpiece in this room is the **Woman with a Veil★** by *Raphael* (1516). There is a magnificent portrait "La Fornarina"; this is the artist's celebration of the beauty of the woman who inspired so many of his paintings, particularly the "Madonna of the Chair" (see next room).

Hall of Saturn. This room is chiefly devoted to *Raphael*; from left to right: the **Virgin of the Grand Duke★★★** (1504; this was Ferdinando dei Medici's favorite painting); portraits of Tommaso Inghirami (1504) and **Agnolo and Maddalena Doni★** (1506); between them is "The Vision of Ezekiel" (1518), hanging below the "Madonna of the Canopy" (1506; incomplete). After them are the "Portrait of Cardinal Dovizi da Bibbiena" and, finally, the famous **Madonna of the Chair★★** (1515–16), one of the most harmonious, balanced and serene paintings by this artist. It is regarded by many as his masterpiece. Among works by other artists, note: *Andrea del Sarto*, "Dispute over the Trinity"; *Annibale Carracci*, "Portrait"; *Perugino*, "Deposition", "Mary Magdalen"; *Fra Bartolomeo*, "Christ Appears to the Disciples"; *Ridolfo Ghirlandaio*, "Portrait of a Young Man" commonly called "The Goldsmith". There are also works by *Guercino, Carlo Dolci* and *Jacopo Bassano*.

Hall of the Iliad. This room was added in the time of the grand dukes of Lorraine. The frescoes on the ceiling are by *Luigi Sabatelli* (1819); they illustrate episodes from Homer's epic. In the center is a group of Neo-Classical marble sculptures made in 1824 by *Luigi Bartolini* and representing Charity. The major paintings in this room are by the following artists: *Raphael*, the **Pregnant Woman★★** (1506); *Andrea del Sarto*, two paintings of the "Assumption" (one painted in 1526, the other, unfinished, in 1531); *Titian*, "A Gentleman", "Philip II of Spain"; *Ridolfo Ghirlandaio*, "Portrait of a Lady"; *Sustermans*, "Prince Mattias dei Medici", "Portrait of Count Waldemar Christian, Prince of Denmark". There is also a painting by *Velasquez* (rare in Italian galleries), "Philip IV of Spain on Horseback"; and a painting by *Carlo Maratta*, "St. Filippo Neri in Ecstasy".

Reception rooms of the royal apartments

Room of the Niches or Dining room. The Empire décor is by *Giuseppe Maria Terreni* and *Giuseppe Castagnoli*. On the walls there are portraits of the Medici by *Sustermans*. Sèvres porcelain and Chinese vases are also on display.

Green room. The *chiaroscuro* painting on the ceiling is by *Luca Giordano*. Four Gobelins tapestries (18th century), representing the "Story of Esther", adorn the walls. The large Florentine marquetry cabinet was made at the end of the 17th century.

Throne room. The tapestries belong to the Story of Esther series. Portraits by *Sustermans* and *F. Pourbus the Younger* (among others, "Henri IV of France" and "Maria dei Medici"); Empire furniture and oriental vases.

Blue room. Gobelins tapestries (1690–1706); portraits by *Sustermans*; Chinese vases.

Chapel. 'Virgin and Child" by *Carlo Dolci* (the frame is richly decorated with *pietre dure*); portraits of the Medici by *Sustermans*; Florentine cabinet in ebony, ivory and alabaster.

Parrot room. This was the ante-chamber which separated Queen Margherita's apartments from those of King Umberto I (see below). The walls are lined with silk decorated with parrots. Portraits of Giulia Varano, duchess of Urbino, by *Titian*; portraits of François I by *Hans von Aachen*, and of Elizabeth of France, by *F. Pourbus the Younger*. Austrian majolica stove.

Salon and bedroom of the queen and the Oval Room. These were Queen Margherita's apartments. The first two are decorated with splendid Gobelins tapestries (1735–45), based on drawings by *Oudry*, representing Louis XV hunting. The Oval room is entirely hung with embroidered silk (motifs inspired by Chinese art).

The following rooms are open only on request:

Apartments of the king of Italy. All the rooms are decorated with tapestries, portraits by *Sustermans* and beautiful furniture. Particularly worth noticing are the *Sala di Bona* with 17th-century frescoes by *Pocetti*, which show, among other things, the "Battle of Bona" in Africa; chandeliers from Bohemia; and the **White room** or Ballroom with its stucco decoration (1776–80) by the *Albertolli* brothers of Lugano. This room, with its magnificent Venetian glass chandeliers, was once used for balls and parties; today it is used for concerts.

Other rooms of the Pitti Gallery (*not always open to the public*). The most interesting are the **Sala Castagnoli** (communicating with the Hall of Venus), with its inlaid marble table and decoration by *Castagnoli* (1754–1832) — The **Volterrano Apartments:** *Baldassare Franceschini*, called *Il Volterrano* (1611–89), began the decoration; 17th-century Florentine painting by *Salvatore Rosa*. — **Hall of Prometheus:** *Luca Signorelli; Filippo Lippi*, **Virgin and Child**★; *Botticelli*, two portraits, one of which showing a young man, has great expressive force; *Pontormo; B. Peruzzi*, "Dance of Apollo". — **Hall of Justice:** *Titian*, "Portrait of Tommaso Mosti"; works by *Tintoretto, Veronese* and *G.B. Moroni* (1525–78). — **Hall of Flora:** *Canova* (1757–1822), **Venus;** *Andrea del Sarto*, "The Story of Joseph"; *Pontormo*, "Epiphany". — **Hall of the Education of Jupiter:** *Caravaggio*, "Love Asleep"; *C. Allori*, "Judith". — **Stove room:** beautiful mosaic floor; the vaults and lunettes are by *Matteo Rosselli*; the walls are covered with frescoes by *Pietro da Cortona* and are allegorical representations of the "Four Ages of the World" (1640).

The stove room is linked to the vestibule.

In the vestibule: beautiful coffered ceiling and fountain by *F. del Tadda* (the "Child with a Bird" is by *Tribolo*) from the royal villa of Castello. Descending the great staircase, built by *Luigi del Moro* in 1895–97 in the Renaissance style, you will reach the ground floor and the Museo degli Argenti (silver museum).

Museo degli Argenti★★

Visit: Wed and Fri 9 am to 2 pm; Sun 9 am to 1 pm. Ground floor, entrance on the left under the portico.

The museum contains gold- and silverware, vases, ivories, jewels and cameos, chiefly from the Medici and grand ducal collections. Some of these magnificent pieces were made by Florentine workshops from the 15th century onwards; others came from abroad, especially from Germany and Austria through marriage or succession.

The large rooms on the ground floor, decorated with 17th-century frescoes celebrating the glory of the Medici, are used for concerts.

The Giovanni da San Giovanni room. This artist, along with *Furini*, painted the frescoes (1634) on the occasion of the marriage of Ferdinando II and Victoria della Rovere.

The "Dark" room. This room houses one of the most precious collections in the museum: the **vases★★** in semi-precious stone which belonged to Lorenzo dei Medici whose monogram (LAVR MED) can be seen on them.

The next three rooms are decorated with frescoes (1630-44) by *Colonna* and *Mitelli* depicting allegorical scenes and *trompe-l'oeil* architecture. They contain an 18th-century **chiffonnier★** in ebony with *pietre dure* incrustations, an ebony cabinet inlaid with semi-precious stones of the same period and, on the table, a group of cherubs by *Bernini* (16th century). The small adjacent rooms contain a superb collection of 16th- and 17th-century German and Flemish **ivories★**; the amber collection of the grand duke exhibited in curious 18th-century glass cases; objects in lapis lazuli and rock crystal including a **vase★** made for Francesco dei Medici and based on a design by *Buontalenti*.

On the first floor, the treasury contains some rare jewels, especially those which belonged to *Anna-Maria Lodovica*, Electress Palatine and the last of the Medici. The small **casket★** in cut rock crystal by *Valerio Belli* showing the Passion (1533) was a gift from Clement VII to François I on the occasion of the marriage of his son, the future King Henri II, with Catherine dei Medici. There is also German jewelry of the late 16th century, as well as cameos and intaglio work, 54 gilded silver cups from Salzburg, a **precious collection★** of majolica and porcelain from Vienna, Chelsea, Capodimonte, Meissen, the Ginori workshop, China, Japan, and Sèvres, the latter including a piece with the portrait of Napoleon I after *Gérard*.

Galleria d'Arte Moderna★★

Visit: 9 am to 2 pm; Sun 9 am to 1 pm. Closed Mon. Subject to changes or possible closure because of restoration work. Second floor; entrance on the right under the portico.

The gallery was founded in 1860 and has been continually enriched. It is devoted to Italian painting from the beginning of the 19th century to today. There are 30 rooms open at present. They are on the second floor and were once inhabited by the grand dukes of Lorraine. There is a beautiful view of the Boboli Gardens, the city and the hills.

Neo-Classicism. This vast movement, which spread across the whole of intellectual Europe from the end of the 18th century to the middle of the 19th century, was born out of the interest created by the archeological excavations following the discovery of the ruins of Pompeii. It is at once a reaction against the decadence of Rococo and a return to Classicism. The most notable painters of this period are *Andrea Appiani* and *Pompeo Battoni*; there are also numerous sculptors, among them *Benvenuti*, *Camuccini*, *Landi* and, above all, *Canova*, who was the official sculptor of the First Empire.

Romanticism. A movement which opposed Neo-Classicism, characterized in Great Britain by a communion with nature, and in Italy by introspection, sentimentalism and provincialism. Among the works shown here, those of *Hayez*, *Bezzuoli*, *Giuseppe* and *Francesco Sabatelli*, *Luigi* and *Cesare Mussini*, *Pollastrini*, *Cassioli*, *Ussi* and *Ciseri* are of a more academic and intellectual character.

The Macchiaioli (paintings donated by Diego Martelli) was the most productive movement of a not very interesting century in Italy.

The *Macchiaioli* were the painters who, from 1855 to 1860, brought the meaning of painting into question once again. They habitually met in the Café Michelangelo in Florence. They rejected traditional art and "the academic cult of form", because, according to *Adriano Ceciano* who, with *Signorini*, was the theoretician of the group, it was a question of "rendering impressions and perceptions of reality". There is an evident affinity here with the French painter, *Boudin*, precursor of Impressionism, who, during this same period, was attempting to render in paint the misty skies and humid atmosphere of the Normandy coast. The *Macchiaioli* quickly grasped the importance of the Impressionists'' discoveries about the division of light but they did not adopt Impressionist techniques. They remained more figurative and never attained the sensualism of a *Renoir* or the freedom of a *Monet*.

On display here are works by *Fattori*, in particular the famous "Rotonda dei Palmieri" and "Cousin Argia". *Fattori* was undoubtedly the most important figure both of this group and of the whole period, thanks to his masterly touch and the robustness of his temperament. You will also see works by *Zandomeneghi*, a friend of Degas, who exhibited with the Impressionists: "Portrait of Diego Martelli"; as well as paintings by *Lega*: "Walk in the Garden" and "Visit to the Wet-Nurse"; *Signorini*: "Bathing at Portoferraio"; *Puccinelli*: "Signora Marocchi"; and *Abbati*: "At Church".

The Galleria d'Arte Moderna also has canvases by *Boldini*, a talented portraitist of European high society. Paintings by *Tontanesi, Palizzi, Morelli*, etc., represent the Naturalist movement.

The early 20th century. New trends emerged in Italian painting with *Severini* and *Carrà* who, with Futurism, posed problems about the relationship between art and contemporary society. *Carrà* joined *De Chirico* and the Metaphysical painters. In opposition were *Giorgio Morandi*, who concerned himself with the intense, silent world of still-life, and *Felice Casorati*, who adapted Cubist methods to the classical tradition. *De Pisis* is considered to be one of the most important artists of the first half of this century and one of the greatest Italian landscape painters. Among the foreign painters represented in the gallery are: *Dupré, Lenbach, Sargent, Winterhalter, Böcklin* and, above all, *Pissarro*.

Galleria del Costume (MAP II F2)

Visit: Tues, Thurs, and Sat 9 am to 2 pm. Housed in the Palazzina della Meridiana, access beside Boboli Gardens.

This pavilion, built in 1776 at the south-west corner of the Palazzo Pitti, was used as a private residence by the Savoia family. The gallery has 18th- and 19th-century costumes in contemporary décor.

Museo delle Carozze

Collection of carriages, saddlery and sedan chairs. (*Temporarily closed for restoration; entrance at the extreme right of the facade of the palace.*)

THE BOBOLI GARDENS★★
(MAP I F-3. MAP II DE 3-4)

Visit: 9 am to sunset.

Access to *Buontalenti's* grotto and the Boboli Gardens is by the **Bacchus gate** at the extreme left of the facade of the Palazzo Pitti. The gate is so named because of the nearby fountain with a statue of Bacchus (immediately inside the gate on the left) by *Valerio Cione* (1560), which represents the grotesque figure of a dwarf from the court of Cosimo I. The gardens, which cover the hill behind the palace, are a remarkable example of the Italian garden. Concerts and theatrical performances are held there during the "Maggio Musicale Fiorentino", the music festival which takes place each May.

According to Vasari, *Niccolò Pericoli*, known as *Il Tribolo*, was the architect of the garden which was designed to follow the natural lie of the land. The amphitheater, around which the garden is planned, is based on a natural slope, as can be seen from a painting of the Palazzo Pitti showing Florence at the beginning of the 16th century. The garden dates from 1550. *Tribolo* died before completing his work, which was finished by *Ammannati* and *Buontalenti*. Some changes were made in the 17th century, particularly by *Alfonso Parigi*; in place of the plantations ornamenting the highest parts of the amphitheater in the original plan, a wall was built, giving it the aspect of a Roman hippodrome. In the setting of this open-air theater, the great Medici fêtes were celebrated, including the marriages of *Cosimo II*, *Ferdinando II* and *Cosimo III*.

The courtyard of Bacchus is followed by an artificial grotto by *Buontalenti* (1583) which, in its paganism, expresses man's fascination with ancient mysticism and also, perhaps, his instinctive desire to burrow into the earth. The grotto is decorated with frescoes and statues; among the latter there is a **Venus★** by *Giambologna*.

On the right, the **amphitheater** is decorated in the center by a Roman bath and an obelisk from Thebes. To the right stands the Palazzo Pitti and the Artichoke Fountain (1641). At the back of the amphitheater stand Roman statues (Septimius Severus, Ceres, etc.). On the next terrace, there is a fishpond with a bronze Neptune fountain in the center. The statue of the sea god is by *Stoldo Lorenzi* and is Baroque in style. The third terrace has a statue of Plenty, by *Giambologna* and *Tacca*.

Still higher up, you can see the Cavaliere (bastion) garden, decorated with the Fontane delle Scimmie (fountain of the apes) by *Tacca*. From here can be seen one of the most beautiful views of Florence and its surrounding hills. The pavilion in the Cavaliere garden houses the **Museo della Porcellana★** where porcelain from Sèvres and other Parisian manufacturers, as well as those from Chantilly, Vienna, Berlin, Meissen, Worcester, Capodimonte, etc., are displayed.

As you come back down, turn right on the terrace with the Neptune fountain and follow the alley known as the *viottolone*, bordered with cypresses, laurels and pines, which leads by the Prato delle Colonne to the Porta Romana exit. The *viottolone* is bordered on both sides by classical and imitation classical statues. The Piazzale dell'Isolotto, halfway along the walk, is a water garden designed by *Alfonso Parigi*. In its center, there is an islet with the Ocean Fountain by *Giambologna*. Sea monsters, rocks and water create a poetical effect inspired by Hadrian's maritime theater at Tivoli.

━━ *SAN FELICE*
(MAP II F3)

Upon leaving the Boboli Gardens, turn left. The church of San Felice stands a very short distance away. It is a Gothic building with a Renaissance facade attributed to *Michelozzo* (1457).

The interior has some interesting paintings and frescoes. — 1st Altar on the right: "Pietà", a fresco attributed to *N. Gerini*; 5th Altar: "Pietà", in terra-cotta, by *Cieno da Gambassi*; 6th Altar: "Virgin and Saints", by *R. Ghirlandaio*. In the place of the 7th Altar is a lunette decorated with 14th-century frescoes. — Left side: 7th Altar, "St. Massimo Succoured by St. Felice", a fresco by *Giovanni da San Giovanni*. 6th Altar: a triptych by *Neri di Bicci* (1467); on the wall of the nuns' choir, a **Crucifix★** by the school of *Giotto*; 1st Altar: a triptych (1480), school of *Botticelli*.

At the corner opposite the church (n° 8, Piazza San Felice) is the **Casa**

The Boboli Gardens, a remarkable example of the Italian garden.

Guidi where *Robert Browning* and *Elizabeth Barrett* lived after their flight from Wimpole St. in London until Elizabeth's death in 1861.

Visit: Mon to Fri 3 pm to 6.30 pm or by appointment, tel: 28-43-93.

▬▬ THE OLTRARNO★★
(the district on the other side of the Arno)
(MAP II EF 1-2)

What the Trastevere is to Rome, the Oltrarno is to Florence. This is the real heart of the city, where the people are warm-hearted, ebullient and have a teasing sense of humor. Here, the past comes alive. Walking around this district you will find that each piazza with its church is designed as a sun with its "rays", the narrow streets, radiating from it — delightful streets, where you will still find, in Stendhal's phrase, "the imprint of medieval passions". One of the greatest pleasures of Florence is wandering around in the old districts and discovering unexpected palaces with coats of arms emblazoned above their great doors and perhaps a glimpse of a sumptuous courtyard beyond.

The Oltrarno has always been the artisans' district. In the modest studios and workshops slotted between palaces or half hidden at the backs of courtyards where everything blends together in a way peculiar to Italy, the old crafts are carried on as they always were: woodcarving, framing and gilding. The Oltrarno is also the center of the antique trade. The most typical streets are Via Santa Monica, Via Maggio, Via Sant'Agostino and Via de'Serragli but do not neglect Borgo San Iacopo (MAP II E3), Via di Santo Spirito and Borgo San Frediano.

▬▬ *VIA MAGGIO*
(MAP II EF 2-3)

This street, well designed and lined with palaces, is the most dignified of all the roads of the Oltrarno. The **Palace of the Rosselli del Turco family** (15th century) is at n° 40. At n° 26 you can see the **House of Bianca Cappello,** also known as the **Palazzo Buontalenti,** named after the architect who designed it (1566). The facade is decorated from the ground floor up with frescoes. Although weathered by the years, their colors still look bright in the sunlight. Above the entrance, a stone shield in the shape of a hat evokes the memory of *Bianca Cappello* (her surname means hat) who lived here.

Bianca was the mistress of Francesco dei Medici, heir to the Duchy of Tuscany. On the death of Joanna of Austria, Francesco's wife, Bianca, persuaded him to marry her (1578) and became in turn the grand duchess of Tuscany. In doing so, she provoked the fury of her brother-in-law, Cardinal Ferdinando dei Medici, the heir presumptive to the throne.

Francesco and Bianca died after a meal at Poggio (1587). Ferdinando was accused of being behind their sudden deaths. In another version of the story, Bianca was supposed to have prepared a poisoned cake for the Cardinal but she and her husband mistakenly ate the poisoned part. Bianca Cappello was beautiful. The painters of Florence have left numerous portraits of her in the Uffizi, the Palazzo Pitti and the Palazzo Vecchio.

▬▬ *PIAZZA SANTO SPIRITO*★
(MAP II E 2)

This is one of the most charming squares in the city, elongated and irregular in shape. The garden, full of shady trees in the center, was planted in the last century. A market adds a lively note to the whole square and painters often set up their easels there. At the extremities of the square stand the **church of Santo Spirito** and the **Palazzo Guadagni★**, attributed to *Simone del Pollaiuolo,* called *Il Cronaca* (1503). To the left of the white facade of the church (at n° 29) you can see the **Cenacolo di Santo Spirito** (*visit: 9 am to 2 pm; Sun 9 am to 1 pm: closed Mon*), the only vestige remaining of a 14th-century Augustinian monastery. It contains a fresco painted in 1360 by *Orcagna,* who executed a great many works in Florence in the 14th century. The fresco depicts the "Crucifixion" and the **Last Supper★**; in spite of changes made to it, it is considered as one of the Florentine painter's major works. The 14th-century refectory, which was bought by the antiquarian *Salvatore Romano,* also contains collections of sculpture donated by him to the city in 1946. There are works by *Donatello, Jacopo della Quercia, Tino de Camaiano,* etc.

Santo Spirito★★ (MAP II E2)

The church of the Holy Ghost was designed in 1440 by *Brunelleschi*, but the original plan differed considerably from the church we see today which was built by *Antonio Manetti* and various other architects. The church should have faced the river, thus dominating a broad esplanade. The facade was never completed and is all white. The cupola, which was also designed by *Brunelleschi*, was not built until the end of the 15th century.

The bell-tower was built between 1503 and 1517 by *Baccio d'Agnolo*. Although the result does not conform to *Brunelleschi's* original idea, the group has architectural clarity and unity. Along with the church of San Lorenzo, on which the artist worked concurrently, this is one of the most elegant buildings of the early Renaissance.

The interior is magnificently planned. Thirty-five columns rhythmically divide the three naves. Apart from its architectural interest, Santo Spirito is also a veritable art gallery; many valuable works hang in its 40 semi-circular chapels (numbered here from right to left).

Right of nave. 2nd chapel: the "Pietà" (1549), by *Baccio Bigio*, is a copy of the original by *Michelangelo* (in St. Peter's in Rome).

Right transept. 15th chapel: **Virgin with Saints and Donators★** (*c.* 1490), by *Filippino Lippi*; 17th chapel: the sarcophagus of Neri Capponi (1458), attributed to *B. Rossellini*.

Apse. 18th chapel: "Virgin and Saints", school of *Lorenzo di Credi*; 23rd chapel: "Annunciation", Florentine school of the 15th century; 24th chapel: "Nativity", school of *Ghirlandaio*; 25th chapel: "Virgin", by *Raffaellino del Garbo*.

Left transept. 26th chapel: "St. Monica", by *F. Botticini*; 27th chapel: "Virgin and Saints" (1481), by *Cosimo Rosselli*. The 28th chapel (marble architecture and decoration; 1492) is an early work by *Andrea Sansovino*, who also executed the "Last Supper", the tabernacle and the "Life of the Virgin"; the balustrade was made in 1642. In the 31st chapel, you will see a "Virgin with Saints" (1505), by *R. del Garbo*; in the 32nd chapel, a "Calvary" by *M. Ghirlandaio*, and a stained glass window depicting the "Incredulity of St. Thomas".

Choir. The baldaquin (1608) over the high altar, by *Giovanni Caccini*, is not lacking in grandeur but it does not fit in with the style of the church.

Left of nave. 33rd chapel: "Maestà" by *Fra Bartolomeo*; 37th chapel: "Virgin", "St. Anne and Saints" by *Michele* and *Ridolfo Ghirlandaio*; 40th chapel: "Christ Resurrected", by *Taddeo Landini*, based on a work by *Michelangelo* in the church of Santa Maria sopra Minerva, Rome.

On the left side of the nave, below the organ, you will see the late 15th-century vestibule, by *Simone del Pollaiuolo* (called *Il Cronaca*), which precedes the octagonal sacristy (1489–92) by *Sangallo*; the cupola was built in 1497 according to a design by *Simone del Pollaiuolo* and *Salvi di Andrea*. From the vestibule, a door opens into the 17th-century cloister.

▬▬ *SANTA MARIA DEL CARMINE★*
(MAP II E1)

St. Mary of Carmel, usually known as the Carmine, is situated right in the center of the Oltrarno district and is a reminder of the place held by the Virgin in the faith of the hermits of Mount Carmel in Palestine centuries ago.

The interior of the Romanesque-Gothic church of 1268, remodeled during the succeeding centuries, was destroyed by fire in 1771; fortunately the exterior and the sacristy were undamaged. The interior was reconstructed in the 18th century by *Giulio Mannaioni*. The chapel of Sant'Andrea Corsini (bishop of Fiesole, 1301–73), at the end of the left transept, which was built by *G. Silvani* in 1683, and the **Brancacci chapel** at the end of the right transept, also survived the fire.

The **frescoes**✶✶ (under restoration) in the Brancacci chapel constitute the most important work of art in the church. They were begun in 1424–25 by *Masolino da Panicale* and continued by *Masaccio* in 1426 and 1427, then finished by *Filippino Lippi* in 1485. They show, in the main, episodes in the life of St. Peter.

Upper frescoes (from left to right): **Adam and Eve Expelled from Paradise** and **Payment of the Tribute**✶ (*Masaccio*); "St. Peter Preaching" (*Masolino*); "St. Peter Baptizing" and **St. Peter Healing a Cripple**✶ (*Masaccio*); **St. Peter Raising Tobias from the Dead**✶ (*Masolino* and *Masaccio*); **The Temptation of Adam**✶ (*Masolino*).

Lower frescoes (from left to right); "St. Peter Visited by St. Paul in Prison" (*Lippi*); "St. Peter Raising the Emperor's Nephew from the Dead" (*Masaccio* and *Lippi*); "St. Peter in the Pulpit", "St. Peter Healing the Sick" and "St. Peter and St. John Giving Alms" (*Masaccio*); "Crucifixion of St. Peter", "St. Peter Before the Proconsul" and "The Angel Delivering St. Peter from Prison" (*Lippi*).

Although it can be difficult to distinguish *Masolino's* part of the work from *Lippi's*, there is no mistaking the inspiration, style and composition of *Masaccio's*. This chapel is considered to be his masterpiece. We know that he interrupted work on it to go to Rome, where he died two years later in 1429, aged 28. His work is characterized by his sense of space, along with the geometrical abstraction with which the scenes and characters are arranged. It is understandable that this fresco, spared by the fire, should have had such a great influence on Florentine art of the 15th century, and more still on modern painting.

In the choir, look at the funerary monument of Piero Soderini, Gonfaloniere of the Republic (1522; buried in Rome), by *Benedetto da Rovezzano*.

A door on the left of the Brancacci chapel gives access to the **sacristy** (15th century) which has a number of 14th- and 15th-century paintings and frescoes by *Bicci di Lorenzo*. From here you can go into the beautiful 17th-century **cloister** which is also decorated with frescoes, notably by *Alessandro Allori*.

From the steps of the church you can see in the distance the delicate cupola of the church of San Frediano in Castello, built by *Cerruti* in 1698.

ITINERARY F
ARISTOCRATIC FLORENCE

Via de'Tornabuoni, the great palaces, Santa Trinita, Borgo Santissimi Apostoli, Santa Maria Novella.

In Florence, all roads lead to the Duomo; the famous cupola, always visible above the roofs, is a perennial reference point. This itinerary starts from the Duomo and takes you through the elegant district around the Via de'Tornabuoni. This is Florence as one imagines it in all its luxury and refinement. The Renaissance is expressed here in the arrogant nobility of the palaces which leave only a small strip of sky visible between them; the names of these palaces — Strozzi, Rucellai, Bartolini-Salimbeni and Spini-Feroni — evoke the powerful families for whom they were built.

The Florentines observed the construction of these buildings with particular attention and never failed to pass judgement on them in lively terms. The architect *Baccio d'Agnolo* built the Palazzo Bartolini-Salimbeni in a style which left the Renaissance behind in favor of forms that verged on the Baroque. It was more Roman than Florentine and the critics had plenty to say. In the end, the architect avenged himself by placing a stone plaque above the door with the inscription: *Carpere promptius quam imitari* "To criticize is easier than to copy".

At the end of your walk, it is worthwhile to spend a good hour to the church of Santa Maria Novella. For those arriving by train, this is their first sight of Florence. The Cistercian simplicity imported from France blends well with the Renaissance decoration.

Via de'Cerretani (MAP II C4)

This lively street passes **Santa Maria Maggiore,** a 13th-century Gothic church which has often been restored. Its austere interior is decorated with 14th-century frescoes. In the chapel to the right of the choir is a 13th-century polychrome wood relief of the "Virgin and Child", surrounded by paintings. At the corner of the Via de'Cerretani, at the base of the bell-tower, is a late Roman bust familiarly known to the Florentines as *Berta.*

Santa Maria Novella: the facade, inspired by classical architecture.

Piazza Antinori (MAP II C3)

This square takes its name from the **Palazzo Antinori,** built in the 15th century by *Giuliano da Maiano*. The church opposite, **San Gaetano,** was built in 1648 by *Nigetti* and the *Silvanis*. It is a rare example of Florentine Baroque.

Via de'Tornabuoni★ (MAP II CD3)

Since the 15th century, this has been the most aristocratic street in Florence, often called "the city's drawing room". It is broad, though not very long, and is lined with majestic palaces which house world-famous luxury shops such as *Gucci, Ferragamo*, etc. In the evening, sodium lights give the street the unreal atmosphere of a stage set.

▬ THE GREAT PALACES

Palazzo Strozzi★★ (MAP II D3)

This elegant noble residence of the Renaissance period was begun in 1489 according to plans by *Benedetto da Maiano*. After *Da Maiano's* death, *Simone del Pollaiuolo* took over and worked on the building from 1497 to 1504. He added the cornice and the **courtyard★**. It was left unfinished by the Strozzi who, having failed to compete with the Medici in commerce and banking, moved to Lyons in France where they managed to make a fortune.

The building, which is square, opens onto the street through a large portal, forming an arch framed with square windows at the ground level. The upper floors have pairs of arched windows. The construction of the building represents the flowering of an architecture which began with the Palazzo Medici-Riccardi in the 15th century. The torch- and standard-bearers, which only noble families were allowed to possess, were made by the master blacksmith *Niccolò Grosso*, known as *Il Caparra* (*caparra* means advance; the master craftsman would not accept any job without an advance on the payment).

Today, the palace houses various cultural institutes and is used for temporary exhibitions, notably the Biennial Antique Fair (Sept to Oct, every other year on odd-numbered years).

Palazzo Rucellai★ (MAP II D2-3)

Not far from the Palazzo Strozzi at n°18, in the small Via della Vigna Nuova, you can see the beautiful facade of the Palazzo Rucellai, one of the best examples of Renaissance architecture. The architect, *Leon Battista Alberti* (1404–72), drew up the plans for a rich merchant, *Giovanni Rucellai*, in 1446. The building was completed by *Bernardo Rossellino* in 1451.

Here, the break with medieval traditions is complete; the Classical order, inspired by antiquity, prevails. "Without order," said Alberti, "nothing is pleasing to the eye." This first Renaissance palace is exemplary in its clarity of line and suppleness of design; it leaves behind the heaviness of preceding eras. The fortress has lost its *raison d'être* and domestic life begins to be more open to the exterior. Facing the palace is the **Loggia dei Rucellai,** also designed by *Alberti* for fêtes and meetings.

Nearby, in the Via della Spada, the **Rucellai chapel** contains the Holy Sepulchre temple, a small rectangular building in black and white marble of geometric design. This is also by *Alberti* (1467). Not far away stand the abbatial **church of San Pancrazio** (MAP II CD3), with an atrium in front of it, and the monastery which *Alberti* restored for the Rucellai. San Pancrazio is shortly to become a museum dedicated to the works of *Marino Marini* who began his career in Florence.

Piazza Santa Trinita★ (MAP II D3)

In the center of the square stands the column of Justice which came from the baths of Caracalla in Rome. It is a monolithic block of granite that was presented by *Pope Paul IV* to *Cosimo dei Medici*, the first grand duke of Tuscany, who used it as a symbol of his victory over the Sienese coalition, at Scannagallo, in 1554. The statue of Justice was made in 1581 by *Francesco Ferrucci*, also known as *Il Tadda*.

The controversial **Palazzo Bartolini-Salimbeni★** at n° 1, was built by *Baccio d'Agnolo* in 1520. The architect's mocking plaque in answer to his critics can still be seen over the door. The courtyard, in particular, shows the elements of the new Baroque style.

To the right of the Palazzo Bartolini, at the corner of the Borgo SS. Apostoli and the Via de'Tornabuoni, stands the **Palazzo Spini-Ferroni,** a sort of three-floored fortress with a crenellated roof. It was built in 1289 on the banks of the Arno and served as a sentinel post from which the recently built Santa Trinita bridge could be guarded. Facing it is the **Palazzo Gianfigliazzi,** built at around the same time as the Palazzo Spini but smaller.

The Via Porta Rossa runs past the Palazzo Bartolini on the left. The severe **Palazzo Davanzati★** (MAP II D3), a perfect example of a 14th-century patrician house, is at n° 9. It is now the **Museo della Casa Fiorentina Antica** (*guided tours: 9.30, 10.30, 11.30 am and 12.30 pm. No 12.30 tour on Sun or holidays. Closed Mon*). The rooms are arranged around a central courtyard lined with colonnaded arcades.

From the courtyard, a staircase leads to the upper floors and a 16th-century covered terrace. In the living rooms and bedrooms, there are paintings, sculptures, furniture, pottery, tapestries, household objects and utensils which recreate Florentine domestic life from the 14th to the 17th centuries. Note the fresco decoration, especially in the **Parrot Room** (sala dei papagali, 14th century).

▬ *SANTA TRINITA★*
(MAP II D3)

Although the facade of the church of S. Trinita was built in 1593 by *Bernardo Buontalenti* in the Baroque style, the church itself is much older, as you will realize on entering it. The present church was built in the 13th century, replacing an 11th-century building which itself was constructed on the site of a 9th-century oratory. The crypt of the 11th-century church is a reminder of the monks of Vallombrosa (the mountain near Florence) who reformed the Benedictine rule under *San Giovanni Gualberto*. The austere life of the monks had a considerable effect on the tone and morals of the city when they settled in Florence.

Once past the facade, the décor changes and, from ostentatious decoration, we come to the simplicity of the shadowy interior, where exuberance gives way to meditation, serenity, purity and humility. There are three naves with five chapels on each side. Frescoes dating from the 14th century are still visible on most of the walls.

Right nave. 1st chapel: 13th-century crucifix (restored). According to tradition, it was carried in the processions organized by the Compagnia dei Bianchi, penitents who wanted to reconcile warring families and end the divisions between political factions by substituting the arms of religion for the poison and knives commonly in use in the city. 3rd chapel: "Virgin and Saints" (1491) by *Neri di Bicci*; 4th chapel: on the altar, **Annunciation★** (1425) by *Lorenzo Monaco*; on the walls, frescoes by the same artist (master of *Fra Angelico*) depicting the "Life of the Virgin" and "Prophets"; 5th chapel: marble altar by *Benedetto da Rovezzano*, and 14th-century frescoes ("Pietà").

Right transept. The **Sassetti chapel★** (2nd to the right of the high altar) is decorated with frescoes (1483–86) by *Domenico Ghirlandaio* depicting various episodes in the "Life of St. Francis", against an elegant background of 15th-century Florentine life; apart from the *Sassetti* family, a number of prominent people of the time figure in this work. Behind the altar in this chapel, you can see depicted the Palazzo Spini-Ferroni and the Piazza Santa Trinita as it was before the addition of *Buontalenti's* facade. Against a view of the Signoria are *Lorenzo dei Medici,* the young *Giuliano dei Medici, Agnolo Poliziano,* the humanist who taught Lorenzo's children and composed poetry both in classical languages and Tuscan, and the poet *Luigi Pulci.* The tombs of Francesco Sassetti and his wife, Nera Corsi (1495), against the walls, are attributed to *Giuliano da Sangallo.* The "Adoration of the Shepherds" on the altar (1495), and the fresco of the Sibyl Tiburtina (on the outside arch) are by *Ghirlandaio.* In the Ficozzi chapel (1st on the right of the high altar), the miraculous crucifix of San Giovanni Gualberto is by an anonymous master.

Choir. On the high altar is a triptych by *Mariotto di Nardo* showing the "Holy Trinity and Saints" (1416).

Left transept. Over the arches of the chapels, there are frescoes (1434) by *Giovanni del Ponte.* The marble **tomb of Benozzo Federighi★,** bishop of Fiesole, with a glazed terra-cotta mosaic border (1456), in the 2nd chapel to the left of the high altar, is by *Luca della Robbia.*

Left nave. 15th chapel: the statue of Mary Magdalen (in wood; 1464) by *Desiderio da Settignano,* was completed by *Benedetto da Maiano* in 1468; 4th chapel: "Coronation of the Virgin", in the style of *Bicci di Lorenzo,* and the tombstone of Dino Compagni (1260–1323), chronicler and friend of Dante; 3rd chapel: on the altar, "Annunciation" (1491), by *Neri di Bicci;* the tomb of Giuliano Davanzati is a Paleo-Christian sarcophagus with added bas-relief work; 2nd chapel: on the altar, the "Mystical Marriage of St. Catherine of Sienna", by *Antonio del Ceraiolo* (16th century); on the walls, two paintings (1503) by *Ridolfo Ghirlandaio,* one of them is an "Annunciation". The crypt (stairs in the nave) has the remains of the 11th-century Romanesque church, which was situated on a much lower level.

▬▬ *BORGO SS. APOSTOLI*
(MAP II DE3)

This street, which faces the church of Santa Trinita, is a perfect example of the medieval streets of Florence. There are still numerous tower-houses from the 13th and 14th centuries. Across from n° 17–19 is the narrow, short Via del Fiordaliso where you can see some interesting overhung houses. N° 17–19 itself is the **Palazzo Rosselli del Turco,** built by *Baccio d'Agnolo* in 1517; at the side of the palace overlooking a little square below, is a Virgin (16th century), sculpted by *Benedetto da Rovezzano.* Next to the palace in this little square stands the **church of SS. Apostoli★,** surrounded by the old houses of the district. It is an 11th-century building with beautiful Renaissance doors by *Rovezzano.*

The interior, with its three naves, is built on the basilica plan; the columns are in green marble from Prato. The capitals were taken from Roman buildings. The terra-cotta tabernacle (on the left of the high altar) is by *Giovanni della Robbia.* Note also the two tombs of the Altoviti, next to the tabernacle (1399) and over the door of the sacristy (1507), to the right. This church houses some pieces of flintstone said to have been taken from the Holy Sepulchre during the first Crusade; each year, at Easter, during the traditional ceremony known as the Scoppio del Carro (explosion of the cart; see p. 50), they are taken to the cathedral where they are used to light the "sacred flame".

▰ *PONTE SANTA TRINITA*★
(MAP II E3)

This bridge, which was rebuilt after the last war, is part of the traditional imagery of Florence. It was built by *Bartolomeo Ammannati* in 1570 in place of an older bridge which was twice destroyed by floods and the ravages of time. In 1608, marble statues of the Four Seasons, made by *Francavilla*, *Caccini* and *Landini* were placed at the four corners.

The bridge stands on two piles, inspired by those of the Ponte Vecchio, and has three arches which seem to play with gravity, giving the impression that the architect was testing geometrical theorems in space. For a long time, people wondered whether his structure would hold. *Ammannati*, ahead of his time, was able to calculate exactly the stress to which the bridge would be subjected and, apparently solving problems as fast as he encountered them, spanned the Arno with a work of architecture, remarkable for its grace and flexibility.

Lungarno Corsini (MAP II D2-3). This stretch of the river bank is named after an illustrious Florentine family who played an important role in the history of Italy. *St. Andrea Corsini* (1301–73), bishop of Fiesole (buried in the church of Santa Maria del Carmine), and *Pope Clement XII* (1652–1740) were among its members. N° 10, the **Palazzo Corsini,** with its statue-filled terraces and its remarkable spiral **staircase★**, is an excellent example of 17th-century Florentine Baroque architecture. The palace houses the **Corsini Gallery★** (*visits by request, tel: 28-76-29; entrance at n° 11 Via di Parione*). This rich, private collection dates from 1765 and is a rare example of the personal museum which amateurs in those days were able to assemble. Apart from beautiful furniture, the gallery contains some unique works by the Florentine school of the 15th and 16th centuries (*Filippino Lippi, Signorelli, Raphael, Pontormo,* etc.), and paintings by Italian and foreign artists of the 17th and 18th centuries. The **Ponte alla Carraia** is at the end of the Lungarno Corsini; the British consulate is at n° 2.

Piazza Ognissanti (MAP II C1). This charming square faces the river (Lungarno Amerigo Vespucci) and offers a fine view of the nearby hills. It is decorated with a piece of modern sculpture, Hercules Fighting the Lion, by *Romano Romanelli*. At n° 2 in the square, on the corner of the Borgo Ognissanti, the 15th-century **Palazzo Quaratesi,** formerly the Palazzo Lensi Busini, houses the French consulate and the French Institute. In the Borgo Ognissanti you can also see the old **Palazzo Vespucci** (until recently it was the hospital of San Giovanni di Dio), where *Amerigo Vespucci* was born in 1454 (see below, church of the Ognissanti).

The church of the Ognissanti (All Saints)★ (MAP II C1-2)

The church was founded in the middle of the 13th century but its Baroque aspect dates from its reconstruction which was begun in 1638 by *Matteo Nigetti* in a manner not at all pleasing to Florentine taste. All that remains of the original building is the beautiful bell-tower and the 15th-century terra-cotta tympanum depicting the **Coronation of the Virgin★** above the main door — the work of *Benedetto Buglioni*.

The interior is a mixture of styles and works of the Renaissance and the 17th century. Above the second altar on the right, there is a fresco by *Domenico Ghirlandaio* depicting the **Madonna of Mercy Sheltering the Vespucci Family★** (*c.* 1470). One of the family, the navigator *Amerigo Vespucci* (1454–1512) was to explore the coast of the New World on behalf of the king of Portugal and give his name to the American continent (1507). The explorer figures in this fresco as the young man in red between the Madonna and an old man; also in the fresco is *Simonetta Cattaneo*, one of the nymphs of *Botticelli's* Primavera, who was a mistress of Giuliano dei Medici. To the left of the altar you can see the tombstone of the Vespucci.

In one of the chapels in the **right transept,** a plaque on the floor marks the corner where *Botticelli* was buried. The frescoes (1617) on the cupola and the high altar below are by *Giovanni da San Giovanni*. In the sacristy, frescoes have been uncovered which are by *Taddeo* and *Agnolo Gaddi*; the "Crucifix" on canvas is by the school of *Giotto*.

From the left transept or, if this access is closed, from the exterior at n° 38, to the left of the church, you can enter the Renaissance **cloister.** The frescoes which decorated it have been removed for restoration. They are by *Jacopo Ligozzi* and *Giovanni da San Giovanni* and depict the life of St. Francis.

The old refectory of the convent is decorated on the far wall with a fresco (1480) by *Domenico Ghirlandaio*: the **Last Supper★** (*Cenacolo del Ghirlandaio*). It is probable that *Leonardo da Vinci* was inspired by this work in his "Last Supper" painted in Milan but the techniques are different: *Ghirlandaio* is less dramatic; his composition is less agitated. The figures are strongly portrayed; with his simple realism the artist has produced a work which is both lyrical and solemn, and which harmonizes well with the surroundings for which it was conceived.

There is also a fresco by *Botticelli* depicting St. Augustin (1480) and another by *Domenico Ghirlandaio* of "St. Jerome at Work" (1480). The refectory contains several other frescoes.

Piazza Santa Maria Novella (MAP II C2-3)

In the Middle Ages, this was the center of a very poor district. The mendicant brothers of the order of St. Dominic, who had come to Florence to preach a renewal of the faith, settled there because there was no place available in the city center. Members of the Church there would have no part of their preaching about poverty. Towards 1246, an old church consecrated to the Virgin was conceded to them. Two architects of the order, *Fra Sisto* and *Fra Ristoro* transformed the small, half-abandoned sanctuary into a magnificent building that could compete with the Cathedral. This was Santa Maria Novella, the church that gives its name to the square. In the center of the square, two marble obelisks resting on bronze tortoises by *Giambologna* (1608) mark the extremities of the space reserved for the Palio dei Cocchi, a chariot race introduced by Cosimo I in 1563 and which took place every year on June 24. Facing the church, the **Loggia di San Paolo** (1496) has beautiful arcades decorated with terra-cottas by *Andrea* and *Giovanni della Robbia*: the 1st medallion on the left outside is a self-portrait of Andrea; the last medallion on the right is his uncle Luca. The lunette beneath the arcade shows the "Meeting of St. Francis and St. Domininic" by *Andrea*.

▬▬ *SANTA MARIA NOVELLA★★*
(MAP II B2–3)

The church was begun in 1246 by *Fra Sisto da Firenze* and *Fra Ristoro da Campi*, but it remained unfinished for a long time: *Fra Jacopo Talenti* was given the job of continuing the construction in 1330 and worked until 1360 when he completed the Romanesque-Gothic bell-tower. The **facade★**, dressed with polychrome marble, was begun in the 14th century (the lower part) and was continued by *Leon Battista Alberti* (1456), for the Rucellai family. *Alberti* designed the upper part of the facade in the style of a Classical temple.

The mixture of the Gothic with the decorative flowering of the Renaissance lends an air of magnificence and joy which blends well with the purity of the lines. To the right of the church lies the old cemetery of the Florentine aristocracy.

The interior of the church is a blend of Florentine Gothic and the Cistercian style imported from France; the generous lines of the former, in particular, add a dimension of space and light to the exhalation of bareness and poverty.

Right nave. Monument (1451) to the Blessed Villana Betti (*d.* 1360), by *Bernardo Rossellino*, and the tomb of the Blessed G. da Salerno (14th century); facing the 5th pillar, the Cappella della Pura, Renaissance period (1474), consecrated to the Virgin (14th-century frescoes and crucifix). From here, you can go out into the old cemetery which stretches along this side of the church. It is now a garden with cypress trees and roses.

Right transept. Tabernacle with a realistic terra-cotta bust of Sant'Antonino (15th century); above, against the wall, the tomb of Bishop Aliotti of Fiesole (d. 1336) is attributed to *Tino di Camaino*. Higher up still, you can see the tomb of Aldobrando Cavalcanti (d. 1279), bishop of Orvieto, by *Nino Pisano*; below is the tomb of Joseph, patriarch of Constantinople, who died during the Ecumenical Council of 1439, which was held in Florence. A small staircase leads up to the Rucellai chapel which bears traces of some 14th-century frescoes on its walls. The "Maestà" by *Duccio di Buoninsegna* used to be here but it is now in the Uffizi. The tomb slab of Fra Leonardo Dati (1425), by *Ghiberti* is on the floor. The Bardi chapel (2nd on the right of the choir) is decorated with 14th-century frescoes; on the pillar to the right of the entrance there is a relief of St. George (13th century); the Strozzi chapel (1st on the right of the choir) is decorated with **frescoes★** (1492–1502) by *Filippino Lippi*: "Life of St. Philip" and "St. John the Evangelist". Here, Botticelli's pupil is moving away from the master and giving his work a movement which anticipates Mannerist and Baroque painting. The tomb of Filippo Strozzi the Elder (1491) is by *B. da Maiano*.

Chapel of the high altar. Also known as the Tornabuoni chapel, it forms the apse. There is a bronze crucifix by *Giambologna* on the altar. The choir stalls and the lectern are by *Baccio d'Agnolo* and *Vasari*. The vault and walls are decorated with **frescoes★** by *Domenico Ghirlandaio*, depicting the "Life of the Virgin" and the "Life of St. John the Baptist" — they were painted between 1485 and 1490. As in the church of Santa Trinita, Florence serves as the background for the various episodes represented, and the people of the city figure in the paintings. The *Tornabuoni* family occupies the most important place. *Ghirlandaio* paid great attention to detail and, in this work, he left a faithful record of his time, his city and its way of life. The women's clothes, which are of an astonishing richness, are rendered with the care of a fashion designer. It is thought that *Michelangelo*, who was attached to this painter's studio at the time, may have worked on these frescoes. The stained glass window (1492) at the back is also by *Ghirlandaio*.

Left transept. The Gondi chapel (1st on left of choir) has polychrome marble decoration (1503) by *Giuliano da Sangallo*; the vault has the remains of frescoes by 13th-century Greek artists; on the back wall hangs a **crucifix★** in wood by *Brunelleschi*, made between 1410 and 1425. The Gaddi chapel (2nd to the left of the choir) has architectural decoration by *Giovanni Antonio Dosio* (1515–77), stucco and frescoes (vault) by *A. Allori* and a painting by *Bronzino*. A staircase leads to the Strozzi chapel: beneath the staircase, there is a 'Descent from the Cross' by the school of *Orcagna*.

The **Strozzi chapel★** is decorated with frescoes by *Nardo di Cione*, Andrea Orcagna's brother, painted between 1328 and 1331. On the far wall is the "Last Judgement"; on the left, "Paradise", on the right, "Hell". These are illustrations of the "Divine Comedy". Dante died a few years earlier. The poet is seen among the people in Paradise. The **polyptych** of "Christ in Majesty" (1357), on the altar, is by *Orcagna*. The medallions on the vault, showing "St. Dominic" and the "Virtues", are by *Nardo di Cione*. A door in the west wall of the transept gives access to the sacristy (1350), built by *Fra Jacopo Talenti*, in which there is a **crucifix★★** by *Giotto* of great dramatic beauty; the slip-decorated terra-cotta lavabo (1498) is by *Giovanni della Robbia*.

Left nave. The wall (under the third section) is decorated with a **fresco★★** by *Masaccio* depicting the 'Holy Trinity', 'The Virgin with St. John the Evangelist' and, under the altar, 'Death' (1426). On each side of this realistic work you can see the two donors. In this fresco, *Masaccio* has applied in painting the architectural ideas of *Brunelleschi*. The pulpit, on the second pillar of the central nave, was designed by *Brunelleschi* and sculpted by *Andrea Cavalcanti* (called *Il Buggiano*), *Brunelleschi's* adopted son, in 1462.

From this pulpit, *Caccini* denounced the theories of *Galileo*. The tomb of the juris-consult A. Strozzi (1524; to the right of the altar in the left nave) is by *Andrea Ferrucci da Fiesole*.

Museum of Santa Maria Novella★ (MAP II B2)

Visit: 9 am to 7 pm; Sun 8 am to 12.30 pm. Closed Friday.

On the left of the church, you will first enter the Romanesque **Green Cloister,** built by *Fra Giovanni da Campi* in 1350. It owes its name to the frescoes (1430) by *Paolo Uccello* and his pupils, in which the dominant colors are green and raw sienna. To protect them from the humidity which has already damaged most of the figures, the frescoes have been detached from the walls. They show scenes from the Old Testament. The better preserved ones: **The Flood★**, the **Story of Noah★**, the "Creation of Adam" and the "Creation of Eve", are on show in the old refectory (entrance in the north-east corner of the cloister) along with the preparatory drawings discovered under the frescoes. Many of them are by *Uccello*.

The Spanish chapel (*cappellone degli Spagnoli*) opens off the cloister on the east side. It is so-called because it was here that religious offices were performed for the Spanish attendants of *Eleonora di Toledo*, wife of *Cosimo I dei Medici*. It is the old Chapter House, built by *Fra Jacopo Talenti* in 1359 in honor of St. Thomas Aquinas. The thoughts of the theologian *Jacopo Passaventi* (1298–1358) inspired the frescoes painted here (1366) by *Andrea di Bonaiuto*, called *Andrea di Firenze*. The artist has illustrated the allegory of "True Penitence", glorifying the Dominican order. On the vault are the basic themes of Christianity: the "Resurrection", the "Ascension" and "Pentecost"; on the facing wall is a "Calvary", a "Crucifixion" and the "Descent into Limbo". On the left wall, "Divine Wisdom" comes to inspire the prophets and saints (among them "St. Thomas Aquinas' Triumph over Heresy"), thus conferring a supernatural value upon human work, of which the liberal arts (right) and the sacred arts (left) are the everyday expression. On the right wall we see the "Church Militant" and the "Church Triumphant" with the symbol of Christian society as it appears through the theological doctrine of St. Thomas Aquinas, with the pope, the emperor and the procession of men. White dogs with black spots, which symbolize the Dominicans, stand guard over a flock of sheep. St. Dominic, St. Thomas and St. Peter help sinners to resist temptation; the mortal sins shown are "Avarice", "Lust" and "Anger". Through confession, the sinners return to the purity of their childhood and, under the protection of the blessed Virgin, can enter Paradise. This complex group has been well restored.

On the altar, there is a 14th-century polyptych by *B. Daddi*.

As you come out of the chapel, you will see immediately to your left, a small corridor leading to the Cloister of the Dead (*chiostrino dei Morti*), a Romanesque construction with tombs of the great Florentine families and the remains of 14th-century frescoes. In a tympanum is a 15th-century fresco of "St. Thomas Aquinas". In the small chapel, a terra-cotta work from the *Della Robbia* workshop can be seen. Entitled "Noli me tangere", it depicts the resurrected Christ meeting Mary Magdalen.

The **Stazione Centrale** (MAP II A2) is behind Santa Maria Novella. It was built between 1932–34 by *Giovanni Michelucci* and members of his studio. It is undoubtedly one of the better examples of Rational architecture in Italy. From the station you have a good view of the apse and bell-tower (1360) of **Santa Maria Novella.**

ITINERARY G
FROM THE MUSEUM OF SAN MARCO
TO THE ACCADEMIA GALLERY

**Museum of San Marco, Accademia Gallery,
SS. Annunziata, Ospedale degli Innocenti,
Archeological Museum.**

Almost a century separates *Fra Angelico* and *Michelangelo* but it is not so much time as their different ways of seeing the world which makes them such opposites. The former, with his simple, happy faith exalts the glory of God and the marvels of creation in his radiant message; the latter translates his life struggles, his revolt and his doubts into artistic terms with works which are charged with great dramatic power. Chance would have it that some of their most important works are geographically close together; the buildings that house them nearly face each other across the Piazza San Marco. As you leave the museum of San Marco and enter the Accademia Gallery, which house the works of *Fra Angelico* and *Michelangelo* respectively, it is like moving out of the sunlight into the shade.

When young couples marry in Florence, they traditionally come to pray to the miraculous Virgin of Santissima Annunziata to ensure their future prosperity and happiness. The sanctuary, which is one of the most venerated in Florence, is covered with gifts to the Virgin, and this intrusive decoration contrasts with the simple elegance of the square where the church stands. This is, without doubt, an urban landscape faithful to the spirit of the Renaissance.

After seeing all the masterpieces in the two museums mentioned above, you will probably not feel like visiting the Archeological Museum. Leave it until the afternoon, or even the next day, if you have time, because it would be a pity to miss such a rich collection of Egyptian, Etruscan, Greek and Roman objects belonging to an era when Florence did not yet exist.

Via Cavour (MAP II B4-5)

This is a continuation of Via de'Martelli (which begins in the Cathedral Square), and is equally busy, at least until it reaches the Piazza San Marco. It is lined with palaces, notably the **Palazzo Medici-Riccardi** (see p. 65) and other noble dwellings of the 17th and 18th centuries.

Cenacolo di Sant'Apollonia⋆ (MAP II A4-5)

Entrance at n° 1 Via 27 Aprile. *Visit: 9 am to 2 pm; Sun 9 am to 1 pm. Closed Mon. Tel: 28-70-74.*

This is the old refectory of the convent of Sant'Apollonia which belonged to the nuns of Camaldoli. *Andrea del Castagno* decorated it with magnificent frescoes, *c.* 1450. The **Last Supper**⋆⋆ (1457), on the far wall, gives us the finest example of the artist's emotive power; it is a work which shows both his sense of drama and an insistent monumental rigidity. These same characteristics, especially an almost harsh severity, can be seen in his equestrian portrait of Niccolò da Tolentino in Santa Maria del Fiore.

The other frescoes depict the "Crucifixion", the "Deposition", the "Resurrection", "Saints" and a "Pietà".

At n° 25 Via San Gallo you can visit a charming and elegant 15th-century cloister belonging to this same convent.

Still in the Via San Gallo, you can see the Loggia dei Tessitori (16th century), the church of San Giovannino dei Cavalieri and the Palazzo Pandolfini (MAP I B4), built in 1520 according to a design by *Raphael*.

Chiostro dello Scalzo (MAP 1 B4)

69 Via Cavour (*temporarily closed; tel: 48-48-08*).

This is a 16th-century cloister decorated with monochrome frescoes depicting the **Life of St. John the Baptist**⋆ in 16 episodes. The frescoes were painted by *Andrea del Sarto* between 1512 and 1514; when he left for Paris in 1515, his pupil *Il Franciabigio* completed two of the frescoes.

Piazza San Marco (MAP II A5)

This is a classically beautiful square which takes its name from the church dedicated to the Evangelist. The adjoining convent is now the Museum of San Marco (or dell'Angelico). On the other side of the square, at the corner of Via Ricasoli, the **Accademia delle Belle Arti** has a 14th-century loggia with terra-cotta decoration by the *Della Robbia* workshop.

The church of San Marco

Built in the 13th century, this church was completely remodeled in 1452 by *Michelozzo* and enlarged by *Giambologna* who added another chapel (1580); it was modified again by *Pier Francesco Silvani* in 1678. The Baroque facade is by *Fra Gioacchino Pronti* (1780).

Inside, at the center of the gilded and coffered ceiling, there is a "Maestà" (1725) by *G.A. Pucci*. Above the portal is a "Crucifix" by the school of *Giotto*. On the 2nd altar on the right is a **Virgin**⋆ by *Fra Bartolomeo* (1508). The **Virgin at Prayer**⋆, on the 3rd altar, is a Byzantine mosaic (705) from the oratory of Pope John VII in Rome. In the left transept, the chapel of S. Antonino by *Giambologna* is decorated with frescoes by *Passignano* ("The Translation of the Saint's Remains"). Sant'Antonino (bishop of Florence and prior of San Marco) is buried beneath the altar.

In the wall on the left of the nave are the tombstones of Pico della Mirandola (1463–94) and Agnolo Poliziano (1454–94).

▬▬ MUSEUM OF SAN MARCO★★★
(MAP II A5)

Visit: 9 am to 2 pm; Sun 9 am to 1 pm. Closed Mon.

The entrance is at n° 3 in the square to the right of the church. The museum is housed in the evocative setting of the 13th-century Dominican convent of San Marco, which was rebuilt for the most part by *Michelozzo* (1452). In the 15th century, it was a notable cultural center: *Fra Angelico, Sant'Antonino, Savonarola* and *Fra Bartolomeo* all lived there. This museum is of exceptional interest: in 1866 almost the whole of Fra Angelico's work, until then scattered among the various churches and galleries of Florence, was assembled there.

Antonino Pierozzi (1389–1450), who was to become Sant'Antonino, was both the archbishop of Florence and the prior of San Marco. He was the one who put *Fra Giovanni* to work with *Michelozzo. Fra Giovanni* was a monk who had studied painting with *Lorenzo Monaco* and various miniaturists of the period and who was to achieve fame under the name of "*Beato* (Blessed) *Angelico*" (1387–1455). *Fra Angelico's* contribution to the building of San Marco was his faith. He was not a decorator but a monk like the others for whom religion impregnated every gesture and thought, influencing every hour of his day. For him, iconography was simply a means to meditation in the Byzantine sense. This collection of a hundred or so works, not all by his hand but all influenced by his inspiration and his personal style, covers the walls of the convent as if to accompany the monks in their daily life and define its purpose. *Fra Angelico* not only found a purpose for his work in each part of the building — the cells, the refectory, the meeting room — he also showed extraordinary skill in utilizing light and in setting his figures in a universe that blended realism and the supernatural. He presents Florence as a celestial Jerusalem. He does it simply and without effort, with a frankness that draws us in, attracted by the sweetness of the images and the freshness of his scenes and landscapes, the spiritual grandeur of his characters. He is a radiant and happy painter. The word "blessed" characterizes him exactly, a life's work illuminated by the most serene faith and created by an imagination to which figurative dramatizations were foreign.

Passing through the vestibule of the convent, you will enter the **Cloister of Sant'Antonino★**, decorated with 16th- and 17th-century frescoes depicting episodes in the saint's life (note the one on the tympanum near the entrance by *Bernardo Poccetti*, where you will see the cathedral of Santa Maria del Fiore). "St. Dominic at the Foot of the Cross" by *Fra Angelico* is on the wall facing the entrance. Above the door of the Pilgrims" Hospice, you can see "Jesus as a Pilgrim being Received by the Dominicans", by the same artist.

The Pilgrims' Hospice. This vast room contains a number of works by *Fra Angelico*, such as the **Tabernacolo dei Linaioli★★★** (commissioned by the linen guild — *Linaioli* — in 1433), a "Madonna and Child Enthroned" and some of his finest angel musicians. The marble tabernacle was made according to a design by *Ghiberti*. "The Marriage of the Virgin" and the "Death of the Virgin"; "The Naming of John the Baptist" (note the Tuscan town in the background); two "Maestàs"; scenes from the life of saints Cosmos and Damien (the burial scene shows Piazza San Marco as it was then) are also here. The 35 small pictures showing the **Life of Christ and the Virgin★** come from a polyptych which was in the church of SS. Annunziata; the scenes showing the "Flight into Egypt", "The Nativity", and "Christ Entering Jerusalem" are by *Fra Angelico*, the others by his pupils (three are by *Alessio Baldovinetti*). Note also the "Madonna of the Star" (1430); a large "Deposition" (1440); the **Last Judgement★** ("Paradise" is entirely by *Fra Angelico* while "Hell" was painted by his pupils); the "Coronation of the Virgin"; an "Annunciation" and an "Adoration of the Magi" (*Fra Angelico* shows himself to be a fine miniaturist here). On the far wall is another **Descent from the Cross★★** (1435) — Joseph of Arimathea is a portrait of *Michelozzo*, the architect of the convent; "The Resurrection", "Noli me tangere" and "The Holy Women" are by *Lorenzo Monaco*.

The Lavatorium. Devoted to works by *Fra Bartolomeo* (1472–1517); note the "Madonna with St. Anne and Saints".

The Great Refectory. On the right wall, there is a large fresco (damaged) by *Fra Bartolomeo* and *Albertinelli* depicting the "Last Judgement". On the far wall, there is a fresco by *G.A. Sogliani* showing the "Crucifixion" and an episode in the "Life of St. Dominic".

The Chapter House. Here you can admire one of *Fra Angelico's* greatest masterpieces: the large fresco of the **Crucifixion★★★** (1442) peopled with numerous saints who founded religious orders. The composition is on a grand scale and the figures are solidly constructed. From this arcade of the cloister, you will enter a corridor. To the left of the stairs is the Small Refectory with a fresco of the "Last Supper" by *Domenico Ghirlandaio* (the artist was to paint this subject again for the refectory of Ognissanti). The "Pietà" in terra-cotta is by *Andrea della Robbia*.

First floor. The cells on either side of the white corridors (note the visible wooden structure of the ceiling) are all decorated with frescoes painted between 1437 and 1445 by *Fra Angelico* and his pupils (though always from drawings by the master). These are probably the artist's finest works. At the top of the staircase, the visitor is welcomed by an **Annunciation★★★** and introduced to *Angelico's* world of mysticism and revelation. Taking the left corridor and beginning with the cells on the left, you will see *Fra Angelico's* beautiful frescoes in the following order: 1) "Noli me tangere"; 3) "The Annunciation"; 4) "The Crucifixion"; 6) "The Transfiguration"; 7) "The Crowning with Thorns"; 9) "The Coronation of the Virgin"; 11) "Virgin and Child with Saints".

At the end of the corridor, the prior's apartment consists of a vestibule and two cells where Savonarola once lived. It contains two paintings by *Fra Bartolomeo*: one is a portrait of Savonarola and the other of "St. Peter the Martyr" with the monk's features; the wooden crucifix, attributed to *Baccio da Montelupo*, was in this room when it was used as a study by Savonarola.

An ardent Dominican, Savonarola was born in Ferrara in 1452 and came to Florence in 1482. The Medici were then in power. The city, at the height of its glory, was the center of a pagan and sensual humanism which the monk condemned as an image of evil, at the same time denouncing the role of the Medici and demanding the creation of a theocratic republic, the advent of which he prophesied in a fever of language which hardly anyone was capable of ignoring. Even Lorenzo respected him. The arrival of Charles VIII, king of France, seemed to confirm Savonarola's warnings of impending punishment. Piero dei Medici left Florence and the city become a Republic, a sort of ideal State where God's rule was law, a terrible God who spoke through the mouth of Savonarola and which ended by alienating the entire population. On April 8, 1498, the convent where Savonarola lived was attacked by the people and the political preacher was hanged and burned in Piazza della Signoria on May 23, 1498. This dramatic event took place against a background of the most charming, gentle paintings ever produced in Italy.

After leaving Savonarola's cell, you will see those of the novices; almost all of the frescoes show St. Dominic at the foot of the cross and are by pupils of *Fra Angelico*. Cell 31 was once inhabited by Sant'Antonino, the one next to it by *Fra Angelico* himself who painted the frescoes in these two and in cells 34 and 35. At the end of the corridor, cells 38 and 39 were used by Cosimo the Elder who liked to retreat here, far from the world, to reflect and pray. They contain a "Crucifixion" and "The Virgin and Saints" by *Fra Angelico* and *Benozzo Gozzoli*, as well as an "Adoration of the Magi" by an unknown artist.

The **library★** (facing the window) was built by *Michelozzo* in 1441–44. It contains illuminated missals, hymn books and psalters and 14th-, 15th- and 16th-century manuscripts.

Museum of San Marco: 'Annunciation' by Fra Angelico.

THE ACCADEMIA GALLERY★★
(MAP II A5)

Visit: 9 am to 2 pm; Sun 9 am to 1 pm. Closed Mon.

The Accademia Gallery, which was created at the end of the 17th century, is as essential a place to visit as the Uffizi is for anyone wishing to know about Florentine painting from the 13th century to the Renaissance. It is a particularly important complement to a visit to the Medici chapel for anyone wanting to study the work of Michelangelo. The museum contains several of his major works.

The art of Michelangelo★★

The gallery, or "salone", is hung with 16th-, 17th- and 18th-century tapestries from Florence and Brussels. It contains some celebrated works by the master, notably the unfinished **Prisoners★** (1518), which should have surrounded the tomb of Pope Julius II in Rome (two other prisoners, almost completed, are in the Louvre). Michelangelo expressed his pain and rage in these extraordinary ghostly figures. Here we see the sculptor at work, trying to create with marble and chisel the forms of his dreams. A sense of the artist's passionate feelings emanates from the work. The statue of **St. Matthew**★ (1505), made to be one of a series of the Twelve Apostles commissioned for the facade of the Duomo is, likewise, unfinished. The **Pietà di Palestrina**★ (1520; destined for the church of Santa Rosalia di Palestrina in Rome, a property of the Barberini) is an undocumented work, no longer considered to be by Michelangelo's own hand.

Perhaps even more than the finished pieces, Michelangelo's unfinished works show an extraordinary exaltation of the subject matter and of the soul which animates the great artistic achievements of the painter of the Sistine chapel. His was a wild and passionate nature, and his life was a constant struggle. In an alcove at the far end is his **David**★★ (1501–04), which once stood in the Piazza della Signoria, until it was replaced, in 1873, by a copy. It is a very·accomplished work, of great dramatic power, which broke with Florentine Renaissance traditions to innovate a new style that was to lead the way to the Baroque. Above all, with its tragic content, it foreshadows the revolt and hardness which were predominant later in Michelangelo's style.

On the right of the David, there is a bronze bust of Michelangelo by his pupil and friend, *Daniele da Volterra*.

The Accademia also has a fine collection of paintings.

Room I. Florentine painters of the early 16th century: *Fra Bartolomeo, Albertini, Filippino Lippi, Perugino, G.A. Sogliani, Francesco Granacci*.

Rooms II–IV. Painters of the Florentine Renaissance: *Andrea di Giusto; Maestro del Cassone Adimari*, an unknown Florentine of the 15th century who painted the **Marriage Chest** (cassone) on which is depicted the "Adimari-Ricasoli Wedding in the Piazza San Giovanni" (note the portraits and costumes of the Florentines of the time); *Domenico di Michelino; Maestro della Natività di Castello; Cosimo Rosselli; Filippino Lippi*: "Annunciation"; *Ghirlandaio* or *Perugino*: "Visitation"; *Lorenzo di Credi; Baldorinetti*: "The Holy Trinity"; three paintings by *Botticelli*: the "Virgin and Child with St. John and Angels", and the "Virgin of the Sea" are the best; *Jacopo del Sellaio*; and *Raffaello del Garbo*.

Rooms V–VII (at present being reorganized). Florentine painters of the 13th and 14th centuries: panels and various crucifixes of the Tuscan school as well as works by *Pacino di Buonaguida; Maestro della Maddalena*, "Mary Magdalen"; *Andrea di Cione*, known as *Orcagna*, "Madonna with Two Angels and Four Saints"; *Nardo di Cione*, "The Holy Trinity"; *Jacopo di Cione*, "Coronation of the Virgin"; *B. Daddi; T. Daddi*, "Scenes from Life of Christ"; *A. Daddi; Giovanni da Milano*, "Pietà".

Room VIII (at present being reorganized). Florentine painters of the second half of the 16th century: *Pontormo, Bronzino, Michele Ridolfo* and *Ghirlandaio, A. Allori*. Three other rooms are to be opened on this floor.

As you leave the Accademia Gallery, you can either go directly to the Piazza SS. Annunziata or make a slight detour by way of the Museum of Musical Instruments and the Workshop of Mosaics and *Pietre Dure*. In this case, turn left as you leave the gallery, then left again into the Via degli Alfani (MAP II B5).

Museum of Musical Instruments

Museo degli Strumenti Musicali; entrance at n° 80 Via degli Alfani. The museum is temporarily closed and the instruments are on display in the Palazzo Vecchio.

Workshop of Mosaics and Pietre Dure

Opificio delle Pietre Dure: entrance at n° 78 Via degli Alfani. *Visit: 9 am to 1 pm. Closed Sun and holidays.*

This unique workshop was founded by *Ferdinando I dei Medici* (1549–1609). The work in semi-precious stones carried out here was used in the decoration of the Medici chapel (Cappella dei Principi) and of numerous churches and palaces in Florence. Craftsmen specializing in this work are still much in demand today.

To get to the Piazza SS. Annunziata, turn left as you come out of the workshop, then turn left into **Via de'Servi** which is lined with interesting palaces. Note particularly (n° 15) the **Palazzo Niccolini,** built by *Baccio d'Agnolo,* with its "graffiti" decorated facade and its loggia. At the junction with Via degli Alfani, there is an octagonal building, the **Rotunda of Santa Maria degli Angeli,** that was begun in 1428 by *Brunelleschi* and left unfinished. Once a church, it is now a lecture hall.

If you want to go to the Piazza SS. Annunziata directly after leaving the Accademia, turn right on leaving the gallery and right again into Via Cesare Battisti. At the corner of this street and the Piazza San Marco stands the **University of Florence,** which houses the following museums (entrance at n° 4 Via La Pira): the **Museum of Geology and Paleontology** (*open Mon 2 pm to 6 pm, Thurs & Sat 9 am to 1 pm, 1st Sun of each month 9.30 am to 12.30 pm; closed July, August and September plus remaining Sundays and holidays; admission free*), the **Museum of Mineralogy and Lithology** (*open 9 am to 1 pm weekdays and the 1st Sunday of the month, Wed 3 pm to 6 pm, closed July, August and September, remaining Sundays and holidays; admission free*). Behind the University are the **Botanical Gardens,** *Giardino dei Semplici,* founded in 1545, with a museum (entrance at n° 3 Via Micheli; *open Mon, Wed and Fri 9 am – 12 noon; admission free*).

PIAZZA SS. ANNUNZIATA⋆
(MAP II AB6)

This is a beautifully proportioned square, designed by *Brunelleschi.* It is decorated in the center with an equestrian statue of Ferdinando I dei Medici, a late work (1608) by *Giambologna,* and with two Baroque fountains (1629) by *P. Tacca.* On the north side of the square stands the church of Santissima Annunziata; on the east side, the Spedale degli Innocenti; on the south side, the **Palazzo Riccardi-Mannelli** (1557–63), formerly the Palazzo Grifoni, by *B. Ammannati* and, to the west, the portico of the convent of the Servite order, built in 1516–25 by *A. Sangallo the Elder* and *Baccio d'Agnolo.*

GALLERIA DELLO SPEDALE DEGLI INNOCENTI⋆
(MAP II B6) 12, Piazza SS. Annunziata

Visit: 9 am to 2 pm in winter, 9 am to 7 pm in summer; Sun 8 am to 1 pm. Closed Wed.

The Hospital of the Innocents has a portico in front of it, designed and begun in 1424 by *Brunelleschi,* then completed by *Francesco della Luna* in 1445. Between the arcades there are terra-cotta medallions (1463), by *Andrea della Robbia,* showing swaddled infants.

The arcaded courtyard has an "Annunciation" in terra-cotta by *Andrea della Robbia* in a tympanum on the left. On the right, at the end of the arcade, you will find the entrance to the **Hospital Gallery of Painting⋆**. It contains works by *Domenico Ghirlandaio*: "Adoration of the Magi" (1448; the second figure to the right of the Virgin is the artist himself); *Neri di Bicci*: "Coronation of the Virgin"; *G. del Biondo*: triptych of the "Annunciation"; *Botticelli*: "Madonna with an Angel"; *Filippino Lippi*: "Virgin and Child with an Angel"; *P. di Cosimo*: "Virgin and Child", "Marriage of St. Catherine"; *Andrea del Sarto*: "Virgin and Child with Angels"; "The Madonna of the Innocents", attributed to *Pontormo,* etc. There is also a large fresco by *Pocetti* ("Massacre of the Innocents") and works by *Luca* and *Andrea della Robbia* and their workshop. One room is devoted to 18th-century painting.

▬ *SS. ANNUNZIATA*★
(MAP II A6)

The church of the Most Blessed Annunciation is undoubtedly the most venerated sanctuary in Florence. It was originally an oratory. Situated in what was then the countryside, it was built in 1250 by the Seven Founders of the Servite order. These were seven rich Florentine merchants who, in 1233, set up the order of the Servants of Mary (*Servi di Maria*) to honor the sorrows of the Virgin and to obtain her intercession in putting an end to the dissensions which were making a bloodbath of Florence. An anonymous artist painted an "Annunciation" in the oratory and the painting quickly acquired a reputation for working miracles.

For a long time, the cult of the Virgin held pre-eminence in the religion of the Florentines. As late as 1750, they still counted the years by starting from the date of the Annunciation, March 25, instead of from January 1 which had, by then, been adopted by most of Europe.

The 13th-century oratory gave way to the present church, built by *Michelozzo* between 1441 and 1455; *Alberti* completed it by finishing the choir with the semi-spherical cupola which crowns it. The peristyle was added by *Caccini*, in 1599. Over the central portal, there is an "Annunciation" in mosaic by *David Ghirlandaio* (1509).

The atrium (1447, by *Manetti*) is decorated with frescoes retracing episodes in the "Life of the Virgin". Starting from the left of the entrance: the "Assumption" (1513), by *Rosso Fiorentino*; the **Visitation**★ (1516), by *Pontormo*; the "Marriage of the Virgin" (1514), by *Franciabigio*; a marble statue of the Virgin, by *Michelozzo*; the **Birth of Mary**★, by *A. del Sarto* (1514; the central figure is Lucrezia del Fede, the painter's wife) and, by the same artist, "The Adoration of the Magi" (1511; note the self-portrait in the corner on the right); the "Nativity" (1460), by *A. Baldovinetti*. After this, you will see frescoes (1476) by *C. Rosselli* depicting the vocation and taking of monastic vows of San Filippo Beniti or Benizzi, who founded the Servite order (1233–85); the "Life of San Filippo" (1509–10) by *A. del Sarto*. The bust (1606) of Andrea del Sarto (who is buried in the church) is by *Caccini*.

The popularity of this sanctuary and the prestige it has always enjoyed with the Florentines, have brought in all sorts of donations; the interior decoration is so smothered in gifts that it is difficult to distinguish *Michelozzo's* beautifully constructed nave. The magnificent ceiling (1664) was frequently remodeled in the 17th and 18th centuries.

To the left of the entrance, the Tempietto della Santissima Annunziata is a little marble temple, built by *Pagno Portigiani* (1448) following a design by *Michelozzo*, to house the miraculous fresco of the **Annunciation.** This fresco, by an anonymous Florentine artist of the early 14th century, had been in the old oratory of the Servites: legend has it that the Virgin's face was painted by an angel while the artist was asleep. The lamps, lights and altar in solid silver (1600) were given by the Medici. The face of Christ, in the adjoining chapel, is by *Andrea del Sarto*.

Left nave. The **Feroni chapel**★ (1692) by *Foggini* shows the influence of *Bernini* and *Borromini*; the fresco (1455) is by *Andrea del Castagno*. In the next chapel, one door (often closed) gives access to the Cloister of the Dead (see page 122) and another to the sacristy by *Pagno Portigiani* based on plans by *Michelozzo*; 5th chapel: fresco of the "Assumption" by *Perugino*.

Left transept: terra-cotta statue of "St. John the Baptist" by *Michelozzo*.

Tribune. The 17th-century fresco in the cupola ("The Coronation of the Virgin") is by *Volterrano*; on the floor is the tombstone of Andrea del Sarto (1486–1530). Also note the high altar with its silver ciborium (1656).

Accademia: "David" by Michelangelo.

The chapels of the apse. Here you can see the tomb of Bishop Angelo Marzi dei Medici (1546), by *Francesco da Sangallo*; "Resurrection", by *Bronzino*; San Rocco, sculpted in wood by *Veit Stoss* in the 16th century; tomb of Donato dell'Antella, by *G.B. Foggini*. The median **chapel**★ was reconstructed by *Giambologna* in 1594–98 as a tomb for himself (*d.* 1608) and other Flemish artists who died in Florence; the bronze relief and crucifix are also by *Giambologna*.

Right transept: "Pietà" (1559), in marble, is by *Baccio Bandinelli* (*d.* 1560) who is buried here with his wife.

Right nave. 5th chapel: monument to Rolando dei Medici (1456), by *Bernardo Rossellino*.

Outside, to the left of the church, is the entrance to the **Cloister of the Dead,** or Cloister of St. Luke (15th century) which owes its name to the number of graves there. The frescoes which decorate it ("History of the Servite Order", by *Poccetti, Matteo Rosselli* and others) are not particularly interesting. However, before you get there, look at the tympanum of the door opening into the left transept of the church to see *Andrea del Sarto's* sensitive painting of "The Virgin with a Cushion". The cloister of St. Luke is to the left of this door in the same arcade. From 1561, it belonged to the "Artists' brotherhood"; many of its members are buried here, such as *Benvenuto Cellini, Pontormo, Franciabigio, Perugino* and *Bartolini; Andrea del Sarto, Giambologna* and *Baccio Bandinelli* are buried inside the church. In this cloister, which bears the name of the patron saint of artists, the Florentine painters of the Renaissance used to show and sell their works.

▬ *ARCHEOLOGICAL MUSEUM*★★
(MAP II B6)

Visit: 9 am to 2 pm; Sun 9 am to 1 pm. Closed Mon. Entrance at n° 38, Via della Colonna. *The museum is undergoing renovation and some parts may be closed.*

The Florence Archeological Museum was founded in 1870 in the beautiful 17th-century Palazzo della Crocetta, surrounded by a charming garden. It is chiefly devoted to Etruscan antiquity. Apart from a unique collection of primitive Tuscan pieces, there are numerous Greek and Roman exhibits, bronzes, ceramics and coins. There is also an interesting Egyptian collection, the product of Franco-Tuscan excavations carried out in 1829 in the Nile Valley. The various sections of the museum are arranged on three floors.

Ground floor

In one of the two small rooms which are open at present you will see the **François vase**★★, named after its discoverer. It is an Athenian krater made by the potter, *Ergotimos*, and the painter, *Clitias*. A masterpiece of ancient pottery, it bears witness to the importance accorded Greek pottery in Etruria as early as the beginning of the 6th century B.C. Numerous scenes are depicted on it: "The Companions of Theseus Disembarking", "The Fight with the Centaurs", "The Marriage of Thetis and Peleus", "The Return of Hephaistos into Olympus", etc.

Rooms I to IX: **Greek and Roman sculpture.** Among the most interesting works here are Artemis Laphria, a copy of a 5th-century B.C. statue; a 6th- or 5th-century B.C. statue of Apollo di Milani; and a beautiful 4th- or 3rd-century B.C. stone lion guarding the entrance to an Etruscan tomb.

Rooms X to XLIX: **Topographical Etruscan Museum.** The classification and presentation of these objects allows an overall vision of the unity of Etruscan thought and art over a vast region, and an understanding of the different means of expression owing both to dissimilar traditions and materials or techniques. The Etruscan civilization was essentially urban and was composed of rich cities, each autonomously governed. The style of the different Etruscan city-states is emphasized here by the geographical and historical grouping of the collections.

Given that the Etruscan language has never been deciphered (chiefly because of a lack of texts), and given that Rome destroyed the Etruscan civilization after conquering it, the Florence museum, even more than the one in the Villa Giulia in Rome, offers a collection of documents and works of the greatest interest. Finds made by chance or during excavations are presented in relation to their place of origin.

It is not possible to give a complete list of the collections here but some objects merit particular attention: Rooms XII to XIV (Tarquinia): funerary urn with a crested bronze helmet. This was the traditional headdress of the Tuscan hoplites. The urn probably contained the ashes of a soldier killed in battle. — Rooms XV to XVI (Tuscania): 4th- or 3rd-century B.C. lion, an example of the animal sculpture or paintings standing guard on a number of tombs. — Room XVIII (Orvieto): funerary column of the 6th century B.C. with a warrior's head. A very moving sculpture; the dead man seems to express the inner peace he has found beyond death. — Room XIX (Vulci): lion. — Rooms XXV to XXVIII (Velutonia): a group of objects discovered in 7th- and 6th-century B.C. tombs. — Rooms XXXIX to XLVI (Chiusi): statue of the Etruscan sea goddess seated on a throne (5th century B.C.). — Room XLIX (Luni): terra-cotta pediments from two Etruscan temples (2nd century B.C.); polychrome decoration has been restored in part by reassembling such pieces as they were found.

In the **garden** of the museum, you can see reconstructions of various types of Etruscan tombs: with pointed roofs, in the form of a well, with a chamber beneath a tumulus, or with a circular chamber, the roof of which is supported by a central pillar. These reconstructions were made from original materials uncovered on excavation sites. They give a very clear idea of what Etruscan necropolises were like at different periods.

First floor★

The **Egyptian collections.** Note, in particular (Rooms I to VIII) a fragment from a granite statue of Hathor the Cow Goddess Giving Milk to the Pharaoh Horemheb (14th century B.C.), who came into power after the death of Tutankhamun; bust of an unknown pharaoh in rose-colored basalt (7th–6th century B.C.); polychrome reliefs from the tomb of Pharaoh Seti I (13th century B.C.); two polychrome statuettes of servants, one preparing beer, the other grinding flour (2625–2475 B.C.); a wood and bone chariot from a Theban tomb (14th century B.C.).

Rooms X to XXII contain Greek, Etruscan and Roman exhibits which, at times, are interrelated. Among the more interesting exhibits are: the sarcophagus of Ramta Uzenai (4th century B.C.), and numerous bronzes. There is also a remarkable bronze statue, the **Arringatore★** (The Orator) from the 3rd century B.C., discovered at Sanguineto. This was the funerary statue of Aulo Metello. The drapery of the toga is not only decorative but also very realistic. As for the face, it is evidently a portrait of a particular man. With this work we are at the beginning of Roman art. Strictly speaking, The Orator is neither Etruscan nor Roman but marks a crossroads between two civilizations and two styles.

The **Chimera of Arezzo★★** is one of the most celebrated works of Etruria, though its origin is still under discussion because it could possibly be Greek. This bronze monster, dating from the middle of the 5th century B.C., could be a local product strongly influenced by archaic Greek art or by the art of Magna Grecia. The beast — a lion with a ram's head on its back and a serpent's head at the end of its tail — grips the floor with narrow paws and is frighteningly realistic despite the stylized forms and the fantastic aspect of the whole. It is evidently a beast mortally wounded, suffering, but still trying to defend itself. This beautiful bronze was discovered near Arezzo in 1555. The serpent's head on the tail has been restored and *Benvenuto Cellini*, in his memoirs, claims to have done the work but his story has been discredited by modern art historians.

On the same floor there is a collection of coins and also the *Collezione di Preziosi*, a magnificent collection of jewels, precious stones and cameos.

Second floor

Greek, Etruscan and Roman exhibits. — Rooms I to VI have some beautiful works of the 2nd millennium from southern Italy, Cyprus, Greece, the Aegean Isles and Rhodes. — Rooms VII to XV have terra-cotta ware, **Greek vases**★ and Italic and Etruscan pottery. — Rooms XVII to XXX have frescoes detached from Etruscan tombs and reproductions of tomb paintings. There is also a **sarcophagus**★ in polychrome terra-cotta from Lartima Seianti (3rd – 2nd century B.C.) whose style is disputed by experts.

Via dei Servi (MAP II B5).

This street is a direct link between Piazza SS. Annunziata and the Cathedral Square.

Church of Santa Croce: the building, which became the Florentine Pantheon, did not get its marble facade until the 19th century.

ITINERARY H
RENAISSANCE SCULPTURE
AND THE FLORENTINE PANTHEON

**The Badia, the Bargello Museum, Santa Croce,
and the Pazzi chapel.**

Via del Proconsolo. The fact that the district crossed by
this street is called "Dantesque" has nothing to do with
its décor or its atmosphere, which in no way inspire solemn
sentiments. However, there are numerous souvenirs of the
great Italian poet and the Casa di Dante passes for his
birthplace.

In the Bargello Museum, with a silhouette that is a
modest evocation of that of the Palazzo Vecchio nearby, you
will find the great names in Florentine sculpture: *Michelangelo, Cellini, Donatello,* whose work you have already
admired in the churches and other museums throughout the
city.

Your last stop on this walk, the church of Santa Croce
with the adjoining Pazzi chapel, conceals behind its banal
19th-century facade a magnificent nave of surprising ampli-
tude and solemnity. It has been called the Florentine
Pantheon because a great number of famous people of the
arts and sciences are buried there.

The district is a lively one and it is no rarity for the
venerable vaults of Santa Croce to resound with the noise of
the pop groups that play in the square in the summer months.
The souvenir shops around the square are crammed with
plastic Davids and formica Madonnas in an almost surrealist
hodgepodge. Even so, it is delightful to wander the old
streets between Santa Croce and the Uffizi.

▬▬▬ *VIA DEL PROCONSOLO*
(MAP II CD5)

This is one of the oldest Florentine streets, the main road of this district. N°
12, the 16th-century palace known as **Palazzo Nonfinito** because it

was never completed, now houses the **Museum of Anthropology and Ethnology.** The museum was founded in 1869 and contains some interesting collections of the Paleolithic and Neolithic Ages as well as objects of folklore (*visit: 9 am to 1 pm weekdays and the 3rd Sunday of each month; admission free*). It is separated from the Palazzo Pazzi by the **Borgo degli Albizi** which is lined with beautiful old houses.

The **Palazzo Pazzi-Quaratesi**★ (MAP II D5) was designed by *Giuliano da Maiano* between 1462 and 1472, according to an original plan (1445) by Brunelleschi. On the corner, there is a sculpture of two dolphins, the family symbol. Beyond the main doors a spacious courtyard can be glimpsed. A little farther on, the **Via Dante Alighieri** is on the right, leading to a picturesque little square dominated by a medieval tower and surrounded by the Alighieri family houses (Casa degli Alighieri; MAP II D5), which have been reconstructed. **Casa di Dante** (at n° 1 in Via Santa Margherita) is the one in which the poet is supposed to have been born. Inside there is a small museum (*visit: 9.30 am to 12.30 pm and 3.30 to 6.30 pm; Sun 9.30 am to 12.30 pm. Closed Wed. Admission free*).

▬▬ THE BADIA★
(MAP II D5)

This is the church of an old Benedictine abbey founded in the 10th century by *Willa*, marchioness of Tuscany. The Badia has undergone a number of transformations since the 13th century. The **campanile**★, which was begun in 1310 in the Romanesque style, was completed in the Gothic style in 1330. The original aspect of the church was completely transformed during the Renaissance. The exterior of the Gothic apse by *Arnolfo di Cambio* is all that remains of the 13th-century church. In 1627, the interior was remodeled by *M. Segaloni*. The main doors (1475) are by *B. da Rovezzano*, who also designed the vestibule (1495); in the tympanum of the main doors there is a slip-decorated terra-cotta Virgin by *B. Buglioni*, a pupil of the *Della Robbia* studio. From Via Dante Alighieri you can go into the cloister by a 15th-century door and, from there, into the church.

The interior of the church, in the form of a Greek cross, has a beautiful ceiling (1625) but its main attraction lies in its statuary and bas-relief work. One of *Filippino Lippi's* finest works is to the left of the entrance: "The Virgin Appearing to St. Bernard" (1480); on the right is the tomb of Gianozzo Pandolfini (1456) by the *B. Rossellino* studio; beside it, a "Virgin and Child with Saints" (1469) in bas-relief by *Mino da Fiesole*. The tomb of Bernardo Giugni (1468; in the right transept) with its allegories of "Justice" and "Faith", is by the same artist. The **tomb of Ugo**★, marquis of Tuscany (d. 1006) and son of the founder of this church, is in the left transept. *Mino da Fiesole* worked on it from 1469 to 1481, and it may well be the greatest work of this refined sculptor, who also made the tomb of Paul III in Rome. The tomb is decorated with a statue of Charity (the marquis's charity was legendary in Florence).

To the right of the choir you can go down into the **Chiostro degli Aranci** (Cloister of the orange trees, 1440, by *B. Rossellino*). The frescoes on the upper gallery depict the "Legend of St. Benedict" and were painted in the 15th century by the Portuguese artist, *Giovanni Consalvo*.

▬▬ IL BARGELLO (National Museum)★★
(MAP II D5)

Visit: 9 am to 2 pm; Sun 9 am to 1 pm. Closed Mon. Entrance at n° 4, Via del Proconsolo.

The Palazzo del Bargello or del Podestà is, after the Palazzo Vecchio, the most beautiful civic building of the Florentine Middle Ages. It is an austere building, begun in 1254 and frequently enlarged and restored. The last restoration work dates back to the 19th century. The crenellated tower 175 feet/57 m tall standing next to it is called the **Volognana**. The palace now houses the National Museum which has a magnificent collection of Tuscan sculpture of the 14th to the 17th centuries. The museum's collection of *objets d'art* is equally remarkable.

The palace was once the seat of the Capitano del Popolo, and of the Podestà, the ruling power in Florence from 1261 to 1502. Then, until 1574 it was the seat of the Council of Justice, after which the Capitano di Giustizia, (or Bargello) was installed there. The Bargello was the chief of police and part of the castle served as a prison which came to be known as the Bargello. It was the scene of many torturings and hangings. The Bargello became a museum of sculpture in 1859.

The courtyard. The beautiful courtyard is irregular in shape. On one side, an external staircase by *Neri di Fioravanti* leads up to the loggia. On the walls are the shields of the Podestàs and the Councils of Justice (the Ruota). A well is in the center of the courtyard where torturings took place. Under the portico there are statues by *Ammannati* and *V. Danti* and the Neapolitan Fisher Boy by *Vincenzo Gemito* (1917). Note also the St. Paul cannon (1638), decorated on the breech with the head of the apostle.

Michelangelo and 15th-century Florentine sculpture. These sculptures are exhibited in a large vaulted room on the ground floor. Works by Michelangelo: a **David★** (or Apollo) which is unfinished (1530) and not to be confused with the one in the Accademia; a beautiful marble bust of **Brutus★★** (1540); "Drunken Bacchus with a Young Satyr" (1496); and a medallion showing the "Virgin Instructing her Child, with the Infant St. John" (1504). Much space is also given to the works of *Benvenuto Cellini* (1500–71), goldsmith, sculptor and adventurer, and writer of adventure stories on occasion, who was a protégé of the Medici and found refuge at Fontainebleau. Works which may be seen here: bust of Cosimo I, Jupiter, a bronze model of the famous **Perseus★**, Minerva, Apollo, **Narcissus★**. Here, there are also works by *Ammannati, B. Bandelli, V. Danti* and an allegorical group by *Giambologna*. The bust of Michelangelo is by *Daniele da Volterra*.

14th-century Florentine sculpture. The room at the bottom of the courtyard contains the works of *Paolo di Giovanni* ("Virgin with St. Peter and St. Paul", from the Porta Romana); *Tino di Camaino*, "Virgin and Child". Another room has international Gothic pieces.

First floor

Under the loggia there are sculptures by *Giambologna*: **Winged Mercury★** in bronze, the Turkey, the Eagle and the Satyr as well as some 16th- and 17th-century Tuscan sculptures.

General council room. In this room you will find works by *Donatello* and other artists of the 15th century.

Donatello (1386–1466), whose work can also be seen in the Duomo and the Baptistry, is represented here by a magnificent **St. George★★** (1416), in marble, which was made for one of the niches of the church of Orsanmichele and replaced by a copy. Other works by Donatello include busts of **Niccolò da Uzzano★** and **Giovanni Antonio da Narni★** and the **Marzocco★**. The latter is a stone lion whose attribution is disputed. The lion is a symbol of the people of Florence and once stood in front of the Palazzo Vecchio; it has now been replaced by a copy. Note also the **Young David★★**, in bronze and made for Cosimo dei Medici (1430); the marble **David★** and the marble **St. John the Baptist★**; the **Infant St. John★**, Cupid, and **Cherub★**, all in marble. The tragic Crucifixion in gilded bronze is a work from the artist's last period (1458). In the same room there are some Florentine coffers from the 15th century and works by *Luca della Robbia*, not only in slip-decorated terra-cotta for which he was famous (see the "Virgin with an Apple") but also some bas-reliefs in marble. After these come bas-reliefs by *Desiderio da Settignano*, an **Infant St. John★**; by *Agostino di Duccio* and *Michelozzo*. The two **bronze panels★★** by *Brunelleschi* and *Ghiberti* illustrate the Sacrifice of Abraham, they were entered for the Baptistry doors competition of 1401; note also the funerary monument of Mariano Sozzino by *Lorenzo di Pietro*, known as *Il Vecchietta*.

The tower room. This room contains a large collection of seals (both religious and lay) and papal and Venetian bulls; on the walls, there are French tapestries and fabrics from the Carrand collection (see below).

Room of the Podestà. Bust of Louis Carrand (*d*. 1888), a wealthy French collector who left to the city of Florence the marbles, paintings and rare and precious objects from France, Italy, Belgium and the Orient. These are on show in this room and those following it. Worthy of mention are the **Limoges enamels★** (13th – 16th centuries), Byzantine enamels (12th century), goldsmiths' work (12th – 16th centuries), crystalware from Murano (16th century), French and Spanish wrought iron work (15th and 16th centuries), jewelry and some 15th-century paintings. The chimney-piece was made in 1478.

Chapel of the Podestà. On the altar, there is a triptych by *Giovanni Francesco* (15th century) depicting the Virgin and Child between St. Francis and St. John the Baptist. On the walls, there are frescoes by the school of *Giotto*; above the altar, "Paradise", attributed to *Giotto*; at the bottom right, portrait of Dante (dressed in dark red behind the kneeling figure). Below the "Paradise" fresco, on the left, "St. Jerome", by *Bartolomeo di Giovanni*; on the right, "Madonna and Child", by *Mainardi*. The fresco on the wall of the entrance shows "Hell"; on the side walls, "Life of the Virgin, Mary Magdalen and Christ". The carved marquetry pews and the lectern, from San Miniato, are by *Bernardo della Cecca* (1439–98). The glass cases contain goldsmiths' work.

Room of the ivories. A continuation of the **Carrand collection★**: caskets, statuettes and carved ivories, Roman, Byzantine, Arabian, French, Spanish, Italian and Flemish; 14th- to 16th-century statues in wood from Florence, Siena, Pisa and Umbria.

Room of goldsmiths' work. Ecclesiastical ornaments and reliquaries.

Room of majolica. Majolica from Urbino, Pesaro, Faenza, Montelupo, etc. Florentine and Hispano-Moresque lustre ware (14th – 15th centuries).

Second floor

Giovanni della Robbia room. Slip-decorated terra-cotta ware by *Giovanni della Robbia* (1469–1529) and *Benedetto Buglioni*, who was the last representative of this art form of the Florentine Renaissance. Two statues of Ganymede by *Benvenuto Cellini*, one bronze, the other marble.

Andrea della Robbia room. Several Virgins, the bust of a child, a portrait of Andrea della Robbia (1435–1528); also a "Virgin and Angels", by *Antonio Rossellino*, a "Virgin with the Infant St. John", by the school of *B. da Maiano*, and two works by *Giambologna*.

Verrocchio room. This room is dedicated to the work of *Verrocchio* (1435–88). His **David★** in bronze (1476) was probably inspired by that of *Donatello* but shows a more marked sensitivity and sensuality. Among the works on display are a bust of Piero dei Medici, a polychrome terra-cotta of "The Resurrection", "Woman with a Bouquet", "Death of Francesca Tornabuoni-Pitti", "Two Virgins", etc. In the same room there are several works by *Mino da Fiesole*, among them a tabernacle and a bust of Rinaldo della Luna. The bust of the young warrior is by *Antonio del Pollaiuolo*.

Armour room. Collection of arms and armoury of the Medici and the Della Rovere families.

PIAZZA SAN FIRENZE
(MAP II D5)

The piazza takes its name from the large 18th-century building which was once the convent of San Firenze, the church of which has a Baroque facade. Opposite is the **Palazzo Gondi★**, a beautiful Renaissance residence by *G. da Sangallo* (1494) with a harmoniously designed courtyard. South of the square you can see the 16th-century facade of the Palazzo Vecchio.

PIAZZA SANTA CROCE
(MAP II E6)

This vast, rectangular square extends in front of the church of Santa Croce. In the Middle Ages, this famous square held the enormous crowds who came to hear the disciples of St. Francis preach, to watch the tournaments and games of *calcio* which took place there, or to join in riots. Around the square are typically Florentine palaces; n° 1 is the **Palazzo Cocchi Serristori★**, built in the late 15th century by *Baccio d'Agnolo*, n° 21 is the **Palazzo dell'Antella** (1619), which has a corbelled facade and is decorated with frescoes by *Giovanni da San Giovanni* and his pupils.

SANTA CROCE★★
(MAP II E6)

This is the most important Franciscan church in the city. It was built outside the city walls in the district inhabited by the dyers and tanners and was the principal sanctuary of the monks who had been sent to Florence by St. Francis of Assisi. At first, it was just a small chapel dedicated to the Holy Cross. Towards 1228, the chapel was enlarged and came to be frequented more and more by the Florentines who, despite their greed for money and pleasure-loving ways, were attracted by the preaching of the Franciscans and the ascetic ideas of the *poverello* who had passed through their city in 1211. The present church, which was begun in 1294, was consecrated in the middle of the 14th century. *Arnolfo di Cambio* was probably its chief architect. The white facade, designed by *N. Matas* in the Neo-Gothic style so dear to the last century, was added in 1857. S. Croce is a veritable necropolis where many famous Florentines are buried. For this reason it is sometimes known as the Florentine Pantheon.

The interior. The three-nave, church is built on a T-shaped plan with the addition of the chapel of the high altar, which is flanked on each side by five smaller chapels and covered with a beautiful open-timber roof. The building is spacious and simple. The colors of the stained glass windows give it warmth, but the general effect is of Franciscan austerity.

There are a number of tombstones on the floor. In the 16th century, *Vasari* added the altars which stand against the walls and plastered over a number of frescoes.

The nave. On the third pillar, note the **pulpit★** by *Benedetto da Maiano* in marble (1476); the panels illustrate the life of St. Francis.

Right nave. This side houses a large collection of tombs of famous men and works of art. On the first altar, "Crucifixion" by *Santi di Tito* (1579); facing this on the first pillar, "Madonna 'del latte'" by *Antonio Rosellino* (1478), a charming bas-relief. **Michelangelo's tomb★** by *Vasari* (1570), is decorated with statues symbolizing Painting (left, by *G.B. Lorenzi*), Sculpture (middle, by *Valerio Cioli*), and Architecture (right, by *Giovanni dell'Opera*). The bust of the artist was made using his death mask. The fresco with a "Pietà", above the bust, is by *Vasari*. Michelangelo wanted the "Pietà" which is now in the cathedral museum for his tomb. Next follow: Dante's monument, by *Stefano Ricci* (1830; the poet died in exile in

Ravenna in 1321); the tomb of the poet Vittorio Alfieri (d. 1803) by *Canova* in 1810; the **tomb of Niccolò Machiavelli** (d. 1527), by *Spinazzi* in 1787; Renaissance tabernacle with an **Annunciation**★ (1430), by *Donatello*; the 15th-century **tomb of Leonardo Bruni**★, humanist and chancelor of the Florentine Republic, by *Bernardo Rossellino*; the **tomb of Rossini,** who died in Paris in 1868, by *Cassioli* in 1887; the tomb of Ugo Foscolo (1939), by *A. Berti*.

Right transept. The **Castellani chapel**★ (right) is decorated with frescoes (1385) by *Agnolo Gaddi* (son of Taddeo) and his pupils: on the right wall, "Life of St. Nicholas of Bari" and "Life of St. John the Baptist"; on the left wall, "Life of St. Anthony the Abbot" and "Life of St. John the Evangelist"; altar relief by a pupil of *Nicola Pisano*; small marble tabernacle by *Mino da Fiesole*; "Crucifix" (1386) by *Niccolò di Pietro Gerini*; statues of St. Francis and St. Dominic by the *Della Robbia* workshop. The **Baroncelli-Giugni chapel**★ is at the end of the transept. Here the walls are decorated with famous frescoes depicting the "Life of the Virgin" (1332–38) by *Taddeo Gaddi*, *Giotto's* greatest pupil. "The Coronation of the Virgin" on the altar carries *Giotto's* signature but it is probably by *Taddeo*. The tomb of the Baroncelli-Giugni family (1328) is by the Sienese *Balduccio*.

To the left of the Baroncelli-Giugni chapel, a beautiful doorway by *Michelozzo* gives access to a corridor leading to the **Medici chapel** or Chapel of the Novitiate (1434) also by *Michelozzo*. On the altar, there is a "Virgin and Child" in terra-cotta by *A. della Robbia*. On the left is the sacristy, its right wall decorated with a 14th-century fresco. Note also "Crucifixion" by *Taddeo Gaddi*; "The Ascent to Calvary", probably by *Spinello Aretino*; "Ascension and Resurrection" by *Niccolò di Pietro Gerini*; cupboards and chests by *Giovanni di Michele* in 1440; missals and sacred ornaments (15th – 16th century) and a bust of the Redeemer, by *G. della Robbia*. A wrought iron grille (1371) separates the sacristy from the **Rinuccini chapel** which is decorated with frescoes portraying scenes from the life of the Virgin and of St. Mary Magdalen (1366), by *Giovanni da Milano*; the polyptych (1379) is by *Giovanni del Biondo*.

The corridor leads to the salesroom of the leatherworkers' school.

Chapels to the right of the choir. 1st chapel: **Scenes from the Life of St. Francis**★★ (1317), by *Giotto* and on the altar there is a painting by an anonymous Florentine of the 13th century "Life of St. Francis"; above the outer arch, "St. Francis Receives the Stigmata" also by *Giotto*.

2nd chapel: *Giotto* painted the **Scenes from the Life of St. John the Baptist**★ (left) and the "Life of St. John the Evangelist" (right) in 1320.

3rd chapel: on the right, tomb of Julie Bonaparte-Clary (d. 1845), by *Luigi Pampaloni* in 1847; on the left, tomb of Charlotte Bonaparte (d. 1839), by *Lorenzo Bartolini*.

Choir. On the altar, there is a large 14th-century polyptych: "Virgin and Child with Saints", by *Niccolò di Pietro Gerini*, and "Four Doctors of the Church", by *Giovanni del Biondo*. Note the large painted crucifix, attributed to the "*Maestro di Figline*", an important follower of Giotto. The vaults and walls are decorated with frescoes by *Agnolo Gaddi*, depicting the legend of the Holy Cross (1380–85); the stained glass is also attributed to *Agnolo Gaddi*.

Chapels to the left of the high altar. 1st chapel: over the outside arch, "The Assumption", studio of *Giotto*; on the altar, polyptych (1372) by *Giovanni del Biondo*, with a predella of a later date by *Neri di Bicci*.

4th chapel: slip-decorated terra-cotta altarpiece by *Giovanni della Robbia*. On the walls, frescoes (1330) by *Bernardo Daddi* depict the martyrdom of saints Laurence and Stephen.

5th chapel: **frescoes**★ (1340) of the "Life of St. Sylvester, the Pope", by *Maso di Banco*, who was known as *Giottino*, a pupil of *Giotto*. The master's influence is evident.

Left transept. Chapel at the far end (1579): the frescoes (1660) are by *Baldassare Franceschini*, known as *Il Volterrano*. The **Crucifix★** in wood (1425), by *Donatello*, was criticized by Brunelleschi for its realism. (He justified his criticism by making a crucifix himself which can be seen in S. Maria Novella.) In the chapel on the left, rebuilt by *G. Silvani* in 18th century, the tomb of Princess Zamoyska Czartoryska (*d.* 1837) is by *Lorenzo Bartolini*. At the corner of the transept and the left wall of the nave is the monument to the Florentine musician, Luigi Cherubini (1760–1842, born at n° 22, Via Fiesolana, not far from Santa Croce), by *O. Fantacchiotti*.

Left of nave. On the altar, "The Pentecost", by *Vasari*; in the three medallions, memorials to Christopher Columbus, Amerigo Vespucci and the astronomer Toscanelli; **tomb of Carlo Marsuppini★** (*d.* 1453), humanist and secretary of the Florentine Republic, a masterpiece by *Desiderio da Settignano* in 1460. The artist took his inspiration from the tomb of Bruni, by *Rossellino*, which faces it. On the floor is the tombstone of Gregorio Marsuppini, Carlo's father, also by *Desiderio*; "Pietà", by *Bronzino*; great tombstone of Lorenzo Ghiberti, buried here with his son Vittorio; commemorative plaque to Raphael who is buried in the Pantheon in Rome and to Leonardo da Vinci (buried at Amboise, in France); near the exit, **tomb of Galileo** (*d.* 1642), by *G.B. Foggini* and *G. Ticciati*.

Interior facade. Left of the door, tomb of G. Battista Niccolini (*d.* 1861), historian and tragic poet, by *Pio Fedi* (1883), with the beautiful Statue of Liberty which inspired *Bartholdi* when he made the Statue of Liberty for the port of New York.

Museo dell'Opera di Santa Croce★★

Visit: 9 am to 12.30 pm and 3 pm to 6.30 pm (Mar 1 – Sept 30); 9 am to 12.30 pm and 3 pm to 5 pm (Oct 1 – Feb 28). Closed Wed. Entrance to the right of the facade of the church.

The first cloister, or Arnolfo's cloister, was built in the 14th century. Under the arcade on the left, frescoes, *c.* 1350, and tomb of Gastone della Torre (*d.* 1317) attributed to *Tino di Camaino*; under the arcade on the right, commemorative monument to Florence Nightingale, born in Florence in 1820. At the far end of the cloister, the graceful bell-tower by *Baccani* (1865) and the **Pazzi chapel★**, a beautiful Renaissance building by *Brunelleschi*, (1429–46). Like the old sacristy in San Lorenzo, this is a small building where architecture and decoration blend in perfect harmony. In front of the chapel is a colonnaded portico with a frieze of medallions (cherubs' heads, by *Desiderio da Settignano* from drawings by *Donatello*). The terra-cottas on the arch are by *Luca della Robbia*. The doors are carved to a design by *Giuliano da Maiano* (1472). The somber interior is decorated with terra-cotta friezes and medallions, with "The Evangelists and the Apostles", by *Luca della Robbia*. The altar is from the workshop of *Donatello*. The stained glass window with the figure of St. Andrew is attributed to *Baldovinetti*.

Brunelleschi's cloister (left on leaving the Pazzi chapel). Built in 1453, following a design by the architect shortly after his death (1446), with entrance doors attributed to *Benedetto da Maiano*.

The old **refectory** contains a number of works of art which were once in the church; fragments of a fresco by *Orcagna* depicting, in the form of *danses macabres*, Hell and the **Triumph of Death★**; a **statue★** of St. Louis of Toulouse in gilded bronze, by *Donatello* (1423); the fresco at the far end ("The Tree of Life"and "The Last Supper") is by *Taddeo Gaddi*. The famous painted **Crucifix★**, by *Cimabue*, restored after the 1966 flood, still bears the marks of the catastrophe.

Casa Buonarroti (MAP II D6)

Visit: 9 am to 1 pm. Closed Tues. N° 70, Via Ghibellina.

Since 1965, the house has been used as a center for Michelangelo studies. It was bought by the artist at the end of his life for his nephew, Leonardo.

The house was decorated by Florentine artists at the beginning of the 17th century. Among the exhibits are a bust of Michelangelo, by *Daniele da Volterra*, the **Virgin "of the Staircase"**, a wooden **Crucifix★**, various documents concerning the artist and his work, and an extraordinary collection of drawings.

Via Magliabechi (MAP II E6)

This is another street characteristic of 15th- and 16th-century Florence; n° 10 is the **Palazzo Rasponi-Spinelli** with its decorated façade. The enormous **Biblioteca Nazionale,** the National Library, next to the cloister of Santa Croce, was built at the beginning of this century (entrance n° 1, Piazza de'Cavalleggeri). It is the largest library in the country and the legal repository of every Italian publication.

Museo Horne (MAP II E5)

Visit: Mon to Fri 4 pm to 8 pm; Sat 9 am to 1 pm; closed Sun. Entrance at n° 6, Via dei Benci.

The museum is housed in the **Palazzo Alberti-Corsi,** attributed to *Simone del Pollaiuolo* (known as *Il Cronaca*) or to *G. da Sangallo*. The palace and the collection were left to the city by an English art lover, Herbert Percy Horne (1864–1916). The furniture and *objets d'art* recreate the atmosphere of a 15th-century patrician residence. The picture gallery houses works by *Simone Martini, B. Daddi, B. Gozzoli, Giotto* ("St. Stephen"), *P. Lorenzetti, Sassetta, Filippino Lippi, Beccafumi*, etc., as well as drawings by *Michelangelo, G.B. Tiepolo* and *Raphael*.

Ponte alle Grazie (MAP II F5). The present bridge, rebuilt after the last war, replaced the 13th-century bridge which was the second one to span the Arno. Very attractive view from the bridge.

Museo Bardini★ (MAP II F5)

Visit: 9 am to 2 pm; Sun 8 am to 1 pm; closed Wed. Entrance at n° 1, Piazza de'Mozzi.

The museum stands opposite the two Palazzi Torrigiani, one of which was built by *Baccio d'Agnolo* and his son *Domenico*. The Bardini is one of the most interesting of the small museums in Florence. Its 20 rooms have a rich collection of Etruscan, Greek, Roman and medieval (especially 15th-century) statues in wood, plaster and terra-cotta, by the Florentine and Sienese schools. Note particularly the Charity, a marble group by *Tino da Camaino*; there are also Renaissance paintings and sculptures, Peruvian carpets (16th–17th century) and 17th-century Florentine **tapestries★**. On the second floor, the **Corsi Gallery** (*visit by request*) houses approximately 600 works by various painters of the 12th to the 19th centuries.

The **church of Santa Lucia de'Magnoli** is situated on the nearby Via de'Bardi (MAP II F5). Note the "Santa Lucia" by *Pietro Lorenzetti* on the high altar.

From the Museo Bardini, the Via S. Niccolò leads to the Porta S. Niccolò (1324), a gate in the old city walls. From there you can climb the steps up to Piazzale Michelangelo. In the sacristy of the Renaissance **church of S. Niccolò sopr'Arno** (MAP II F6) there is a fresco by either *Pollaiuolo* or *Baldovinetti* of the "Madonna della Cintola" (1450) under a small tabernacle in the style of *Michelozzo*. Facing the church, the street climbs up to the Porta S. Miniato (14th-century city gate) and the Forte di Belvedere.

ITINERARY I
THE FORTE DI BELVEDERE

Viale dei Colli, Piazzale Michelangelo, San Miniato.

The Viale dei Colli was designed by Giuseppe Poggi in 1865. Even though horse-drawn carriages have been replaced today by cars and motorbikes, it is still one of the most beautiful avenues in Florence, offering a splendid view over the town with its ochre-colored roofs and its bell-towers. Cypresses, lime trees, plane-trees and holm oaks add a touch of green and freshness which is lacking in the city streets below. The hillside is dotted with elegant villas half hidden by their gardens. This is a residential area which must be extremely pleasant to live in.

On the Piazzale Michelangelo, packed with noisy coaches, there stands a monument dedicated to the great sculptor which would probably horrify him if he were to return to this world. From here you can go up to San Miniato, one of the masterpieces of Florentine Romanesque architecture. If you choose the right time (early in the morning) you will find the same atmosphere of peace and serenity which attracted the Benedictine monks who built the church.

If you are short of time, just go straight to San Miniato: bus n° 13 from the Central station, going through the center and stopping at Piazza dei Giudici (MAP II E4), by the Arno behind the Uffizi. You can also climb the steps which start from Porta San Niccolò (MAP II F6).

▬▬ *VIALE DEI COLLI*★★

The Viale dei Colli is 4 miles/6 km long and, under various names: Viale Michelangelo, Viale Galileo, Viale Machiavelli, it connects Piazza Ferrucci (MAP I D5) with Porta Romana (MAP I E3) near the entrance to the Boboli Gardens.

▬ *PIAZZALE MICHELANGELO*★★
(MAP I E5)

Standing about 328 feet/100 metres above the Arno, the Piazzale Michelangelo offers a marvelous **view**★★ of one of the most beautiful towns in the world. In the background you can see the Apennines; in the middle of the square, a monument dedicated to Michelangelo. This shows reproductions of some of the artist's most famous statues and is of rather dubious taste.

San Salvatore al Monte (MAP I E5)

At the back of the Piazzale Michelangelo, steps flanked by cypresses will take you up to a Renaissance church built by *Simone del Pollaiuolo*, in 1475 on the site of a former oratory. Michelangelo nicknamed this church: "a nice little country girl". Inside, you can see a terra-cotta roundel by the *Della Robbias'* workshop, showing a "Descent from the Cross" (2nd altar on the left), along with a "Pietà" attributed to *Neri di Bicci* (5th altar on the right).

▬ *SAN MINIATO AL MONTE*★★★
(MAP I E5)

Miniatus, the first Florentine martyr, was buried here in the 3rd century, on the site of a pagan sanctuary. Charlemagne came to this place on a pilgrimage, and the Benedictine monks found here the peace they needed for meditation, which the city could not give them. *Michelangelo* built fortifications round the sacred hill, the ruins of which you can see as you climb to the top of the hill (height: 453 feet/138 metres).

In 1018, *Bishop Hildebrand* decided to have the present church built to replace an old chapel dedicated to the martyr **San Miniato.** It is one of the masterpieces of Florentine Romanesque architecture. The 12th-century **facade**★ is faced with white marble and decorated with a large mosaic on a gold background (13th century), representing Christ between the Virgin and St. Miniatus. The top of the facade is crowned by an eagle, symbol of the guild of the Calimala. The bell-tower was built in 1518 to a design by *Baccio d'Agnolo.*

The interior has the usual severity of Romanesque churches. Like the facade, the walls are decorated with green and white marble in a somber geometric pattern. The nave has a truss ceiling with polychrome decoration. The center of the **marble floor**★ (1207) is decorated with the signs of the Zodiac. The columns are all different, having been taken from Roman monuments. San Miniato is an astonishing building, difficult to compare with any other.

The walls of the aisles are covered with 15th-century frescoes. The **ciborium**★ or "Chapel of the Crucifix" was built at the end of the nave in 1448 by *Michelozzo* to hold the miraculous Crucifix (now in Santa Trinita) of San Giovanni Gualberto, founder of the monastery of Vallombrosa. The vaults of the ciborium are decorated with slip-decorated terra-cotta by *Luca della Robbia.* The paintings on the small doors of the tabernacle are by *Agnolo Gaddi.*

The **chapel of the cardinal of Portugal**★ is in the left aisle. This magnificent Renaissance chapel was built between 1459 and 1466 by *A. Manetti*, a pupil of Brunelleschi. The chapel was constructed to house the tomb of Jacopo di Lusitania, cardinal and archbishop of Lisbon, nephew of King Alfonso of Portugal, who died in Florence in 1459. The vault is decorated with medallions by *Luca della Robbia.* The painting of saints Vincent, James and Eustace, above the altar, is a copy of the original by *Antonio* and *Piero del Pollaiuolo* now in the Uffizi. On either side of the painting the same artists have painted frescoes of two angels. On the right of the chapel you can see the tomb of the cardinal (1461), by *Antonio Rossellino*. In the left niche above the bishop's chair there is an "Annunciation" (1467) by *Alessio Baldovinetti*.

At the back of the nave, a wrought iron gate (1388) leads to a crypt with 7 naves (11th century) where the relics of the martyr are kept. The vaults show remains of frescoes (1341) by *Taddeo Gaddi*.

The raised **choir**★ is enclosed by a balustrade and decorated with marble mosaics (1207). A terra-cotta "Crucifix" by the *Della Robbia* workshop hangs over the 12th-century altar. The inlaid wooden stalls of the choir were made in 1470. In the apse, a mosaic (1297), represents Christ between the Virgin and St. Miniatus. The windows are made of slabs of pink alabaster.

A door on the right of the choir leads to the **sacristy** (1387) built in the Gothic style and decorated with contemporary frescoes by *Spinello Aretino*, describing the **Life of St Benedict**★. In the lunette there is a 15th-century "Pietà" by *Alessio Baldovinetti*. The carved wooden stalls are also from the 15th century. The sacristy is connected to the cloister (*permission to enter must be obtained from the monks*) which was decorated with frescoes by *Paolo Uccello* but only fragments of these remain today.

The Palace of the Bishops (*Palazzo dei Vescovi*, 1295) is on the right of the church. This austere, crenellated building used to be the summer residence of the bishops of Florence. It then became a hospital and is now part of the convent of the Olivetan monks.

Behind the church, on the left, on the site of fortifications built by *Michelangelo* in 1530, there is a vast cemetery, the Porte Sante (Holy Doors), which was built in 1839. Many Florentine artists and writers are buried here.

Via San Leonardo (MAP I E4)

From the Viale dei Colli (in the section called Viale Galileo) the street leads on the left to Arcetri, Florence's observatory of astrophysics. It is one of the largest observatories in the world. On the right, the Via San Leonardo is an enchanting country road lined with beautiful villas which are surrounded by trees. This leads to the Porta San Giorgio (1224) close to the Forte di Belvedere. On the way you can see the Romanesque church of **San Leonardo in Arcetri** (13th-century tribune and 14th-century paintings from the Tuscan school).

Forte di Belvedere (MAP I DE4)

The *Medici* ordered the construction of this fortress in order to protect the Palazzo Pitti in case of uprisings against the grand dukes. In 1590, *Bernardo Buontalenti* drew up the plans for the buildings according to the concept of military architecture of the time. If necessary, the grand dukes could reach the fort through the Boboli Gardens or, so it is said, through secret underground passages. Today, the Forte di Belvedere houses temporary art exhibitions. Free access to the terraces. Panoramic **view**★★ of the town and the hills.

MORE TO SEE
IN FLORENCE

The various itineraries suggested in the previous chapters do not pretend to be an exhaustive list of the treasures of Florence. You will probably have discovered for yourself places which no guide-books mention but which you have found interesting. This is part of the charm of Florence.

Having described what we feel are the most important works of art and curios, there are still a number of other villas, churches and museums which we have grouped together in this chapter.

The Cascine (MAP I BC1)

Bus n° 17 from the center.

This broad park was designed in the 18th century on farmland belonging to the grand dukes. It is a favorite spot with Florentines (accessible by car), and stretches 1½ miles/3 km west of the town along the right bank of the Arno. There are restaurants, cafés, a race-course, a stadium and various sports facilities. At the end of the park, where the Mugnone joins the Arno, you will find an unexpected **monument** dedicated to the **maharajah of Kalipur** who died in Florence in 1870 and was cremated here.

Stibbert villa and museum

Entrance at n° 26 Via Stibbert, on the right of Via Vittorio Emanuele II, 1½ miles/3 km north of the center (MAP I A4)

Bus n° 1 from Via dei Cerretani (MAP I D1)

Visit: 9 am to 2 pm. Sun 9 am to 1 pm. Closed on Thurs.

The villa and the collections were donated to the town by Frederick Stibbert (1838–1906). A vast quantity of furniture, paintings and curios, from different periods and countries, are on show in the 60 rooms of the museum. The main attraction, however, is the collection of arms and armoury, both European and Oriental.

Museo di Storia della Scienza★

Entrance at n° 1 Piazza dei Giudici (MAP II E4)

Visit: winter 9.30 am to 1 pm daily; Mon, Wed and Fri 2 pm to 5 pm. Summer 9.30 am to 1.30 pm daily; Mon and Fri 3.30 pm to 7 pm.

Panorama of the Duomo and the Palazzo Vecchio, seen from the Forte di Belvedere.

The work of Galileo Galilei (born in Pisa in 1564) has a privileged position in this museum dedicated to physics. You can see the telescope with which he was able to discover the four satellites of Jupiter, as well as a splendid collection of measuring instruments, calculators from the 17th century to the 19th century, microscopes, and astronomical instruments. A large part of the collection comes from the Medici and the dukes of Lorraine, who had a great interest in the sciences. An alchemist's laboratory has been reconstructed on the ground floor.

The church of Sant'Ambrogio (MAP I C5)

Several artists are buried in this old church: *Leon del Tasso, Mino da Fiesole, Verrocchio, Francesco Granacci.*

On the right of the choir, in the chapel of the Miracle (where, in 1230, a miracle took place), there is a beautiful tabernacle (1481) by *Mino da Fiesole* with, on each side, angels holding candelabras made by the *Della Robbia* workshop in 1513, and a fresco of "The Procession of the Miracle" by *C. Rosselli* in 1486. Next to it is a "Virgin" by *Graffione* and "Saints" by *Alessio Baldovinetti.* On the 3rd altar on the left, "Virgin and Saints" by *C. Rosselli.* In a niche, statue of St. Sebastian by *Leon del Tasso.*

The church of Santa Maria dei Pazzi (MAP I C5)

58 Borgo Pinti.

Visit: 9 am to 12 noon; 5 pm to 7 pm.

The church was rebuilt in 1492 by *Giuliano da Sangallo.* There is a pretty courtyard with a portico in front of the church. Inside, the 15th-century chapels have remained untouched. From the church, you can go into the cloister and proceed from there into the chapter room which is decorated with a large, impressive fresco by *Perugino* showing "The Crucifixion". The figures of Mary Magdalen, the Virgin, St. Bernard, St. John the Evangelist and St. Benedict are all portrayed.

Walking down Borgo Pinti, take a look at n° 68, the **Palazzo Panciatichi-Ximenes**, built by *Giuliano* and *Antonio da Sangallo* in 1479, which was enlarged in 1605; and at n° 97 the **Palazzo della Gherardesca**, which has a charming garden. Borgo Pinti leads to the **Piazzale Donatello** (MAP I C5) and the **Protestant Cemetery★** (19th century) surrounded by cypresses. Since many well-known English people are buried there, including *Elizabeth Barrett Browning*, it is generally known as the **English Cemetery.**

Cenacolo di San Salvi (MAP I D6)

Temporarily closed.

The refectory of the old abbey of San Salvi is decorated with a fresco of the "Last Supper" by *Andrea del Sarto*, painted in 1519.

Museo di Firenze com'era (MAP II C5)

Entrance at n° 24 Via dell'Oriuolo.

Visit: 9 am to 2 pm; Sun 8 am to 1 pm. Closed on Thurs.

Housed in the former convent of the Oblate, the **Historical Museum of Florence** illustrates the story of the city with prints, paintings, engravings and photographs.

Next to it, at n° 21 Via Sant'Egidio, is the **Museum of Prehistory.** *Visit: 9.30 am to 12.30 pm. Closed Sun. Admission free.*

Ospedale di Santa Maria Nuova (MAP II C5-6)

Opposite the Museo di Firenze com'era.

The hospital was founded in 1286 by *Folco Portinari*, father of *Dante's* beloved, *Beatrice.* On the front, a portico designed by *Bernardo Buontalent,* was added in 1611. The center of the portico opens into the **church of Sant'Egidio,** rebuilt in 1419. Inside, there is a terra-cotta Virgin by *Andrea della Robbia* on the right of the altar. In the cloister (14th century) on the right of the church, you can see a "Pietà" by the *Della Robbia* workshop.

Cenacolo di Foligno (MAP II A3)

Entrance at n° 42 Via Faenza.

Temporarily closed.

Perugino painted a fresco of the "Last Supper" in the refectory of the former convent of Sant'Onofrio. This fresco was once attributed to *Raphael.*

Museo Zoologico "La Specola" (MAP I D3)

Entrance at n° 17 Via Romana.

Visit: Zoology: Tues 9 am to 12.30 pm; Sun 9 am to 12 noon. Anatomy: Sat 3 pm to 6 pm (summer); Sat 2 pm to 5 pm (winter). Admission free.

Housed in the **Palazzo Torrigiani,** the museum stands on the site of a former astronomical observatory. Besides the zoological collections, you can see a small vivarium and a beautiful room, the Tribuna di Galileo (1841), decorated with marble, mosaics and frescoes.

The church of San Giovanni Battista

On the Autostrada del Sole (A1), exit Firenze Nord.

This church by *Giovanni Michelucci* is one of the most original of the modern buildings in the outskirts of Florence. The roof is built like a tent and the interior space is divided rhythmically into smaller spaces.

THE OUTSKIRTS
OF FLORENCE

It is impossible to write about Florence without mentioning the surrounding hills. Town and country have been carrying on a harmonious dialogue over the centuries during which the landscape has become as civilized, ordered and intelligible as a garden. Stately cypresses and twisted olive trees give contrasting patches of light and dark colors, just like the walls of the Duomo and of the Baptistry. The geometrical balance on the facades of the Florentine churches is repeated in the Italian gardens of the beautiful Tuscan villas. The roofs of Florence reflect the same colors as the soil of the Chianti vineyards.

▬ 1 — SAN DOMENICO DI FIESOLE — FIESOLE

How to get there: Fiesole is 5 miles/8 km north-east of Florence.

San Domenico di Fiesole is an old village which has become a famous residential area of Florence. It is half-way up the hill to Fiesole. The terminus of bus n° 7 is in the village, leaving from Florence's Central station. By car: leave the city by Viale Alessandro Volta (MAP I AB6).

San Domenico di Fiesole

The church of San Domenico was built in 1435, a portico was added in 1632 and a bell-tower by *Matteo Nigetti* in 1613. In the adjoining convent in 1406, *Sant'Antonino* (*Antonino Pierozzi* 1398–1450) — see p. 115 — and *Guidolino di Pietro* took their religious vows. The latter took the religious name of *Fra Giovanni da Fiesole*, better known as *Fra Angelico* (1387–1455), and he left two beautiful works of art there: a **Madonna with Saints**★ (1430, first chapel on the left) and a **Crucifix**★ (in the refectory of the convent). The church has many other fine pieces.

Turn left almost opposite the church and walk down along the Via Badia dei Roccettini for five minutes to get to the **Badia Fiesolana,** former cathedral of Fiesole. In 1208, the Benedictine monks turned it into an abbey and kept it until 1437. In 1456, the church was rebuilt in the style of *Brunelleschi.* The marble facade of the old Romanesque church, which was smaller, was integrated into the unfinished facade of the Renaissance church. To the right of the church, you can enter the abbey, which is well worth a visit.

Fiesole★★

Province of Florence. Pop 14,800; height 968 feet/295 metres.

Anybody who walks to the top of the city and up to the convent of San Francesco will understand how Fiesole, though never an important town,

The Tuscan landscape has the ordered elegance of a garden.

remained an independent stronghold for such a long time. Its exceptional position accounts for this. At less than 6 miles/10 km distance, you can identify all the monuments of Florence, spread out before you in the valley below. Olive groves, vineyards and gardens surrounding luxurious villas divide the big city from this favorite suburb of the Florentines.

All the names of the Renaissance are evoked here. In the "Decameron", *Boccaccio's* characters take refuge in Fiesole. The Etruscans were the first (or among the first) to settle here, and they founded *Faesulae* in the 5th or 6th century B.C. There are remains of the walls built to protect the town against the Celts. In 80 B.C., at the time of *Sylla*, Fiesole became a Roman town.

Piazza Mino da Fiesole is named after the famous sculptor (*b.* Poppi *c.* 1430–84) who later settled in Fiesole. The site of the Roman forum is now the center of the town. It is bordered on the western side by the seminary and the Bishop's Palace, on the northern side by the Duomo, and to the east by the Palazzo Pretorio (14th–15th centuries), now the town hall, and the **church of Santa Maria Primerana.** This church has a painted Crucifix (14th century) on the right of the nave; "Crucifixion" and "Saints" in terra-cotta by the *Della Robbia* workshop; on the walls of the choir, fragments of frescoes by the school of *Giotto.*

The Duomo★ is a Romanesque building (1208), enlarged in the 13th and 14th centuries, dominated by a crenellated bell-tower (1213).

The interior has the austere aspect of a basilica, with three naves and a raised choir over the crypt. A statue of the church's patron, San Romolo, made in terra-cotta by *Giovanni della Robbia*, stands above the main portico.

Choir: on the high altar, note the triptych (*c.* 1450) by *Bicci di Lorenzo.* The wall of the apse bears a fresco by *Nicodemo Ferrucci* and on the left wall of the high altar a triptych (1372) depicts the "Crowning of the Virgin" by *Giovanni del Biondo.*

The Salutati chapel★ is to the right of the choir. There are 15th-century frescoes by *Cosimo Rosselli* and three works, all done around 1465, by *Mino da Fiesole*: the tomb of Bishop Leonardo Salutati, a **Virgin**★ and the **bust of the bishop**★, one of the artist's masterpieces.

In the chapel to the left of the choir, the altar (1494) with statues of San Romolo and San Matteo is by *Andrea Ferrucci.*

The crypt has a baptismal font (1569), wrought iron altar (15th century) and gate (14th century). Frescoes (15th century).

Next to the Duomo, the Via Dupré will take you to the entrance of the gardens which contain the archeological museum, the Roman theater and various Roman and Etruscan ruins.

The archeological museum (*visit: summer 10 am to 12.30 pm and 2.30 pm to 6 pm; winter 9 am to 12 noon and 2 pm to 5 pm. Closed on Mon*) contains some Etruscan, Roman and Barbarian objects; in particular, statues, steles, funerary urns, fragments of the temple of Bacchus and of a frieze from the theater, and a bronze sculpture of a she-wolf (1st century B.C.).

The theater★ has 19 terraces that could seat up to 3000 spectators. It was built at the time of *Sylla* (1st century B.C.) and was modified by *Claudius* and *Septimius Severus.* There were also Roman baths. The temple was altered by the Romans but retained influences from the Etruscan period, as far as we can judge by the few remains. Take a look at the remaining stretch of the Etruscan walls.

The Bandini museum. *Same visiting hours as the archeological museum. Closed on Sun. Entrance to the right when you come out of the garden.*

It contains terra-cottas by the *Della Robbia* workshop, a statue by *Nino Pisano* and paintings from the Tuscan school (mostly 14th and 15th centuries) by *Agnolo Gaddi, Giovanni da Ponte, Jacopo del Sellaio, Lorenzo Monaco, N. Bonaccorsi, Andrea Rico da Candia*, etc.

Sant'Alessandro and San Francesco★

Between the seminary and the Bishop's Palace, take the Via San Francesco. After a steep walk, you will reach a terrace offering one of the best **views★★** of Florence and its surroundings. You will pass, on your right, the **church of Sant'Alessandro★**, built in the 6th century on the site of a temple dedicated to Bacchus. The interior is divided into three naves and contains the 16 columns taken from the former temple and the basilica in the forum.

If you go farther up, you will reach the top of the hill (1132 feet/345 metres), the former site of the ancient Etruscan acropolis. Here stands the **convent of San Francesco★** (15th century).

The church (c. 1330) has an interesting facade (15th century). The main door is protected by a small roof; above, there is an attractive rose-window, and below, a fresco representing St. Francis (15th century).

The interior of the church is in the Gothic style, decorated with many paintings (some of them are being restored): above the high altar, an "Annunciation" by *Raffaellino del Garbo*; above the altars on the right, the "Mystic Marriage of St. Catherine" (Florentine school, 15th century) and a "Crucifixion" by *Neri di Bicci*; on the left, "Adoration of the Magi" by *C. Rosselli*, and "Madonna with Child and Saints" (*Perugino* school).

On the left of the nave, a door leads to the cloister (18th century) and to a room in which you can see a Neapolitan terra-cotta crib. This room also houses the museum of Franciscan Missions (objects from the Far East). On the other side of the church, there is another quiet and peaceful cloister (14th century). The first floor is occupied by the monks' cells.

If you are driving, you can go back to Florence by the Via Boccaccio to see the **Villa Schifanoia** (beautiful garden — seat of the **Pius XII Institute**) and, farther on, the **Villa Palmieri** where *Boccaccio* took refuge during the plague in 1348 and where he wrote the "Decameron".

▬ 2 — CERTOSA DEL GALLUZZO — IMPRUNETA

How to get there: the Certosa of Galluzzo is 3½ miles/6 km south of Florence. Bus n° 36 and 37 from Piazza Santa Maria Novella (MAP II C2–3) If you are traveling by car, leave the town from Porta Romana (MAP I E3) and take the road towards Siena as far as Galluzzo (3 miles/5 km). Once past the village, a small road on the right leads up to the monastery.

To Impruneta, (9 miles/14 km from Florence) take the coach from C.A.P. (coach company), 13r Via Nazionale (MAP II B3). By car, continue on the road towards Siena for about 1 mile/2 km, leaving the motorway entrance to your right and go towards Tavarnuzze. In the village, a road on the left will take you up the hill to Bagnolo and Impruneta. Beautiful drive.

Certosa del Galluzzo★ — also called *Certosa di Val d'Ema*.

This monastery was founded in 1342 by the Florentine banker *Niccolò Acciaiuoli*, a friend of *Petrarch* and *Boccaccio*. Later on, further donations were made to the monastery which was enlarged and transformed several times, so that today it is a mixture of various styles of architecture. In 1958, the Carthusian monks left the monastery and the Cistercian monks took it over.

Opening hours: summer 9 am to 12 noon and 3 pm to 6 pm; winter 9 am to 12 noon ·and 2.30 pm to 5 pm. Closed on Mon. A small donation is expected.

Palazzo degli Studi. There is now a museum here containing the detached frescoes by *Pontormo* of "Scenes from the Passion of Christ" (inspired by *Dürer*). They were painted in 1522 when the artist had taken refuge in the

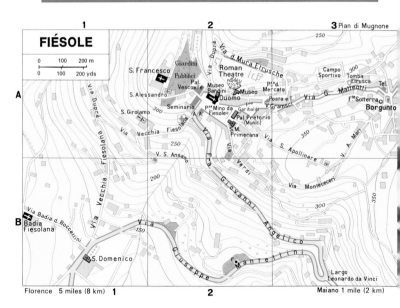

monastery from an outbreak of plague in the city. The frescoes were originally in the cloister. The museum also contains paintings by *Mariotto di Nardo, Masolino* and *Ridolfo Ghirlandaio.*

The church. The building is in the Gothic style but a new facade was built in the 16th century. The interior, with cross vaults, is divided into two parts by a tribune according to the rule of the Carthusian order, one for the monks and the other for the lay brothers. In the monks' choir, there are beautiful wooden stalls (1570–91); on the altar, a marble tabernacle. From the choir, steps lead to a subterranean chapel containing the tombs of Cardinal Agnolo Acciaiuoli (16th century) and Niccolò Acciaiuoli (d. 1365).

You can also visit the Chapter room ("Crucifixion" by *M. Albertinelli,* 1506), the refectory, the pharmacy (where liqueurs, honey and lavender may be bought from the monks), three cloisters of which the largest is decorated with 66 medallions by *Andrea* and *Giovanni della Robbia;* and some monks' cells.

Impruneta *(Pop 14,500; height 902 feet/275 metres)*

This is an agricultural town in the Chianti area. It holds the famous festival during the grape harvest. On October 18, St. Luke's day, there used to be a market for horses and mules which was one of the most important in Europe. Jacques Callot, the French engraver, made a series of prints in 1620 depicting the fair. The Venetian painter *Domenico Tiepolo* came to the market several times in order to make drawings of donkeys.

Impruneta is also an important center for the production of terra-cotta pots and tiles, and for straw hats. The main square is bordered by arcades. The **church of Santa Maria dell'Impruneta,** founded in the 11th century and rebuilt in the 15th century, was restored after the Second World War. The bell-tower was built in the 13th century and the portico outside the church was built in 1634.

Inside, *Michelozzo* added small chapels (1455) on each side of the choir. The Chapel of the Cross (right) has a majolica ceiling, a marble frieze and a terra-cotta tabernacle by *Luca della Robbia.* The Chapel of the Madonna (left) has a similar decoration and terra-cotta statues of St. Paul and St. Luke by *Luca della Robbia.* Inside the tabernacle there is a painting of the Virgin in the Byzantine style (13th century). In a niche, marble predella (15th century). On the high altar, large polyptych of the Florentine school (14th century). Cloister (14th century) on the right of the church.

From Impruneta you can reach **Siena** (35 miles/57 km) going through the valley of the Greve. Take road S.S. 222 through the Chianti hills and the famous vineyards producing the *Chianti Classico* (Greve, Castellina, Radda, Gaiole), the best vintage wine.

▄▄ 3 — THE FLORENTINE VILLAS

Florence is surrounded by many villas in the midst of beautiful gardens, which you can visit on guided tours in the summer. This is the only possibility of access without special permission. Apply to the travel agencies.

Villas to visit:

The villa di Poggio Imperiale, built at the beginning of the 15th century, was confiscated by *Cosimo I dei Medici* in 1565 and then enlarged several times between the 17th century and the beginning of the 19th century.

The Medici villas of Petraia and Castello: Petraia was originally a castle. It was rebuilt in 1575 for Cardinal *Ferdinando dei Medici* by *Bernardo Buontalenti.* Later it became a royal residence. It has one of the most beautiful Florentine gardens.

The villa of Castello was acquired by *Lorenzo the Magnificent* in 1477. It was damaged during the siege in 1530 and then restored for *Cosimo I* by *Bronzino* and *Pontormo.* The garden was designed by *Tribolo* in 1540.

▄▄ 4 — POGGIO A CAIANO

How to get there: the town is 11 miles/18 km west of Florence.

Coach company CO.PI.T., departure 22 Piazza Santa Maria Novella (MAP II C2), or C.A.P., 13r Via Nazionale (MAP II B3). By car, go from Porta al Prato, Via delle Porte Nuove (MAP I B2-3) and leave the city by road S.S. 66, following signs for Pistoia.

Poggio a Caiano (*pop 5900; height 187 feet/57 metres*)

This town, at the foot of **Monte Albano,** is famous for the Medici villa, probably the best that was built for this family.

Visit: villa 9 am to 1.30 pm; Sun 9 am to 12.30 pm. Closed on Mon. Admission free. Garden 9 am to sunset.

The villa was bought by *Lorenzo the Magnificent* in 1480, and was rebuilt by *Giuliano da Sangallo* between 1480 and 1485. *Francesco I dei Medici* and his wife, *Bianca Cappello,* died there in mysterious circumstances on October 19, 1587. The apartments are beautifully decorated. The walls of the great *salone* are covered with 16th-century frescoes depicting scenes from Roman history chosen as parallels to the life of Cosimo the Elder and Lorenzo the Magnificent. They were painted by *Andrea del Sarto, Franciabigio, Pontormo* and *Alessandro Allori.*

In the village of **Comeana,** 1½ miles/3 km south of Poggio a Caiano, you can visit the monumental Etruscan tomb of Montefortini (7th century B.C.). From there, go 2½ miles/4 km south and you will reach the beautiful villa of Artimino which was built in 1594 by *Bernardo Buontalenti* for Ferdinando I dei Medici. The village of **Artimino** is enclosed by medieval walls. There is an interesting church (12th century). Nearby, you can see the **Etruscan Necropolis of Pian di Rosello** (7th century B.C.) which was discovered in 1970.

5 — SESTO FIORENTINO

How to get there: Sesto Fiorentino is 5½ miles/9 km north-west of Florence on the way to Prato, Calenzano. Bus n° 28 from the Central station. By car, take the Via del Romito (MAP I AB3) and drive through the suburb of Rifredi (13th-century church with decoration by the *Della Robbia* workshop).

At 2½ miles/4 km: **Il Sodo.** The road on the right leads to **Castello** and the Medici villas of Petraia and Castello (see p. 145).

At 5½ miles/9 km: **Sesto Fiorentino** (pop 44,500, height 181 ft/55 m). This is an industrial town producing porcelain and ceramics. In Via Gramsci (north-east side of town), the Porcelain Manufacture of Doccia (Richard Ginori Company) was founded by Marquis Ginori in 1735.

Visit to the museum: 9.30 am to 1 pm and 3.30 pm to 6.30 pm. Closed on Mon.

In Quinto, you can see the impressive Etruscan tomb of the Montagnola (7th century B.C.), at n° 97 Viale Fratelli Rosselli.

From Sesto Fiorentino take the panoramic road of the Colli Alti (High Hills); (going east) 8 miles/13 km farther east, between Pratolino and Montorsoli, you will join the S.S. 65 which goes from Florence to Bologna via the Futa Pass (height 3007 feet/903 m).

6 — SETTIGNANO

How to get there: Settignano is 12½ miles/18 km east of Florence. Bus n° 10 from the Central station or from Piazza San Marco (MAP II A5). By car, go to Piazza Alberti (MAP I D6) and take the Viale De Amicis. After passing the flyover, turn right into Viale D'Annunzio which goes all the way to Settignano.

This charming village is on the top of a hill and it became famous for its tradition of sculpture: *Desiderio da Settignano* (1428–79), *Bernardo Gamberelli* (1409–64). *Michelangelo* spent his youth here in the **Villa Buonarroti.** In the main square, there is a statue of the writer Niccolò Tommaseo (*d.* 1874), and the **church of the Assunta** (16th century) with a Madonna by the *Della Robbia* workshop; pulpit by *G. Silvani* from a sketch by *Bernardo Buontalenti.*

There are various interesting villas in the neighborhood: **Villa Gamberaia** (17th century; superb garden), Villa Capponcini which once belonged to Gabriele d'Annunzio and Villa I Tatti.

7 — THE MUGELLO

A 62-mile/99-km trip in a very beautiful Tuscan valley. All distances are from Florence.

Leave Florence by the Lungarno C. Colombo (MAP I D6) and the S.S. 67 in the direction of Forli and Arezzo, going up the Arno valley.

At 11 miles/18 km: **Pontassieve** (pop 19,800; height 331 feet/101 m). This small town is an agricultural and industrial center. Wine trade. The Arno is joined here by the River Sieve and the town is at the crossroads between the Forli–Ravenna and Arezzo–Cesena roads.

Approximately 1½ miles/2.5 km south-west of Pontassieve, on the other bank of the Arno is the Benedictine **monastery of Santa Maria di Rosano** (12th century). Modified in the 16th and 18th centuries, the church has a fine collection of sculptures and paintings (14th and 15th centuries).

In Pontassieve, ignoring the road to Arezzo on your right, take the S.S. 67 which turns left to go up the narrow valley of the Sieve.

At 16 miles/26 km: **Rufina,** surrounded by vineyards.

22 miles/35.5 km from Florence is **Dicomano,** boasting a splendid Romanesque church. On your right, the S.S. 67 goes to **Forli** (46 miles/73.5 km) passing **San Godenzo** (6 miles/10 km; height: 1270 feet/385 m) church of the Benedictine Abbey (11th century). Alternatively, in Dicomano, turn left and take the S.S. 551 which follows the valley of the Sieve across the **Mugello,** one of the most characteristic valleys of Tuscany, known for its good farming and vineyards.

Vicchio stands at 27 miles/44 km, hometown of the Domenican painter *Giovanni da Fiesole,* known as *Fra Angelico* (1387–1455). The sculptor *Benvenuto Cellini* once owned a farm here.

At 29 miles/47 km you come to **Vespignano,** here you can visit the house *Giotto* (1266–1337) was born in; museum.

At 32 miles/51 km: **Borgo San Lorenzo** — Cross the S.S. 302 for Faenza (right) and Florence (left).

At 36 miles/57 km you will cross the River Sieve at **San Piero a Sieve;** 16th-century church with a 15th-century terra-cotta baptismal font by the *Della Robbia* workshop.

Scarperia (2½ miles/4 km north-east of San Piero, turning right onto the S.S. 503 towards Imola) is a small town, known for its traditional production of cutlery. The Palazzo Pretorio (1306) has a typical facade decorated with coats of arms. The oratory of the Madonna di Piazza is covered with 14th-century frescoes. On the road from San Piero to Scarperia a small road on the left leads, after 2½ miles/4 km, to an isolated Franciscan convent: **Bosco ai Frati;** beautiful buildings (15th century), crucifix attributed to *Donatello.* Back in San Piero a Sieve, turn left on road S.S. 503.

After 37 miles/59 km, you come to **Novoli;** here, a road lined with cypresses leads to the **Castello del Trebbio** (15th century) where *Cosimo I* spent his childhood. At 1 mile/2 km north of Novoli, on the S.S. 65, you will find the **villa of Cafaggiolo,** built in 1451 by *Michelozzo* for *Cosimo the Elder.* In Novoli turn left and take the S.S. 65.

At 44 miles/71 km: **Pratolino** (height 1570 feet/476 m). In the park of the Villa Demidoff (16th century) there is a monumental statue by *Giambologna* representing the Apennines. *Opening hours of the park to be checked on the spot.*

In Pratolino, take a small road on the left up to **Bivigliano** (48 miles/77 km); summer resort (height 1914 feet/580 m). From there, take a road on the right to the convent of Monte Senario, motherhouse of the Servite order (Servants of Mary) which was founded in 1233 (height 2689 feet/815 m). From the convent you can see a vast panorama over the valley and the Apennines. The church was rebuilt in the 18th century, and contains many paintings and a crucifix by *Tacca.*

Go back to Pratolino and return to Florence on the S.S. 65 (62 miles/99 km) passing through Montorsoli.

If you have not yet visited **Sesto Fiorentino** (see p. 146), you can, between Pratolino and Montorsoli, take the panoramic road of the Colli Alti on the right which will take you there (8 miles/13 km).

8 — THE PRATOMAGNO AND THE CASENTINO

Interesting excursion, 62 miles/99 km, recommended to people going to Arezzo.

From Florence to Pontassieve (11 miles/18 km; see n° 7).

In Pontassieve, leave the S.S. 67 and take first the S.S. 69 (on the right, direction Arezzo) which you will leave shortly after, to your right. You continue on road S.S. 70 (towards Consuma). After approximately 1½ miles/2.5 km, take a small road on the right towards the mountains of Pratomagno (signs for Pelago/Vallombrosa). Following this road you will come to **Pelago** (at 14 miles/23 km); **Tosi** (17 miles/27 km) and finally to **Vallombrosa-Saltino** (21 miles/33 km). This summer and ski resort is situated on **Monte Secchieta** (height 4781 feet/1449 m). The town is well placed on the western side of Monte Secchieta, in the middle of a splendid pine forest. The resort is divided between the old village of Vallombrosa (height 3161 feet/958 m) built round the abbey and, less than a mile/1.3 km farther on, the new resort of Saltino (height 3283 feet/995 m).

The famous **abbey of Vallombrosa** was founded in 1036 by *San Giovanni Gualberto*. It is the seat of the congregation of the Vallombrosan order. The main buildings date back to the 16th and 17th centuries, (13th-century bell-tower; 15th-century tower). To the south-east, the whole area of the Pratomagno offers many walks and excursions in the mountains (max. height 5280 feet/1600 m).

Montemignaio, 3 miles/5 km north-west of Vallombrosa. Romanesque church (13th century).

Driving through the forest, you climb a narrow valley and meet the S.S. 70 for Arezzo. At 27 miles/43 km, you will arrive in **Consuma,** a summer resort (height 3382 feet/1025 m) just below the pass (height 3498 feet/1060 m) dividing the mountains of Pratomagno (south) and of Falterona (north).

At 33 miles/52.5 km: pass the bridge over the Arno and turn left towards Stia. The road to Stia climbs the higher valley of the Arno, the *Casentino*. After 4 miles/6 km, **Pratovecchio.** This was the fief of the Ghibelline family of the *Guidi*. *Dante* was welcomed here when exiled from Florence. The Castello di Romena was the castle of the counts of Guidi. It was founded in about 1000. It dominates the village of Pratovecchio where you can visit the Pieve di Romena (height 1570 feet/476 m). This church was built in 1152 on the remains of a sanctuary (10th century). Admire the apse and a painting from the 12th century by the *Maestro di Varlungo*.

At 5 miles/8 km from the turning, you arrive in **Stia** (pop 3000, height 1455 feet/441 m) at the foot of **Monte Falterona** (height 5458 feet/1654 m). There is a Romanesque church (12th century) with beautiful capitals and some paintings: "Virgin with Child" by the *Maestro di Varlungo*; "Assumption" by the Florentine school, and a "Madonna" by *Andrea della Robbia*. Stia is the starting point for walks on the Falterona mountain where the Arno has its source. A road leads to the Passo della Calla (9 miles/15 km), where a pass connects Tuscany and Romagna (height 4276 feet/1296 m). From there a small road (1 mile/1.5 km) goes to the refuge of **La Burraia** (height 4775 feet/1447 m) where people ski in the winter. This road ends up at the top (3 miles/5 km) of the **Monte Falco** (height 5471 feet/1658 m).

Once you are back on the S.S. 70, you go down the **Casentino** towards the **plain of Campaldino** where a column was erected to commemorate a battle in 1289, between Florentines and Ghibellines from Arezzo, in which *Dante* participated.

Poppi (pop 5800, height 1442 feet/437 m) stands at 39 miles/62 km from Florence. This used to be the capital of Casentino. It has kept its city walls. The **Castello Pretorio** was the castle of the counts of *Guidi*, once feudal lords of the area. It is an impressive castle (13th and 14th centuries) with a tower on the facade. The courtyard is decorated with coats of arms. On the first floor (*apply to the custodian*) you can see the main rooms, decorated with paintings and frescoes of the Florentine school (15th century), and the chapel (14th-century frescoes). Poppi is the birthplace of the sculptor *Mino da Fiesole* (1430–84).

Leaving Poppi, the road continues to **Bibbiena,** the largest town in Casentino (at 42 miles/67 km); at **Borgo a giovi** (57 miles/92 km), the road leaves the valley of the Arno and crosses the plain to **Arezzo** 62 miles/100 km from Florence.

BIBLIOGRAPHY

Avery, C.B.: *The New Century Italian Renaissance Encyclopedia* (Appleton-Century Crofts Meredith Corporation, London, 1972)

Blue Guide: *Florence* (Ernest Benn, London, 1984)

Burke, Peter: *Culture and Society in Renaissance Italy 1420–1540* (Batsford, London, 1972)

Cochrane, E.: *Florence in the Forgotten Centuries 1527 – 1800: A History of Florence and the Florentines in the Age of the Grand Dukes* (University of Chicago Press, 1973)

Coughlan, R.: *The Life and Times of Michelangelo 1475 – 1564* (Time-Life International, New York, 1975)

De Tolnay, Charles: *The Sistine Ceiling* (Princeton University Press, 1969)

Detroit Institute of Art: *The Twilight of the Medici: Late Baroque Art in Florence 1670 – 1743* (Detroit Institute of Art Catalogue, 1974)

Fremantle, R.: *Florentine Painting in the Uffizi: An Introduction to its Historical Background* (Leo S. Olschlei Editore, Florence, 1971)

Goldscheider, L.: *Leonardo da Vinci* (Oxford University Press, 1944)

Gunn, P.: *A Concise History of Italy* (Thames and Hudson, London, 1971)

Hall, Marcia B.: *Renovations and Counter Reformation, Vasari and Duke Cosimo at Sta Maria Novella and Sta Croce 1567 – 1577* (Oxford Clarendon Press, 1979)

Kauffman, G.: *Florence: Art Treasures and Buildings* (Phaidon, London, 1971)

McCarthy, M.: *The Stones of Florence and Venice Observed* (Penguin, London, 1986)

The Palatine Gallery, Palazzo Pitti, Florence (Institute Geografico de Aquastini, Florence, 1957)

Phumb, J.H.: *The Penguin Book of the Renaissance* (Penguin, London, 1964)

Posner, K.W.G.: *Leonardo and Central Italian Art: 1515 – 1550* (New York University Press, 1974)

Pullan, B.: *A History of Early Renaissance Italy* (St. Martin's Press, New York, 1972)

Raison, Laura (ed): *Tuscany — an Anthology* (Ebury Press, London, 1983)

Rubinstein, N.: *The Government of Florence Under the Medici 1434 – 1494* (Oxford University Press, 1966)

Schevill, F.: *Mediaevel and Renaissance Florence* (Harper Torchbooks, New York, 1963)

Vasari: *Lives of the Artists* (many editions)

Wasserman, J.: *Leonardo* (H.N. Abrams, London, 1975)

White, J.: *The Birth and Rebirth of Pictorial Space* (Faber and Faber, London, 1972)

Whitney, P.: *Visitor's Guide to Florence and Tuscany* (Moorland Publishing and Co. Ltd, London, 1986)

Wickman, C.: *Early Mediaeval Italy* (Macmillan Press Ltd, London, 1981)

▬ USEFUL VOCABULARY

Common words and phrases

Yes	*Sì*
No	*No*
Sir	*Signore*
Madam	*Signora*
Good morning	*Buongiorno*
Good evening	*Buonasera*
Good night	*Buona notte*
Good bye	*Arrivederci*
I am sorry	*Mi scusi*
Please	*Per favore*
Thank you	*Grazie*
Please, do not mention it	*Prego*
Why?	*Perché?*
What?	*Che cosa?*
Where?	*Dov'è?*
Who?	*Chi?*
When?	*Quando?*
Far	*Lontano*
Near	*Vicino*
More	*Ancora*
Can you tell me?	*Può dirmi?*
Do you have?	*Ha?*
I do not understand	*Non capisco*
Speak slowly	*Parli lentamente*
A lot, very	*Molto*
Few, a little	*Poco*
Too much	*Troppo*
Enough	*Abbastanza*
All, everything	*Tutto*
Nothing	*Niente*
How much?	*Quanto costa?*
It is too expensive	*E' troppo caro*

Numbers

One	*Uno*
Two	*Due*
Three	*Tre*
Four	*Quattro*
Five	*Cinque*
Six	*Sei*
Seven	*Sette*
Eight	*Otto*
Nine	*Nove*
Ten	*Dieci*
Eleven	*Undici*
Twelve	*Dodici*
Thirteen	*Tredici*
Fourteen	*Quattordici*
Fifteen	*Quindici*
Sixteen	*Sedici*
Seventeen	*Diciassette*
Eighteen	*Diciotto*
Nineteen	*Diciannove*
Twenty	*Venti*
Twenty-one	*Ventuno*
Twenty-two	*Ventidue*
Thirty	*Trenta*
Forty	*Quaranta*
Fifty	*Cinquanta*
Sixty	*Sessanta*

Seventy	*Settanta*
Eighty	*Ottanta*
Ninety	*Novanta*
Hundred	*Cento*
Two hundred	*Duecento*
Three hundred	*Trecento*
Thousand	*Mille*
Two thousand	*Duemila*
Three thousand	*Tremila*
One million	*Un milione*

At the station, at the airport

A ticket to	*Un biglietto per*
At what time does it leave?	*A che ora parte?*
At what time does it arrive?	*A che ora arriva?*
From what platform does the train leave?	*Di quale binario parte il treno?*
To arrive	*Arrivare*
To change	*Cambiare*
Couchette	*Cuccetta*
Guard	*Controllore*
To leave	*Partire*
Left luggage office	*Deposito*
Luggage	*Bagagli*
Platform	*Binario*
Porter	*Facchino*
Station	*Stazione*
Stop	*Fermata*
Suitcase	*Valigia*
Taxi	*Taxi* or *tassi*
Taxi stand	*Posteggio di taxi*
Train	*Treno*
Ticket	*Biglietto*
Timetable	*Orario*

Driving

Air	*Gonfiaggio*
Attention danger	*Attenzione pericolo*
Car	*Macchina*
Car wash	*Lavaggio*
Entrance	*Ingresso*
Exit	*Uscita*
Forbidden	*Vietato*
Grease, lubrication	*Lubrificazione*
No parking	*Divieto di sosta*
Oil	*Olio*
Parking	*Parcheggio*
Pay toll	*Pedaggio*
Petrol, gas	*Benzina*
Right	*A destra*
Left	*A sinistra*
Road under repair	*Lavori in corso*
Slippery surface	*Fondo sdrucciolevole*
Tyre	*Pneumatico*

In town

Alley	*Vicolo*
Avenue	*Viale*
Cemetery	*Campo Santo, cimitero*
Church	*Chiesa*
Cloister	*Chiostro*
Courtyard	*Cortile*
Garden	*Giardino, orto*

Market	*Mercato*
Museum	*Museo*
Palace	*Palazzo*
Ruins	*Rovine*
Square	*Piazza, largo*
Square (large)	*Piazzale*
Stairs	*Scala*
Street	*Via*
Walk	*Promenade*

Time

Monday	*Lunedi*
Tuesday	*Martedi*
Wednesday	*Mercoledi*
Thursday	*Giovedi*
Friday	*Venerdi*
Saturday	*Sabato*
Sunday	*Domenica*
Spring	*Primavera*
Summer	*Estate*
Autumn	*Autunno*
Winter	*Inverno*
Today	*Oggi*
Yesterday	*Ieri*
The day before yesterday	*Ieri l'altro*
Tomorrow	*Domani*
The day after tomorrow	*Dopo domani*
In the morning	*La mattina*
In the afternoon	*Nel pomeriggio*
In the evening	*La sera*

At the hotel

Inn, Bed & Breakfast	*Locanda*
Hotel	*Albergo*
Boarding-house	*Una pensione familiare*
I would like a room	*Desidero una camera*
With one bed, with two beds	*A un letto, a due letti*
Room with bath	*Camera con bagno*
On the street	*Sulla strada*
Not on the street	*Interna, sul cortile*
What is the price, including tax and service?	*Qual'è il prezzo, servizio e tasse comprese?*
English breakfast	*Colazione all'inglese*
What time is lunch served?	*A che ora è il pranzo?*
And dinner?	*E la cena?*
Wake me up at ... o'clock	*Mi svegli alle ... ore*
I would like the bill	*Vorrei il conto*

At the restaurant

Apple	*Mela*
Beer	*Birra*
Bread	*Pane*
Butter	*Burro*
Cheese	*Formaggio*
Chicken	*Pollo*
Chocolate	*Cioccolata (in tazza)*
Coffee	*Caffé*
Coffee (white)	*Cappuccino*
Cover charge	*Coperto*
Dessert	*Dolce*
Egg	*Uovo*
Fish	*Pesce*
Fork	*Forchetta*

Fruit	*Frutta*
Fruit juice	*Succo di frutta*
Glass	*Bicchiere*
Grapes	*Uva*
Ham	*Prosciutto*
Knife	*Coltello*
Lamb	*Agnello, abbachio*
Main course	*Pasto*
Meal	*Pasto*
Menu, list	*Lista*
Mustard	*Mostardo*
Mutton	*Castrato*
Omelette	*Frittata*
Orange	*Arancia*
Pasta	*Pasta*
Pepper	*Pepe*
Plate, dish	*Piatto*
Pork	*Maiale*
Potato	*Patata*
Salad	*Insalata*
Salami	*Salame*
Salt	*Sale*
Simple restaurant	*Trattoria*
Soup	*Zuppa, brodo*
Spoon (teaspoon)	*Cucchiaio (cucchiaino)*
Starter	*Antipasti*
Steak	*Bistecca*
Sweet	*Dolce*
Sugar	*Zucchero*
Tea	*Tè*
Veal	*Vitello*
Veal chop	*Costata di vitello*
Vegetables	*Verdura*
Waiter	*Cameriere*
Water	*Acqua*
Wine (red)	*Vino (rosso)*
Wine (white)	*Vino (bianco)*

The outskirts of Florence

Historical figures